D0056409

MESSENGERS
^{OF} THE WIND

970.1
K159

MESSENGERS OF THE WIND

*Native American Women
Tell Their Life Stories*

EDITED BY

JANE KATZ

ONE WORLD

BALLANTINE BOOKS · NEW YORK

LIBRARY ST. MARY'S COLLEGE

A One World Book
Published by Ballantine Books

Copyright © 1995 by Jane Katz
Map by Mapping Specialists, Ltd.

All rights reserved
under International and Pan-American Copyright Conventions.
Published in the United States by Ballantine Books,
a division of Random House, Inc., New York,
and simultaneously in Canada
by Random House of Canada Limited, Toronto.

Library of Congress Cataloging-in-Publication Data
Messengers of the wind : Native American women tell their life stories /
edited by Jane Katz.
p   cm.
Includes bibliographical references.
ISBN 0-345-39060-1
1. Indian women—North America—Biography.   2. Indian women—
North America—Social life and customs.   I. Katz, Jane B.
E98.W8M47   1995
970.004'97—dc20
[B]   94-21938
CIP

Text design by Ruth Kolbert

Manufactured in the United States of America

First Edition: March 1995

10 9 8 7 6 5 4 3 2 1

For all the women
who led the way into the heart of Indian Country.
This is your book.

CONTENTS

III

MENDING THE TEARS, WEAVING THE STRANDS

IV

THEY ALWAYS COME BACK TO THE REZ

V

GO SOMEWHERE ELSE AND BUILD A McDONALD'S

ACKNOWLEDGMENTS

Over the years, so many people have lent their energy and encouragement to this project, helping to bring it to life. First of all, my husband Jack has provided financial and psychological support, he has encouraged me to travel and to dare, and thus has made all my work possible.

The following people read all or part of the manuscript, and offered invaluable critique and support: Paula Gunn Allen, Gretchen Bataille, Marilyn Bentz, Pauline Brunette-Danforth, Priscilla Buffalohead, Heid Erdrich, Louise Erdrich, Carole Miller, Jean O'Brien-Kehoe, Barb Raygor, Jack Weatherford, and Flo Wiger. Others offered suggestions and support: Joan Calof, Janet Donaldson, Helen Howard, Lyane Iglitzin, Debbie Linoff, Fran Munnings, Margaret Raymond, Jane Regan, and Steve Tiger. Andrea Webster transcribed tapes and edited copy with intelligence and skill. My agent, Jeannie Hanson, and my editors, Joëlle Delbourgo and Phebe Kirkham, believed in the book and nurtured it with loving care. To all of you I am indebted.

As a way of acknowledging the contributions that have been made by Native American women, I will be donating a portion of my proceeds from the sale of this book to Migizi Communications and other grassroots Native community groups.

———————

"... Daughters, the women are speaking.
They arrive
over the wise distances
on perfect feet.
Daughters, I love you."[▽]

—LINDA HOGAN,
Chickasaw

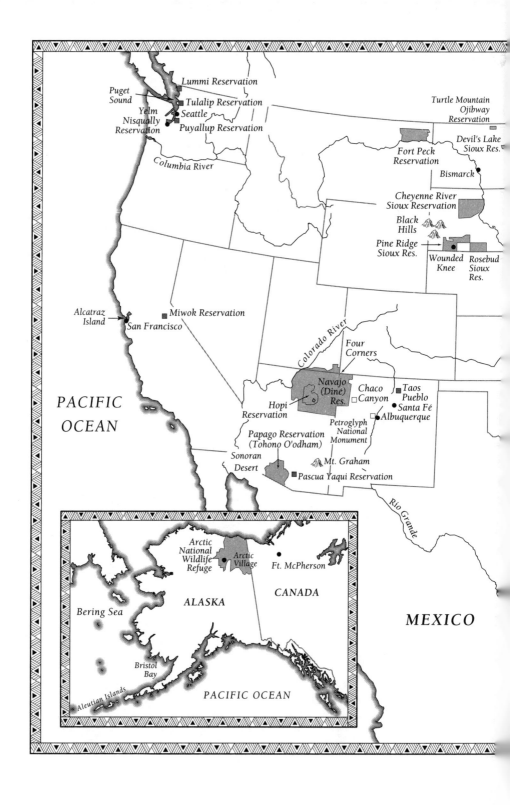

Lummi Reservation

Puget Sound

Tulalip Reservation

Yelm
Nisqually
Reservation

Seattle

Puyallup Reservation

Columbia River

Turtle Mountain
Ojibway
Reservation

Devil's Lake
Sioux Res.

Fort Peck
Reservation

Bismarck

Cheyenne River
Sioux Reservation

Black
Hills

Pine Ridge
Sioux Res.

Wounded
Knee

Rosebud
Sioux
Res.

Alcatraz
Island

Miwok Reservation

San Francisco

PACIFIC
OCEAN

Colorado River

Four
Corners

Navajo
(Diné)
Res.

Chaco
Canyon

Taos
Pueblo

Santa Fé

Albuquerque

Hopi
Reservation

Petroglyph
National
Monument

Papago Reservation
(Tohono O'odham)

Sonoran
Desert

Mt. Graham

Pascua Yaqui Reservation

Rio Grande

Arctic
National
Wildlife
Refuge

Arctic
Village

Ft. McPherson

CANADA

ALASKA

Bering Sea

Bristol
Bay

Aleutian Islands

PACIFIC OCEAN

MEXICO

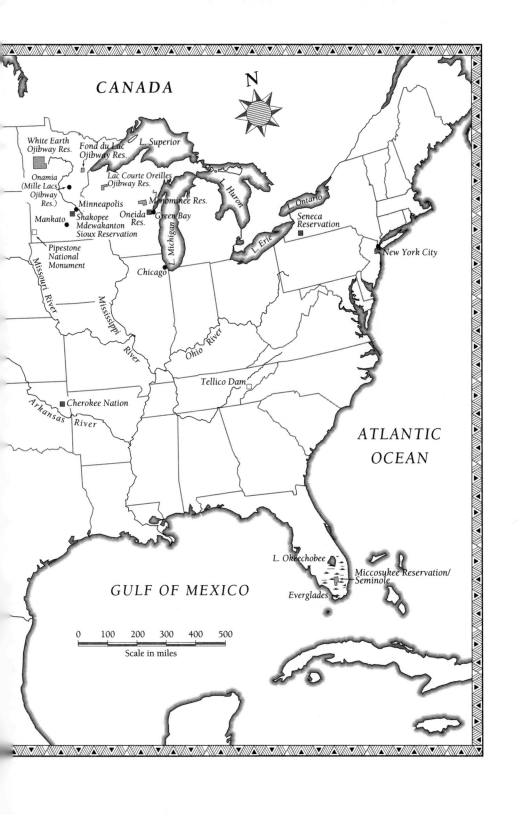

CANADA

N

White Earth
Ojibway Res.

Fond du Lac
Ojibway Res.

L. Superior

Onamia
(Mille Lacs
Ojibway
Res.)

Lac Courte Oreilles
Ojibway Res.

Minneapolis

Menominee Res.

L. Huron

Mankato

Shakopee
Mdewakanton
Sioux Reservation

Oneida
Res.

Green Bay

L. Ontario

Seneca
Reservation

L. Erie

Pipestone
National
Monument

L. Michigan

New York City

Missouri River

Mississippi

River

Chicago

Ohio River

ATLANTIC
OCEAN

Arkansas

River

Cherokee Nation

Tellico Dam

GULF OF MEXICO

L. Okeechobee

Miccosukee Reservation/
Seminole

Everglades

0   100   200   300   400   500

Scale in miles

Introduction

THIS BOOK RECORDS THE VOICES OF WOMEN I ENCOUN-
tered as I followed the many diverse but interconnecting paths
Native American women walk today. Equipped with a tape
recorder and a rental car, a number of years ago I began traveling
down the city streets and back roads of First Nations communities hoping to gain some insight into the challenges and choices
facing indigenous women.

I had no conception of the enormity of the subject, or of the
pitfalls I would encounter as an outsider venturing into "another
country." Fortunately guides appeared along the way. No, they
were not wise women of the woods imparting mystical messages,
but real Native women willing to illuminate aspects of their lives
and share their personal stories.

In a dimly-lit pub in the midst of an urban reservation in
Washington State, Ramona Bennett, former chairwoman of the
Puyallup Tribe, taught me a history lesson:

> When white people came here, they pointed up at the
> Mother Mountain [Mount Rainier] and said, "Who owns
> that?" And the Indians cracked up—what a funny idea, to
> own a mountain! For us, the Mother Mountain is for every-
> one. It brings fresh water, it's where our river comes
> from. . . . It's sacred. Then the white people wrote up title to

the mountain, they cut roads and put ski slopes on it. . . . It's like putting a recreation center on the Virgin Mary's breast.

Bennett recounted the theft of land from her forebears. She spoke of Indians locked out of the job market because of institutional racism. She showed me the graves of babies who died because of malnutrition. She spoke of children virtually kidnapped and sent to orphanages or boarding schools that separated them from family and tribe, leaving them culturally bereft. These were not nightmare scenarios, they were the stories of real people trying to survive in a society that wanted them to disappear.

On a Dakota reservation in Minnesota, Rose Bluestone talked about her ancestors, who, like the Puyallup, had been deprived of land and livelihood and felt betrayed by whites. For their part in the U.S./Dakota Conflict, they were forcibly removed to a concentration camp environment. Rose Bluestone had come to terms with personal tragedy, sustained by the power of prayer. She derived strength from her heritage.

Other women reflected on episodes in tribal history that they perceived as attempted genocide: the Spanish assaults on the life and culture of the Pueblos, the forced removal of the Cherokee known as "The Trail of Tears," the massacre of hundreds of unarmed Lakota at Wounded Knee. These stories are not mere litanies of loss; they chronicle a people's ability to surmount huge obstacles, and endure.

I talked with mixed-blood women who recalled growing up on the margin with the sense that they were invisible, that they didn't belong in either Indian or white society. To fill the empty places in their lives, they joined with other Native people in social service, art, and ceremony, forms of ritual that heal. Their stories affirm human potential. These women are re-creating community. They are remaking their world.

I visited women in traditional, relatively cohesive communities that have managed to hold on to land and culture. In the

Northwest, Lummi weaver Fran James showed me the baskets she weaves just as her ancestors did generations ago and proudly modeled a dress woven from cedar-bark strips. In Taos Pueblo, Southwest arts specialist Soge Track spoke of dealing with "the western mind" in town, then returning to her adobe village to dance, giving energy to Mother Earth. Said Soge Track, "We have children growing up here at the pueblo who follow our life way."

Whether they remain within reservation borders or move beyond them, Native people often find it hard to uphold their time-honored traditions. The contemporary Native woman may find herself navigating in unfamiliar waters without channel markers, forced to make her own way in the world. Some adapt and build bridges between worlds. They come to see traditions as living and breathing entities that can be molded to fit the times. Nevertheless, many Native Americans have been torn apart by value and identity conflicts.

Listening to the voices of women reflecting divergent views and lifestyles, I found myself confronting seemingly endless contradictions. Why is it that Indian and Native Alaskan women have been viewed by the larger society as passive when in fact they often play major roles within their communities and on the national scene? Why is it that indigenous people with deep roots in this land often feel like exiles? Why do some tribal members put their lives on the line to oppose gaming and the appropriation of sacred lands by government and industry, while others sanction these practices? I asked questions, but there were no simple answers.

Gradually I became aware that Native Americans possess a worldview quite different from that of Euramericans. Said Standing Rock Sioux scholar Flo Wiger, "We not only have a different value system; we inhabit a different universe. We don't adhere to rigid standards of right and wrong. Let's face it, on our reservations, we haven't had jobs, we haven't had choices. We will do whatever we have to do to survive."[1] I realized that what seems contradictory to the outsider may make some sense when viewed against the backdrop of Indian history and experience.

Unraveling that complex web of history and experience was a task I was not prepared for by background or training. I grew up in New York City virtually insulated from people of color. In the 1960s I moved to Minneapolis and taught English. I began exploring ethnic cultures and created a black studies course. I left teaching for motherhood. With my children I attended a Native American powwow. After the dancing, an Ojibway elder named Rose Mary Barstow spoke of her journey from tribal circle to Catholic school. She seemed gifted with total recall as she captured the sights, the sounds, and even the voices of her childhood world in vivid detail, making it live. I was in her power.

I included Rose Mary Barstow's account in my 1977 anthology, *I Am the Fire of Time: The Voices of Native American Women*, in which American Indian and Inuit women gave their perspectives on tribal and contemporary life in poetry, prose excerpts, and brief interviews. Native women told me the book echoed their experiences. They gave it to their mothers and grandmothers. One said the book gave her the courage to come out of the closet as a writer.

Moving on to other projects, I collected the life stories of Native Americans in the arts, Holocaust survivors, and refugee artists from many nations. Whether I was talking to a Navajo weaver, a writer who had survived Hitler's death camps, or a painter-turned-freedom-fighter from the hills of Afghanistan, I observed a common obsession: those who had lost their homeland turned to art and storytelling as a way of preserving and passing on their heritage.

The subject of Native American women still called to me, and in 1988, I began a new book focusing on the life stories of Native women. At a dinner party someone asked, "What is the premise of your book?" I replied, "I'm interested in cultural survival, but I don't begin with a hypothesis and then look for data; the knowledge and concerns of Native women will determine the direction of the book." For background I read books on tribal history, I read Indian magazines and newspapers, but I kept the focus on women's personal testimonies, for these put a human face on history. As each woman shared her tribal legacy and communal values, she was in her way celebrating cultural survival.

To gain a sense of the many dimensions of this subject, I looked at the available literature on Native American women. Indigenous communities had been described and dissected by white men—explorers, traders, missionaries, and scholars—whose observations sometimes revealed more about their own cultural biases than about Native people. Misperceptions of Indian women were rampant because they were held up to the patriarchal model. Euramericans expected men to be the providers and defenders of the family while women were supposed to be adjuncts to their husbands, dependent and frail. Among the affluent, those who did manual labor had inferior status. Even an Ojibway Indian turned Christian missionary viewed his own people through that distorted lens. Reverend Peter Jones wrote in the mid-nineteenth century:

> The Indian men look upon their women as an inferior race of beings, created for their use and convenience. They therefore tend to treat them as menials, and impose on them all the drudgeries of a savage life . . . all the hard work falls upon the women, so that it may be truly said of them that they are the slaves of their husbands.[2]

White observers rarely knew Native languages and thus remained outsiders. They did not ask Indian women how they perceived their own status. In fact Native women did work hard, but labor is not necessarily servitude; most were partners with men in the business of survival.

One indicator of a woman's status is her role in economic endeavors. Within the matrilineal Iroquois nations, the fact that women controlled food distribution meant that they wielded considerable political and economic power: they could prevent war expeditions, for example, by denying supplies of dried corn and meat to the men.[3]

The sex roles of Native women were subject to scrutiny. Indigenous women were often pictured by whites as promiscuous. Looking back at their traditions, Native women tell us that their tribes valued purity and held special rituals honoring chaste women. Polygamy was practiced by some Plains tribes, but this is not necessarily an indication of women's low status. In fact some Indian women have spoken or written of the advantage of having cowives as coworkers; one hypothesized that the marriage of one man to sisters allowed the women to present "a united front" to their husbands. Furthermore, writes scholar Katherine M. Weist:

> in some tribes, especially the Crow, women had freedom in selecting their marriage partners, divorcing their husbands, and controlling their own sexuality. That women of their own accord sought liaisons with white traders and travelers without fear of punishment speaks of a high rather than low status.[4]

Movies perpetuated shallow and derisive images of Indian women. The buckskin-clad "squaw" of western films who trod the earth, a respectful distance behind her husband, did not speak her own language; she was never heard to complain about fatigue, backache, or bunions. Cut to the tipi. She prepared food, smoked fish, skinned animals, tanned hides, and stoically bore the pain of childbirth alone.

We did not see her making medicine to heal a sick child, or praying. We did not see her addressing a tribal council or planning military strategy.

Stories of "relationships" between Indians and whites abounded on the screen. An Indian woman paired with a white man was likely to be portrayed as a "princess"—that, supposedly, gave her the dignity and status she was not presumed to have in her own right. No matter that Indian people did not adhere to the European concept of "royalty." In countless films a white man treated an Indian woman as property, using her "primitive" state to justify rape.

The 1990 film *Dances with Wolves* represented a departure from the old stereotypes in its attempt to portray Lakota women with some dignity—they even speak their language. Nevertheless, the movie's only fully developed female character is a white woman adopted into the tribe. With the film *Geronimo* in 1994, Hollywood returned to the image of Native woman as object. The movie portrays Apache women as voiceless victims of white man's violence; it negates their traditional roles as teachers and carriers of tradition. Novelist Sherman Alexie, a Coeur d'Alene Indian, writes of this film that women, both Indian and white, "are the murdered corpses that provoke the surviving men, Indian and white, to commit further acts of violence."[5]

Literature and films reflect pervasive societal attitudes. In the real world, Native American women still find themselves type-cast, burdened by white people's unrealistic images. An educator reported that she feels she is caught in a time warp: "I was asked to give a talk about Indian women, and when I didn't show up in buckskin and moccasins, the audience was disappointed; I felt like they didn't really hear what I had to say."

White people are intrigued by tribal ceremony, which often incorporates music, dance, masks, mime, and colorful attire along with references to sacred stories. But this is not theater designed for the amusement of curious white folks. It is part of the fabric of the lives of tribal people, the way they express their connection with the sacred world, a relationship that is both powerful and private. Some Indians believe the presence of outsiders at ceremonies dilutes their power.

Native Americans are still viewed by many as artifacts, their ceremony as spectacle. The "wise-Indian myth" is packaged and sold. Images of the sacred being Spider Woman appear on greeting cards. Attend a high-priced retreat or workshop, sit on the floor or on a futon, smoke a peace pipe, do a round dance, and you will be treated to revelations ostensibly emanating from a "shamaness"—no doubt named Flying Elk or White Crow Woman. Look around. There is no Indian in the room, only white people searching outside their own culture for spirituality or a new identity.

Mysticism is only one aspect of the multifaceted world of Native women. To get beneath the surface, I steeped myself in the oral narratives of tribal women. Native women's autobiographies were recorded in the late nineteenth and early twentieth centuries by white ethnographers and anthropologists. Some of these scholars learned the languages and produced collaborative works conveying valuable information about tribal customs and values; others, hampered by their own biases and limited knowledge of the languages, perpetuated distortions. Even when Natives translated, the finished work often failed to convey the subtle nuances of the speaker.

As Native American women became fluent writers of English, they began publishing their own life stories. Such works as Anna Moore Shaw's *A Pima Past*, Beverly Hungry Wolf's *The Ways of My Grandmothers*, and Maria Campbell's *Halfbreed* give the reader an authentic look at women's roles within their own societies.

Groundbreaking books focusing on many aspects of the lives and literary traditions of Native women appeared in the 1980s. Lakota anthropologist Bea Medicine published her pioneering research about self-actualizing Plains Indian women in *The Hidden Half*. Gretchen Bataille examined Indian women's autobiographies in *American Indian Women*. Paula Gunn Allen explored the oral and written literature of First Nations women in *The Sacred Hoop*, demonstrating how their sacred traditions shape their worldviews.

Leslie Marmon Silko's novels and poems celebrated the restorative power of the oral tradition; Louise Erdrich's novels orchestrated the voices of grassroots Indian women with humor and compassion. Chapbooks by Wendy Rose, Linda Hogan, Joy Harjo, Roberta Hill Whiteman, Mary TallMountain, and others appeared on bookstore shelves, introducing readers to Native poets with powerful and passionate voices.

What was my rationale for undertaking another book when Native American women were expressing their own vision, reclaiming their traditions, defining themselves?

Blessed
are those who listen
when no one is left to speak.[6]

Hypnotic words from the Chickasaw poet Linda Hogan, a reminder that the elders were dying and with them their memories of worlds in transition. It seemed imperative to go beyond the written literature, to go to the women themselves and listen to their voices. They had stories to tell; I knew how to listen.

I found that not only elders but younger Native women see themselves as carriers of culture passed down orally for countless generations. Storytelling helps the modern Indian woman "mend the tears in the web of being from which she takes her existence," writes Paula Gunn Allen:

> My mother told me stories about cooking and childbearing; she told me stories about menstruation and pregnancy; she told me stories about gods and heroes, about fairies and elves, about goddesses and spirits; she told me stories about the land and the sky. . . . She told me European stories and Laguna stories; she told me Catholic stories and Presbyterian stories; she told me city stories and country stories; she told me political stories and religious stories. She told me stories about living and stories about dying. And in all of those stories she told me who I was, who I was supposed to be, whom I came from, and who would follow me. In this way she taught me the meaning of the words she said, that all life is a circle and everything has a place within it.[7]

The Indian and Native Alaskan women I talked to have integrated the wisdom of the ancients passed down orally, using it to adapt to a changing world. As they speak out in defense of land,

culture, natural law, and sacred traditions, they often acknowledge the influence of the old ones. Women old and young report
that ancestral voices are a palpable presence in their lives.

When I first began gathering this material, I sought out
prominent Native American women. Then an Indian woman I
talked to said, "Women like that get plenty of recognition. Go
and find those behind the scenes doing the work that keeps our
communities together." She and others provided leads. I found
that "ordinary" women can be extraordinary. I found that younger
women moving in new directions possess vision and commitment. I included the voices of women of all ages and walks of life,
representing as many communities as possible.

I looked for interviewees who were connected to their people, but soon learned that such connections can be tenuous.
Mixed-blood poet Wendy Rose returned to her father's Hopi
community in search of family only to be relegated to the outer
fringes because her mother was not Hopi. Nevertheless, her poetry affirms a profound sense of oneness with Native people.

I asked the women what it was like to walk the precarious
path between Indian and white value systems. Flo Wiger told me,
"I always felt like I had to be an interpreter. I still do." I asked
mixed-blood women what it was like being an outsider in two
worlds. Wendy Rose offered this perspective: "We are part of an
additional mainstream . . . we carry the blood of the oppressors as
well as of the oppressed."

In their quest for self-definition, Native women have had to find
a way to reconcile traditional tribal perceptions of women with the
sometimes conflicting standards of the dominant society. Pursuing
this theme, I asked a few questions about home, family, and community to provoke thought, then listened intently, picking up
threads as they emerged. As each woman indicated what was important to her, that became the focal point of the interview.

Women shared stories about their female role models. Con-
tradicting that docile Indian woman myth, they cited instances of

women past and present accorded respect as decision makers, active in governing councils of their nations and in ceremony. Said painter Emmi Whitehorse, who grew up in the fifties and sixties on the Navajo Reservation: "The female owned everything, the woman ran everything." Said another Navajo woman, "For the most part, they still do."

Sometimes spontaneously, sometimes in response to my questions, the women reflected on the messages imparted by parents and grandparents that gave direction to their lives, as well as the constraints imposed on them by community and church. They seemed genuinely challenged by the process of looking at old practices, trying to determine why some had been relinquished, some preserved, still others adapted for today. I asked, "To what extent did you remain within the pathways set down for you? To what extent did you break away and forge your own path?" The responses of Indian and Native Alaskan women reveal a remarkable ability to adjust to changes in the outside world while remaining rooted.

In the Everglades, Miccosukee Virginia Poole spoke of ancient spiritual values and teachings that she is passing on to her progeny. "Is child rearing a community responsibility?" I queried. "Oh it is," she replied. "We're responsible for human beings. We try to teach the children what we were taught . . ." Gladys Alexie, a Gwich'in woman, gave this glimpse of her community's child-rearing customs:

> I adopted my child when he was five days old. My brother and sister-in-law were having their fourth child and asked me if I wanted the baby. In our culture, if you have children and someone in your family like your sister can't have a child, you give her one of yours. Or you may give your first child to the grandparents so they are not alone. That's our tradition.[8]

Native women were forthright about indicating which aspects of their spiritual realm can be discussed, which are inviolate. Said one woman: "I feel connected to our spiritual traditions, but because I don't know our language, I don't like to talk about them; I'm not a spokesperson."

Some of the women shared their creation stories embodying images of women. Origin stories reflect the highest ideals of a culture, as well as its most corrupt elements, thus serving as vehicles for presenting moral choices. One Lakota creation story speaks of woman as "the maker of choices." Another, told by a Lakota woman in this book, tells how a holy woman brought the people the sacred pipe and taught them how to live in harmony. Some of the women's life histories highlight the Native American mode of understanding the world through story, dream, and prophecy, which is so different from the Euramerican analytical worldview.

Collecting life stories from those who are witnesses to history, one wrestles with the issue of credibility. We all view the past through the sometimes flawed lens of memory. Even a much-respected tribal historian may omit crucial details, his or her perspective may be based on apocryphal stories or colored by emotion. Inherent knowledge of tribal teachings may be obscured by "education" in mission or Bureau of Indian Affairs schools. There is no way back, no sure way to verify what happened in the past.

Ultimately I decided not to mediate between individual perceptions and information that is public knowledge; I decided not to undermine the power of the spoken word. I provide brief passages of historical background to make it clear that the women's stories are firmly grounded in the real world. I offer testimonies coming from different vantage points, trusting the reader to continue the search for information.

There is an information gap. Native Americans themselves admit to being part of the conspiracy of silence that has excluded their voices from the history books. Some bought into the white man's paradigm and accepted their assigned role as victim. Facing the extinction of their Indian identity in government and mission schools, feeling like "nonpersons," they submitted in silence to a system they felt powerless to change. A conversation with Flathead painter Jaune Quick-to-See Smith shed light on this subject:

> Growing up in an Indian community, we learned to say yes to everything so we'd be agreeable; that's what you had to do to get by when you were dealing with a government agency, a welfare worker, the church.[9]

The silence of Native people was often misread by whites as stoicism. Hoping to get behind the myth of "the wooden Indian," I paid attention to the emotional climate each woman created as she told her story. Rose Mary Barstow recalled traumatic events with intense emotion. Rose Bluestone told of the hanging of her great-grandfather in 1862 following a trial many considered a travesty. She heard about it from her grandmother. "It made me feel so sad," she told me, but she did not verbalize anger. Upper Skagit elder Vi Hilbert said that when she had marital troubles she told no one, not even her relatives. "Was it considered a weakness to express emotion?" I asked. "No," she said, "but I was taught to keep my emotional life in perspective, not to let my feelings take over."

Some women were less guarded. Assiniboine physician Lois Steele talked about suicidal "games" played by young Native Americans on her reservation and about the fight against disease and drug addiction. Steele is a raconteur with an ironic sense of humor. "Did your sense of humor help you to cope with job stress?" I asked. "If you live in an Indian community, being able to laugh at yourself is survival," she replied. She also shared stories that show how Indians use humor as a secret weapon against manipulative white people.

Some women tended to choose their words carefully because a verbal misstep could embroil them in controversy.[10] Tulalip Janet McCloud, however, spoke her mind irreverently, exposing abuse and sham, attacking commercialism in both Native and white society. McCloud, like Ramona Bennett and Lois Steele, couched anger in biting humor.

Some individuals chose to focus on personal, formative experiences. Others emphasized the larger issues of tribal sovereignty and the survival of the planet. Each interview uncovered another layer of a world that is richly textured. I felt honored by the women's candor and awed by the strength of their convictions.

A woman telling her life story often weaves a design out of the fragments of her experience. As she highlights events having special meaning, calling attention to patterns and motifs, she reinvents herself. The most memorable interviews were those in which I was able to remain in the background, listening, while an individual took charge of her life story.

All the interviews were conducted in English; all were taped. They took place in homes, offices, restaurants, occasionally over long-distance telephone. An individual's home provided the best setting because then there was a comfort level—we drank tea, I met dogs, parrots, and children, we laughed together. Forming relationships with the women, promising to let them review the text and make corrections before publication helped build trust.

Working from transcripts, I included the women's words as spoken. Here and there I corrected a departure from Standard English because the women asked me to, I omitted a digression, condensed, grouped related passages together so the narrative would be readable while meticulously preserving the language, ideas, and conversational flavor of each interviewee. Because my questions interrupted the flow of the narrative, I deleted most of them. When part of a story needed clarification, I went back to the women if it was feasible. I included a few of my own observations in order to give an outsider's perspective. I sent or brought the text to each woman for her changes and approval.

The last process is the most critical of all. Indigenous women are not "informants" or remnants from some exotic world. They do not need an omniscient interviewer to interpret for them or transform their stories; they are articulate individuals quite capable of speaking for themselves, but many have not had the access to the media that they deserve. Native women shared with me a part of themselves. At all times when doing this work, I feel ethically bound to set down their stories faithfully.

The six chapter headings of the book serve as structural devices but may not satisfy those demanding narrowly focused categories. Life stories range over many different time periods, subjects, and themes and thus do not fit into neatly designed compartments.

Common threads do tie the chapters together. The first introduces women grounded in tradition, comfortable with both continuity and change. Chapter two records the stories of women displaced from land and culture, finding their way back. They see the government policy of relocation and "reeducation" of Indian people as an attempt to make reservations and their residents obsolete; unwilling to fade away, these women share their strategies for surviving. The third chapter highlights women repairing the ruptures in urban Indian communities through their pioneering efforts in community service, creating colleges, making art, and "making relatives." Chapter four introduces reservation voices: a former tribal chairwoman currently a child advocate, a shopkeeper, a physician, a poet; women who live on the Rez or revisit it often for it is their "home" and the people are the source of their strength.

Tribes are sovereign nations, their rights protected by treaties that are under assault by government and industry. Many nations that have submitted to pressures to amend or abrogate treaties have seen their economic and political strength eroded along with the land base. Chapter five brings into sharp focus the issue of the appropriation of the culture and resources of indigenous people. Treaty activist Ojibway Esther Nahgahnub voices her concern about the despoiling of the environment: "Someone should declare the earth a sovereign Nation."

The last chapter features women who are the bearers of sacred traditions that have changed little through the centuries. As they describe participation in sweat lodges, Sun Dances, and blessing ceremonies on sacred ground, they affirm their connection to the earth and to the human community.

In a sort of counterpoint, certain motifs are introduced, with variations recurring throughout the book. There is wide agreement that Native people must look within themselves for solutions to their problems, that entrepreneurship will make men and women self-sufficient, that culture and language are cohesive forces contributing to the survival of Native communities.

Native American women value their roles as mothers and grandmothers, as teachers, storytellers, and healers. At the same time, they are moving into nontraditional roles, working as environmental scientists, physicians, engineers, construction workers, attorneys, corporation executives. They design and implement progressive programs in their communities. Speaking out in Congress and the United Nations, they influence national policy and global awareness.

The reader looking for "the truth" about Native American women will not find it here or within the pages of any book. But journey with me from tribal school in the woods to "sister school," from the pueblos to the Arctic, from past to present to a vision of the future. You will have a sense that you are viewing women's lives through a kaleidoscope highlighting shifting perspectives and variegated colors.

Throughout *Messengers of the Wind*, First Nations women reach into the deepest part of themselves, telling us who they are and where they are going. If we listen to their voices, we will hear their spirits singing and healing. If we heed their messages, we may learn how to repair the tears in the world so their children, and all children, will find a safe haven on earth.

Editor's Note: Tribal affiliations were provided by the interviewees.

NOTES

1. From a conversation with the author, March 8, 1994.

2. Reverend Peter Jones, *History of the Ojibway Indians*, 60 (London, 1861), cited in Priscilla Buffalohead, "Farmers, Warriors, Traders: A Fresh Look at Ojibway Women," *Minnesota History* (Summer 1983), pp. 236 ff.

3. Katherine M. Weist, "Beasts of Burden and Menial Slaves," in Pat Albers and Beatrice Medicine, *The Hidden Half: Studies of Plains Indian Women* (Lanham, Md.: University Press of America, 1983), p. 42.

4. Weist, p. 45.

5. Sherman Alexie, "A Tale of Two Geronimos," *Seattle Weekly*, January 5, 1994.

6. Linda Hogan, "Blessings," *Songs from This Earth on Turtle's Back*, ed. Joseph Bruchac (New York: Greenfield Review Press, 1983), p. 117.

7. Paula Gunn Allen, *The Sacred Hoop: Recovering the Feminine in American Indian Traditions* (Boston: Beacon Press, 1986), p. 46.

8. From a (telephone) conversation with the author, June 9, 1994.

9. From a conversation with the author, July 14, 1990.

10. In the interviews, women described interactions they have had with those representing "the system," whether it was white- or Indian-dominated. They recalled conflicts within tribal communities exacerbated by changing values and by outside forces. On reading the text, some deleted these observations. Those in public life are most likely to feel vulnerable. One told me, "I'm being considered for a major job within the Bureau of Indian Affairs, and they're going over everything I said or wrote." Another woman said, "If you speak out against the regime in power on the Rez, you won't get a job or a house with indoor plumbing." Today, as in the past, internecine struggles plague the tribes; one who takes a stand against the establishment may face repercussions.

GLADYS ALEXIE AND CORY   *Photo by Dick Bancroft*

I

Walking the Trail from Yesterday to Today

I work in an office. I sit on our band council. Weekends in the summer we go about twenty-five miles up the Peel River to fish camp. We camp alongside a creek near the stony riverbank. The hills on both sides of the river are in bloom with spruce, birch and willow trees. It's quiet and serene. You go there and forget everything. It's always been like that . . .

GLADYS ALEXIE
GWICH'IN▽/ATHABASCAN▽

1

We Have to Have Ceremonies

SOGE TRACK
TAOS PUEBLO[1]

Taos, in northern New Mexico, is the home of the Ia sla pi, the Red Willow People. In the shadow of the Sangre de Cristo Mountains, they live in a walled, five-story adobe "apartment complex" called "the village," which has changed little since its construction in 1100 A.D. There is no running water or electricity. What binds the people of Taos Pueblo together is a belief in the sanctity of their life on the land and the determination to hold on to their forests and sacred Blue Lake high in the mountains above Taos, both sources of life-giving nourishment.

Soge Track grew up in the village, but when we met, she was living in a small stucco house nearby on Pueblo land, where, she said, "the sagebrush and piñon meet the mountains." A potter and a skilled communicator, she was then curator of Native American arts at the Millicent Rogers Museum in Taos. As we sat in front of her house and talked, children played in the sandy earth, meadowlarks sang, and Soge Track spoke about her people, who try to live each day as if it were a prayer.

THERE ARE ABOUT ONE HUNDRED PEOPLE LIVING IN the village today. Most have day jobs in the town, but they supplement their income by doing pottery, silver jewelry and beadwork that is sold in the village.

My family has always lived in Taos Pueblo. I have relatives living in the village. We are a close family, very traditional. We speak the Tiwa language.[2]

When I was a child, my grandparents lived all winter in three rooms in the village. Grandmother took care of the house—it was immaculate. Nothing was ever out of place. My grandfather raised cattle and horses outside the pueblo walls. He walked into town every day to garden for a white man. During the 1930s, he earned fifty cents a day at that job.

My grandparents had a summer house near here where they lived all through the summer until fall. My grandmother built it out of adobe—just one little room. She hauled the water for the adobe. My grandfather put the roof on it and other people helped, so it was a team effort. They had a garden. Grandfather planted maybe five or six acres of alfalfa. He did all the heavy work—the plowing and irrigating. Grandmother helped with the hoeing and weeding.

My grandmother didn't speak English. Her whole life was here at the pueblo. She grew up in a time when men were important: women took care of them. She didn't like to go very far away, but I remember once she went to Oklahoma for a powwow.

My mother grew up in the village, she graduated from the 12th grade at the Santa Fe Indian school, and went to work in people's homes. When she went away to California to work, she met my father and they were married there, but because he was in the service, she came back home. My father came to Taos looking for his wife, Veronica Suazo, and was confronted by tribal officials. Although he was in his army uniform and in a jeep, they put him in jail. They were so closed to outsiders at that time, they put him in jail. His commanding officer had to come from Santa Fe to get him out. So right from the beginning he had real strong feelings about this place.

My father was Sioux, from Fort Thompson, South Dakota. Our tribe is patrilineal, and there's the belief that a woman

SOGE TRACK

Photo by Julie Webster

should live with her husband's people, but my mother didn't want to live in South Dakota, so my parents settled here. My grandfather added on a room for them on the second level of the family home.

Since this is such a small community, everybody gets involved in your life. That probably bothered my father—it probably affected his machismo. He was from a tribe that moved from place to place, and I think that's why he never really settled down. I think maybe the mountains bothered him. These are very powerful mountains. I think maybe he missed the starkness of the landscape up there—I don't know. But on a whim he'd go to South Dakota and stay there for a while, and then come back. He was a mechanic; he had jobs here working in service stations.

My mother continued working in homes. I think my mother always felt she was in her right place doing what she was doing: working, and taking care of her family. That's the mentality she grew up with. In the western mind, everything is taken apart and examined under a microscope to see what works, what doesn't work. But in the Native mind, it's all part of a continuum. Women have their capabilities, men have theirs, and neither can really function without the other.

I think it was that way historically in the village. I remember as a child going with my grandmother to visit other people in their summer homes. You'd hear the birds. The husband would be outside hoeing, the wife was inside cooking. People greeted each other formally, but there was real gentleness, a sense of being connected to other people.

Men made most of the decisions and they still do. They're the ones who run the government. But I think a man is only as strong as the woman behind him, or with him, because she can certainly influence him. We all have to coexist. It's a simple way to live, based on respect for life, for humanity. The most successful relationships are those based on respect for each other's space. A man will say, "I'm going up to the mountain today." And the woman will say, "Let me pack you a lunch," without asking questions. You know, he's gone, and you just have to let him go. And you have your own things to work on. So there's an interchange.

That's how our ceremonies are. You hear about how they are conducted by men, but they're not. Men have their ceremonies, women have theirs, and sometimes we come together. It is our strong sense of ceremony and ritual that keeps my people together.

Our ceremonies are about time, and the seasons. We think about how we're going to survive, how we're going to make things better for our children in the future. There are ceremonies almost every day. We have to have ceremonies: planting ceremonies, healing ceremonies, ceremonies about taking care of life.

We have ceremonies of rejoicing at the time of a birth. Our names have special meaning for us. When a child is born, family members get together to compose a new name for that individual. Our way is different from western society: our names are not inherited or passed down.

We have ceremonies of transition to acknowledge the changes one goes through from birth to old age. A young woman is nurtured by her aunts and grandmothers who share with her the traditional ways. The way one acquires knowledge is by being alert and aware, and listening. At family gatherings, at feast days, a lot of things are passed on. As you grow up, you are given information about who you are, your family history. The whole area is a place of instruction.[3]

From ancient times, our ceremonies have been continuous, but they are always being interrupted because of the westernization of cultures. Our ceremonies have been threatened since the Spanish arrived in the pueblos in 1540. They tried to force us to live their way.

The Spaniards came to the pueblos in search of gold. Disappointed, they attempted colonization at gunpoint, which they termed "pacification." The Pueblos joined with their ancient enemies the Apaches and fought back, but the Spaniards prevailed by sheer force, killing warriors in their kivas, enslaving women and children, converting Indians to Catholicism.

That was a terrible time, a bloody time. They tried to control us. They tried to force their religion on us. You know, during the Pueblo revolt, 150 women and children took sanctuary in the church, thinking this symbol of the Christian God would protect them, but they were killed. My grandfather always said, "My ancestors were not meek people, they were strong people, survivors. They put up a fight; they died fighting."

I think that in spite of the intervention of the missionaries, we continued to have our songs and our prayers—they are a part of our daily lives. We continued to practice our ceremonies secretly in our own language. We still live close to the land. We continue to believe that our ceremonies are for us—they must be kept sacred and secret. The reason we have survived is because we have been so secretive.

There's a time and place where you give thanks, where you ask for things, where you give things. Taking in, giving out and sharing with people—that is the breath of life. There isn't any huge mystique or formula that one follows. It's where your heart is, it's how you feel about nature, how you treat other people.

When I plant my garden, I give an offering to Mother Earth, and pray for a good crop. Everyone has their own way of doing it. I put myself in a space where I have no anger, because however you feel is the energy you're putting into that seed in the ground. You can't be upset, you can't be rushing off to an appointment. You have to be in a calm state of mind. It's almost a meditation. You pray that you will have a good harvest, that you will have gentle rains, that your crop will grow to be beautiful and nourish you and your family and friends. You pray that the earth will feel good.

I witnessed the annual Corn Dance in the pueblo. About fifty women of all ages, some with wrinkled, brown faces, assembled in the sunlit square attired in brightly colored mantas,[4] necklaces of silver and turquoise, deerskin leggings, and moccasins. They carried garlands of orange and purple flowers. Just one young man—his body painted, his hair plaited in a long braid with feathers—joined the dancing, shaking a rattle. They danced in a circle while in the background, against the adobe walls, older men, their heads and shoulders covered with shawls, sang and drummed.

The Corn Dance is not done as entertainment or on whim. It is an annual ceremony. By now, people have put their corn in, and so the dance, the drum, the movement of the moccasined feet, those are all movements of prayer. The drumbeat represents the heartbeat—when you stand close, you can feel it go through the earth.

My people dance in celebration of life. We have the strength, we have the power to touch the earth with the blessing of new life.

I was born in 1949. I was given a name by my relatives. Your name is very special—that's who you are. My Tiwa name is Ta uh sema. I'm spelling it phonetically—the language is not written. It means something like "Be happy to dance." My grandmother gave it to me.

I went to BIA [Bureau of Indian Affairs] and Catholic schools, and to Taos High School. I did my postgraduate work at the Institute of American Indian Arts in Santa Fe, studying ceramics, writing and theater.

I was fortunate at a young age to be exposed to the world outside the pueblo. Because my father was from South Dakota, we traveled there. Going through different towns, I realized there were other ways people lived. I wanted to see the Louvre, so I went to France. I remember my grandmother cried when I left. Another year, I went to Cuba. I was fortunate to be able to travel, but it wasn't always easy to make the transition back to the pueblo.

My life today is so different from my mother's life. I value my independence. I feel that you should be independent, should be able to make your own decisions without asking permission. The men in my life haven't always agreed. [Laughs.] I guess that's why I'm alone now. My daughter's father is from the village. He's a part of our lives, but we don't live together.

When my daughter was little, we lived in the village on the second story. My grandparents were living there then, and I wanted to expose her to traditional ways. It was so nice because whenever people were dancing in the village square, we'd sit on the second story and watch.

One day I was working in clay, and my friend said, "There's a job open at the museum in town; you'd better get dressed up and go down there." I thought, "Get dressed up?" Well, I put on some nylons and heels, I went to the interview and they hired me as assistant curator. I'm involved with Pueblo and Plains arts, I'm an advocate for Indian artists. But it was funny. Each day I'd put on my heels and I'd have to tiptoe on the roof of the pueblo because the heels would sink in, and then my sister would have a fit because her place was leaking. I'd go down the ladder in my heels, stumbling, I'd go to work, I'd come back home and put on my moccasins.

Eventually, I said, "What am I doing?" We moved out and rented this house. When you have a job in town and have to dress a certain way, it certainly does help to have running water and electricity, and not have to keep going up and down the ladder. [Laughs.]

It's so beautiful here. We have Chinese elm, we have chokecherries and wild plums that give off the most wonderful smell. We will dry them in the fall, and will eat them through the winter. I wrote a poem a long time ago about wild plums.

> *Kite flying time in Tibet,*
> *children eating moon cakes,*
> *jumping and laughing.*
> *Plum trees encircle pueblo boy's home.*
> *In the spring, they bloom.*
> *When he goes hunting,*
> *he comes back with a plum blossom hat.*

I've never been to Tibet, but I've always felt a connection. When I was a child, I used to go up to the fifth story of the pueblo on a full moon night, and lie there, just imagining the pyramids in the Yucatán, or some temple in Tibet. I think it was the space, and the mountains.

We've had to protect our forests. That struggle goes way back. When my grandfather was a young man with three children to support, he went hunting in the mountains with two Taos men and they killed a deer. They were confronted by two forest rangers, and were accused of poaching. One of the Indians was badly beaten, all three were arrested. My mother told me that she went to the jail to bring food to her father. My grandfather pleaded guilty, and spent only a few weeks in jail. One of the other men did not, and he served a year in the state penitentiary in Santa Fe.[5] So that's what it was like in that time. The U.S. Forest Service wanted control of this land.

In the 1930s, the government wanted to take over the mountain. That would have killed our animals, it would have destroyed our forests, and the Blue Lake. Water from Blue Lake irrigates the pueblo. That lake is our sacred holy place that we cannot live without, and we refuse to.

If they had taken that land, it would have destroyed our culture, we would have died, it would have been genocide.

We are supposed to have religious freedom in this country. The government had the audacity to say that our lake was just a lake with fish in it, that it was not sacred and had no religious significance. My grandfather Eliseo Suazo was involved in the fight. Paul Bernal, my grandfather's nephew, was interpreter and secretary for the Tribal Council of Elders, and he spent many years fighting the government, going to Washington, going to the Supreme Court, helping to develop legislation.

All the Tiwa people were involved, even the children. We all knew in our hearts it was not right for them to take away our holy place. Everyone was told, "This is a time when you have to put play aside; you are going to sit down with people in the community and support them," and that's what we did. We came together, we put all our energies together. So when we had the hearings in Washington, tribal members went, and our religious leader, the cacique went, and Paul Bernal interpreted, and spoke very touching words to get the Blue Lake back.

On December 2, 1970, HR 471, known as "the Blue Lake bill," passed in the Senate. Taos spiritual leader Juan de Jesus Romero paid tribute to the nation's leaders who took a stand to protect "what this America is—really beautiful, peace, honesty, truth, understanding . . ." Then, tribal members, old and young, took part in a pilgrimage, walking thirty miles up the mountain to Blue Lake—to give energy back to the earth.[6]

We were ecstatic when the bill passed. I remember the celebration in the village, the speeches of all the dignitaries. The bill provided for the return of forty-seven thousand acres of land to the tribe. It set a precedent for other tribes to fight for their endangered holy places. Although the Religious Freedom Act was passed in 1978, there are still hearings involving two thousand acres including roadways leading to the lake. Every day when we say our prayers, Blue Lake is in our minds.

We believe we are a part of nature; we are nature. There's four-leggeds and two-leggeds, and we, the two-leggeds, happen to have intellect, but all of us have to live here, all of us have to respect one another and the earth. That's what our world view is, and our world view is who we are.

The following year, Soge Track left her museum job, and moved back to the village where she lives today, doing pottery.

In this day and age, we have children growing up here at the pueblo who follow our life way; they take part in our ceremonies. Still, they go to public school and learn how to deal with the western mind, just as I did. You know, white people who come here are often surprised that we don't wear feathers!

When I was growing up in the pueblo, all the women did pottery, and I learned from them. I get my clay in the Sangre de Cristo mountains, national forest land. Before I take the clay, I say a prayer. I'd like to get some clay from around here. The older women who know where it is have all passed away, but they're here in the beauty of this place. We are energy moving in different times, and they don't leave us. This is the land they came from and they've gone back to it. Sometimes I feel as if they are talking to me, telling me to hold onto their teaching, to pass it on.

I continue living on the second story of the village. I'm living the way I was raised. Living my life in this place is a ceremony of survival.

From interviews with the author, June 13, 1992, and September 24, 1994.

NOTES

1. The term Pueblo refers to Indian tribes of common ancestry living in New Mexico and Arizona. The Spanish word for *town* is *pueblo*.

2. The Tiwa language differs from Tewa, the language of some other Pueblo peoples.

3. Soge Track spoke of ceremonial practices which prepare young men and women for adult responsibilities, but she explained that this is "sensitive material." Because of the tribe's tradition of secrecy, it cannot be published without authorization from the tribe.

4. The traditional ceremonial dress, which covers one shoulder.

5. This historic event is the basis for the novel *The Man Who Killed the Deer* by Frank Waters (New York: Farrar & Rinehart, 1941).

6. R. C. Gordon-McCutchan, *The Taos Indians and the Battle For Blue Lake* (Santa Fe, N.M.: Red Crane Books, 1991).

See also Cloud Bringing Rain and Marguerite Culp, "Our Blue Lake Lands," *Native Peoples* (Spring 1992), pp. 39–43.

2

Men and Women
Lived with the Seasons

FLORENCE KENNEY
INUPIAT[1]/NATIVE ALASKAN

As a child, Florence Kenney fished for subsistence in the icy waters
of the Bering Sea. Taken to a mission school, she learned powerful
lessons about adult manipulation of children and had to use her wits
to survive.

I met Florence Kenney shortly after she had moved to Seattle at
the age of fifty-eight. She was adjusting to city life: she swam daily in a
chlorine pool, played chess and Scrabble, and sometimes fished in
Puget Sound. As we sat and talked in a gazebo on the grounds of her
condominium, she grew contemplative: "I think the Eskimo[2] people
have a collective memory that has come down through the centuries, a
memory of what to do in certain circumstances."

Florence Kenney is petite, with short brown hair and gentle eyes.
Although at first reserved, she showed me the journals she had kept for
thirty years. "I'd like to write the story of how I was raised," she said,
"but I don't have a typewriter." Then she began telling her story, her
brown eyes lit up, and she came to life.

I WAS BORN IN 1934 IN A PLACE CALLED KANAKANAK,
Alaska. It's near Bristol Bay, a fishing area above the Aleutian
chain. It's a huge area. On my birth certificate, for place of birth
it says "at large." My parents were real nomadic. We traveled

by dog sled. We went to beaver camp in the fall or winter, and fished in the summer. Our life—it was survival, living from year to year.

We lived in the bush. It was flat country with winding streams, wolves, bear, moose, mink and lots of birdlife. We lived in one-room log cabins. People only had ice houses when they were out hunting and could find no other shelter.

We ate little birds. We went out and picked berries on the hillside. I remember my dad would make pancakes—he'd roll them up, put a little jam inside, that was a meal. We drank tea. There were many wild plants—beach grass, heavy sedge—we chopped the bottoms off and used that as a green.

The whole area is one big pharmacy. You could go out and pick up things for stomach cramps, you could get Labrador tea (from the Labrador tea plant) to make yourself sleepy. If you got a headache, you'd take powder from the wild anemone, mix it in a little water and drink it. It works. If you had to have a tooth removed, you'd use a bigger dosage and it would knock you out. If you hated somebody and wanted him gone from your life, you could give him a really large dose, and he'd never wake up. [Laughs.] So it's great stuff!

The jobs of men and women were handed down by tradition. When the man brought in a moose or a fish, he got a lot of glory, he was a "good provider." It was up to the woman to make sure it got on the table. She would cure it to preserve it in some way. If the man was a hunter, the woman didn't say, "Hey, I want my own life, I want to go sell hats." She went with her husband. I don't think anyone thought of disturbing tradition.

My mother made clothing for the family from skins. She had a hand-cranked sewing machine. We had catalogues from Sears and Montgomery Ward, and she sent for some things. When I was about three, my mother contracted tuberculosis and had to go to the hospital. In those days, when you had tuberculosis, you spent years and years away from your family. So I never got to really know my mom.

The way I remember my mom, she was sick all the time, all the time. That's how I remember her.

Did the elders give me support? You could go and get an elder's advice, but I think this elder thing has been blown up out of proportion. If we saw our relatives once a year for a family gathering it was okay because the territory was so vast, people lived so far apart, we traveled by dog sled and boat, so we didn't have close family ties. Our grandma was farther north, twelve hundred miles away. I don't think we were lonely. I don't think that's something my people felt then. Maybe now from being exposed to books and television—all the stress on family togetherness.

My older sister did the cooking and cleaning. After my mom went to the hospital, my father couldn't take care of us, so my brothers, my sisters and I were sent to Holy Cross Mission on the Lower Yukon River. This area was under the jurisdiction of the Catholic Church. The missionaries brought comfort and material goods—cooking pots, clothing, and the people looked up to them. I suppose it was a power play. I think it was the business of the Catholics, taking souls. During the war years, if orphans were found in the villages, or if their parents couldn't take care of them, they were sent to the missions.

Both my parents drank, but I don't like to think about that. My mother brought us to the mission—I remember her down the long corridor smiling and waving. Sure, it must have been hard for her, but she was probably happy too that we would be taken care of, we wouldn't be hungry and cold anymore, we would have a stable environment without moving all over the country. I hardly saw her after that. She died when I was twelve.

I don't remember the transition to the mission being difficult—females are adaptable. It was like another camping ground. I've never become attached to a place, I've never missed a place. I think my people are like that. Home is inside of you.

School separated us; I hardly ever saw my little sister or brothers. We had to speak English, so most of us forgot our language. We couldn't even ask about traditions or stories—nobody did.[3] We didn't have names, we were called by numbers—like I was Miss 14. We looked different from each other, but our souls and spirits were all in the same mold. We were little frozen people. All the time I was growing up, nobody ever hugged me. And you know, I didn't miss it, because I never had it.

We woke up by a bell, we marched to church by a bell, to class, to meals—we lived by bells. We were in class until five-thirty in the evening. The classes were very well run. Nobody even thought about goofing off. We studied and did our work. It seemed like I was born knowing how to read. I loved school. It was a refuge from all the hard work.

After class, we worked on a rotation system—one month we'd cook, the next month we'd empty the buckets for the outdoor toilets and scrub them with lye, the next we'd scrub and wax the church floors, the next we'd take care of the little children. We learned to sew. We planted and harvested vegetable gardens. We were taught to be housewives. But we never had a hammer in our hands, never got to tinker under a car. I always thought it would be fun to take a motor apart.

We were beaten regularly, for anything. When I was maybe fourteen, I went to lay on my bed to read although the dormitory was off limits during the day. One of the nuns, we called her "Mistress," came in and said, "What are you doing, Miss 14?" I jumped off the bed, but she came after me. Beating was part of the program. Years later I had nightmares of running and running from one of the nuns.

We all had long braids. Girls had their braids cut off if they did something wrong. Boys who misbehaved had their heads shaved; they had to wear girl's clothing for three months, and get beaten. My sister and her girlfriend spent the night at an Indian woman's cabin listening to the radio. Next morning, they were seen on the hillside, they had to come down, and for punishment, their hair was cut off. A few days later, I was in a funny mood, and when I passed my sister, I said, "Hey, how do you like your new hairdo?" She turned and slapped my face, she started crying and ran off. That night, our mistress called me into a little cubicle, she said, "Sit here!"—she was in back of me—and suddenly, she cut off one of my braids, then she cut the other one off. I froze. I stayed frozen for a year.

Nobody talked about sexual abuse. Years later, my sister had to go to a psychiatrist and work her way through childhood incidents of sexual abuse by one of the nuns, but I wasn't aware of it at the time. I remember her running away a lot up into the hills, and I had to go and get her and talk her back down, but she never told me. She never told me. In later years, it came out.

I didn't know what sex was. You know, the Catholic Church doesn't teach you about sex. [Laughs.] There were a few girls who married right when they were still in school, married boys from the villages. The night before the wedding, the sister would come with a little black leather book called a *Marriage Manual* and the girl had to read it—everything pertaining to sex, procreation, how to get along with your husband forever.

I remember a group of us girls waiting till a bride to be was asleep, then we crawled along in the dark and felt under her mattress looking for the *Marriage Manual* because we wanted to know what to expect. Birth control? No discussion of that. If you thought of boys, you were called a child of the devil. We were raised to do our work, and keep our mouths shut. Then we were supposed to suddenly get married, and have a lot of good Catholic children.

My girlfriend got these two big adding machine rolls, and we thought we'd make comic books. We drew this girl and boy having a relationship—they kissed and hugged, that kind of stuff. I would draw part of it, I would hand it across the aisle to my girlfriend, and she'd draw a little more. The girl and boy got to the point where they were taking each other's clothes off, but we didn't know what happened after that—we had no idea. So that was the end of the comic. Well, a few days later, one of our mistresses found it. Oh, she called us up before the whole assembly, she said we were followers of Satan, we were going to hell. Nobody was to talk to us or associate with us.

I was embarrassed, I felt ashamed. But it was good artwork. [Laughs.] We never wrote the last chapter of the comic. But I started keeping journals, and writing stories. It seemed like there was always a little ball of fire inside me that never did quite go out. If I needed courage, if I needed companionship, it was there, inside me. Nobody could make it die.

I went to the mission school through eighth grade. I was supposed to go to the Catholic high school, but it was filled, so I never went to high school. I stayed at the mission doing all the dirty work, and taking care of the children. I did artwork too—I designed patterns for fur coats for the women of the village. We weren't allowed in the village often but the sisters brought this work to us.

At fifteen or sixteen, I think I was going through a nervous breakdown. We were still getting beaten. One of the nuns was so cruel, it seemed like everything bad that happened was blamed on me. She did terrible things to me. I remember walking around for a year up and down the hallways, up and down the stairs—tears coming down my face. I would be scrubbing the floors, and I'd be crying. I thought I was going crazy. I'd tell myself I had no reason to cry, but I couldn't stop myself. I quit talking, I quit associating with everybody.

I think it was the sister superior who went and told the father superior that I was having these problems. The priest—he was older, maybe fifty-two—I'd be sent to him for a talk. He would draw the shades in the girls' building, he'd hug and kiss me and rub me and press me to his body. I wouldn't call it sexual abuse because I liked the feeling of his arms around me—nobody had hugged me before. Finally, I was in the fold like the sheep.

Well, I was supposed to marry a village boy. His mother gave me her wedding ring. Then the priest who was hugging and kissing me told me that this boy had a baby by another woman in Anchorage and was no good, and he didn't want me to marry him. So I said okay, and I gave the ring back.

When I was eighteen, I was sent away to take care of a couple of children for a dollar a day in McGrath, on the tundra, a long way from Holy Cross Mission. I think it had come to the point where the priest couldn't handle it. The nuns were afraid that since I was older, things might go farther, so they decided to send me away. I went to my sister in Anchorage, then I got a job, and that was my entry into the world. I didn't know how to use the telephone, I didn't know how an elevator worked. I learned by watching.

Anchorage was rough. There was an air base with thousands of air force and army men, and there was a lot of sexual harassment. In the two years I was there, it seemed like I spent most of it hitting men with my purse just to get away. My girlfriend and I were walking to a show, and all the way, there was this carful of servicemen who kept screaming at us—how they would take us off into the bushes, and what they would do to us—it was frightening. We crossed the street, but they circled back. Finally, we picked up rocks, and when they came along, we shattered their windshield, and ran. That was the end of them.

Was there sexual harassment by Native men? I don't think Eskimo men did that. In the old days, there was a lot of sharing: our people shared their homes and their food. There was no word in our language for stealing, because since everything was shared, nobody had to steal. I think that if a man shared his wife with another Eskimo man, it was with her consent—unless her husband was a cruel man. Generally, a woman's wishes would be considered because she was part of the ongoing process of maintaining life.

Men and women lived with the seasons. A woman's life was hard. She didn't choose to go out and spend days in the snow and ice trying to get a moose or a seal. You know, a woman's a little smarter—she'd do a little trading with her husband: "I'll stay home and sew your clothes." Then she'd stay by the warm fire while he went out and endangered his life getting the food.

I want you to know, Jane, these are my private thoughts after all my years of reading and thinking. I haven't gone back to the villages. Some people may disagree—they're entitled to their opinion. I think our people have a memory white people don't have, an ongoing thing. I can think what a woman thought thousands of years ago—it's trickled down through the Eskimo people.

I used to hear stories of old Eskimo women who stripped themselves naked, and walked off in the snow and ice to freeze to death. They did it so there would be one less mouth to feed. There may have been men who did that, but I never heard about it. The women remembered their grandmothers did it—the storytelling went on from generation to generation. We don't question it because we know it's true.

My mother's father was a medicine man for the Inupiat, a really powerful person. He wanted another man's wife, so when the man was gone, he took this woman and her children, and they went way inland to avoid the husband. He wound up with two wives and eight children, so I've got some half cousins. [Laughs.]

In Anchorage, I met my first husband. He was part American Indian, a half-breed. I married him because he was seventeen years older, and I thought we'd have a stable home life and I wouldn't be poor. We lived in Anchorage. He didn't do steady work. He had odd jobs tending bar, and I worked long hours in a fishing cannery.

That marriage was like stepping into a horror story. Every minute of my time had to be accounted for. He used to play these killing games. He would strangle me till I would pass out, but I wouldn't die—that kind of game. He tried to force me into prostitution. He'd say, "Just for a little while," and he'd drop me off. But I wouldn't do it. I'd make my way back home without money, and he'd beat me up. He broke my finger, he broke my cheekbone. We had two children, a boy and a girl, but finally I left with just the clothes on my back. I got away with my life. I got away from him, I was alive.

My husband's family said they would take care of the children, but they didn't. He went to court and said I was an unfit mother—nobody knew about his abuse—and he got custody of the children. He put them in a church home outside of Anchorage, and they were there for six years.

I went to Sacramento, California, to hide out from my husband—I was terrified that he would find me and kill me. I worked in a bowling alley, and I worked in a home for mentally retarded children.

After I was divorced, I went to Pelican, Alaska, to see my sister, and I met my present husband, Don, there. He's part Norwegian, part Scotch and Irish. I wasn't crazy in love, but I was twenty-seven by then, and I thought we would have some healthy children. And we did—we had two wonderful, healthy boys.

Don was a commercial fisherman. I always liked working with fish. We started out in a little open boat, then the next year we got a covered boat, then we took out a big loan and got a big fiberglass boat with a beautiful hull. We took our boys out of school, we had them on the boat with us in the summer, they did their schoolwork on the boat. They did well. We worked hard way out in the ocean, forty miles offshore. In the fall, we hunted for blacktail deer on Chichagof Island in southeastern Alaska. We lived on meat, fish, crabs, shrimp. We all pitched in, it was give-and-take, a good life.

When my first husband died in a fire in Alaska, I was able to go to court in Anchorage to get my first two children, and bring them into our family. My husband became their stepfather. We had a big two-story home in Pelican, Alaska, where our children grew up. I became president of the Pelican School Board. We fished in Alaska in the spring and summer, then we came to Washington—it's about a 1,200-mile run—to fish in the fall. We did really well.

From white people, Native people picked up the idea—hey, there's this buy-and-sell tradition; let's go for it. So they divided the country into corporations, the white man's way of doing business. They built a lumber company and fisheries, they started trading with Japan. We [the Inupiat] got a big sum under the Alaska Native Claims settlement.

In addition to our house in Pelican, we had a house in Washington near the Canadian border. Then Don got hit by a truck, and the man who did it had no insurance. Don was in a coma for a month and a half. It took him two years to learn to walk straight. Insurance paid all his hospitalization, but we lost every material thing we had. We couldn't make the payments on the fishing boat, or on the two homes, so the bank said they would have to foreclose. I felt bad about it.

Then one day, I was flying into Pelican, I looked down and happened to see our house and lot, and I said to myself, "Look at that little square down there—you're losing it." Then I looked around and saw these huge mountains and forests, I saw the ocean and rivers, I looked up at the sky. And I said, "You're losing the house, but look at what you gain!" It was like a revelation. It changed my attachment to material things.

I went to work in a shelter for abused women. My husband recovered, and got someone to help him fish. The children grew up—two of the boys work in the fisheries. My son from my first marriage went to jail on a robbery and drug charge, and he's still there. My daughter contracted ovarian cancer when she was twenty-five, and died within months.

Don and I were living in the little town of Chatham, Alaska, Don was doing some logging work, and he smashed his hip. They sent him to Seattle for hip surgery. I had to stay in Chatham for three months without seeing anyone. The mail plane came once a month, the pilot dropped off the mail, said hi and flew off again. A preacher flew in to try to save my soul, then flew out. But I was never lonely.

All the years I was in the mission I got in the habit of saying, "There's nothing out there I can trust, there's nothing out there I need, it's all inside of me." I could be my best friend, the one who cheered me on, the giver of happiness. I never felt jealous of anyone, I never felt hatred.

They put metal plates in Don's hip, but it didn't work, and he had to give up his work and the outdoor life, so we moved here. He's on disability insurance. We're taking care of his mother—she's very sick.

Don and I go beachcombing; we like to go look at seals. I enjoy the grocery stores, but I can't abide going to a big store to look for new shoes or a shirt. I get nervous. Up there in the bush, I was more patient. In the deer season, you knew when the deer were going to come down from the high places. You knew when the fish were leaving the streams or coming back. You knew when the berries were ripe.

You learned to wait for the night to be over. You learned to wait through a time of hunger, to wait for an old person to die.

I think our people have an acceptance of life, we have an acceptance of human beings in all their good and bad times, and an acceptance of death. Death is a part of living. When my daughter was dying, she was so courageous. I saw her looking way out in the distance and I said, "What are you looking at, Suzan? What do you see?" She answered, "I see such beautiful things, Mother." That helped me accept the fact that when you die, it's not the end of you.

I think that ninety percent of the Eskimos believe in reincarnation. When you die, your spirit moves on—it can inhabit a still object like a tree. Your soul goes to a waiting place, waiting for another life form to be born. Traditionally, they gave the name of the dead person to a baby who was born with the same physical characteristics—a birthmark, for example. I believe the soul is the energy source for a human being.

I don't remember ever fearing death. Dying should be as acceptable as a birth. A person dying—it's like one door shutting and another opening.

I knew when my father was dying, but I didn't know where he was. You know, a lot of Native people are psychic. Mind reading goes on over great distances. My sons and I send each other these mental messages. I have prophetic dreams, sometimes they come in symbols. In our culture, there's a belief in signs and symbols—what the birds are doing has a certain meaning, for example. If I think about the dreams enough, I can figure out what's going to happen, and to whom.

Recently, my cousin asked me to go to a powwow for Native Americans in this area. He said I should wear his dance blanket. It was the first time I'd ever danced, and I danced for a solid hour. I'll bet people wonder how can those old folks dance for an hour and not get tired? I found out. It was the drums. The drums carry you along, they give you energy.

What's important now is living with truth and openness. My niece once asked me what makes me so strong. I said I think it's just a matter of using your intelligence. When there's a problem, you sit down and look it over, and it becomes a challenge. I think it's the makeup and the spirit of the Eskimo people.

In spite of all the bad times you go through—the darkness, the freezing, the starvation—you know there's going to be a time of plenty, a time of new births, and endless life. You drop the bad things behind you, you look forward to the good things, and you keep going forward.

From interviews with the author, September 4 and 9, 1992.

Editor's note: A year after our interview, I received a note from Florence Kenney, mailed from Coldfoot, Alaska: "Don and I moved from Seattle. We spent a few months in Juneau and are now settling north of the Arctic Circle. The country is hauntingly beautiful, the true Alaskan bush, and we will be living as the old timers did 100 years ago, baking bread, cutting firewood, living semi-subsistence style. I'm so happy to be back. . . ."

NOTES

1. There are four different groups of Arctic peoples: Inupiat, Siberian Yupik, Central Alaskan Yupik, and Alutiiq according to the Alaska Native Language Center in Fairbanks.

2. The term Eskimo is widely used throughout Alaska. In Canada, Eskimo is thought by many to have derogatory connotations and the term Inuit, which means *the people*, is preferred.

3. The Inupiat have a long tradition of communal storytelling, singing, and dancing, which was long discouraged by schools and missionaries but is being revived today. See Charlotte Heth, ed., *Native American Dance: Ceremonies and Social Traditions* (Washington, D.C.: Smithsonian Institution, 1992), pp. 163–64, 167.

3

People Cared About One Another

FRAN JAMES
LUMMI[1]

O*n islands along the Pacific Northwest coast, the Lummi Indians lived in huge cedar longhouses. They carved images of raven and bear on house posts, they wove baskets and clothing out of bark from their lush forests and the wool of mountain goats. In ceremonies they honored the cedar and the year's first salmon. As they gave in to pressures to relinquish territory, their resources dwindled along with their economy; knowledge of the old arts and ceremonies faded. In 1990 political leaders turned over to the Lummi the deed to a thirty-acre tract of land, resolving a long and volatile dispute over the tribe's burial grounds and sacred sites. At the same time, church leaders promised support for the tribe's drive to revive its traditional culture.[2]*

About two hundred Lummi live on a small reservation north of Seattle, near Mount Baker. In Ferndale, near Fisherman's Cove, sits the barn-red house of weaver Fran James. Her picture window overlooks Lummi Bay where her ancestors paddled their dugout canoes and the island where she lived as a child. Fran James greeted me and led me to a spread of smoked salmon, potato salad, cake, and coffee, saying: "We like to feed people who come here." A small, compact, gray-haired, and good-natured woman wearing dark glasses, she appeared to be in her seventies. We sat on her couch surrounded by bas-

kets of all sizes and shapes, and she talked about an art form and life-ways she is perpetuating.

THIS BASKET I'M WORKING ON IS CEDAR BARK. THE others are made from bear grass, wild cherry and rye grass. I like to use just natural materials from the state of Washington. I get some from my sister-in-law's property, back in the woods here.

There are hardly any more trees left. Remember that big storm we had a few years ago? Oh, my gosh, it just destroyed some of the most beautiful trees ever. They were all just laying there. I wanted to go out and gather the bark and roots for my baskets, but it was bitter cold. I had just got my husband home from the hospital, and the storm was blowing so hard, the wires were down, we were without power for four days. You have to take the bark off the tree before it dries, and I missed out on that. But the local mill let us go in and get the bark.

They're always so concerned about the environment. They'll say, "You might kill the tree." You know, we don't kill a tree when we take the bark. Just look at all the telephone poles out there. How many trees does that kill?

Sometimes we get a permit from the forest service, and we go in some place in the mountains where they're gonna clear-cut. We go in a van, a group of us from different tribes, it takes miles and miles of traveling. We take our lunch, we go on a picnic. We stay all day.

Before we take the bark, we always talk to the tree, we tell him we're going to take this bark and make something pretty. We tell him we're not going to abuse him. If the tree doesn't believe you, you get into trouble. If you don't take the bark the right way, the tree might snap or something. [Laughs.] We take just the outer part of the bark, enough to last a whole year. We don't

FRAN JAMES   *Photo by Jane Katz*

waste anything. If we have a little more than we need, we share it
with people that are handicapped or too old to come.

So, you find all these barks from different kinds of trees, you
come back, and hang up the bark to dry for about six months.
[Strips of bark are drying on a line in the next room.] To prepare
for weaving, you have to resoak the bark. I keep a pan of water
on the stove all the time, and I soak it in boiling hot water, then I
can split it—it comes in layers—and thin it down in order to work
it. It's time-consuming.

People wonder why we have to charge so much for baskets. One time we traveled with *Encyclopaedia Britannica*, they put us in a hallway in a mall in Seattle, right smack dab in front of all these Chinese baskets you can buy for a quarter, and people they just walked right past us. They didn't see what goes into making an Indian basket. Well, over the years we became so known for our work that we don't have to go anywhere to sell them. They come right here. See, we got a picture of our work in this book put out by the Smithsonian.

My aunt made this basket. She's ninety-eight; she can't see or hear, but she made it. Some of these were made by my grandmother. They are handed down in the family. When my time comes, I'll give them to my son.

My mother died when I was four. My two sisters and I went to live with my grandmother in her house on Portage Island, just across the bay. So my grandmother brought me up. Boy, she used to feed us good. My gosh, we had a great big bowl of hot oatmeal, bacon and eggs, hot cakes, a glass of milk right from the cow. Grandmother had a great big orchard, with big apples. We had a little house with racks for drying fruit. We had a root house, with bins for apples, carrots, potatoes and squash, and oh, we worked hard in the garden. We had rhubarb, and we'd take it into the store in town and trade it for coffee or whatever we needed. Grandmother showed us which mushrooms were for eating. She had raised fourteen children, and I tell you, she made do with what she had. She lived to be a hundred years old.

Grandmother had about five hundred head of black sheep, and all the grandchildren had their own sheep to take care of. I learned how to shear wool, how to spin and knit, how to make knitting needles out of ironwood. Grandmother taught me how to weave sweaters and baskets.[3]

If we were going fishing or clam digging, we would go out in

the woods to gather material for baskets, and we'd help Grandmother make them. She would go and dig in the root house, and
she'd bring three little potatoes, one for each of us. We'd dig
clams on the beach. Then we'd row our little boat over to Deep
Water Bay. Using the clams as bait, we'd fish for codfish. You use
a hook and line, you dig way down to the bottom, you pull it up
and the fish drag onto it. We'd gather wood, we'd make a fire and
cook the potatoes and cod, and that was our meal. Then we'd row
way out to Gull Rock, where the seagulls would lay big eggs.
We'd gather them in our baskets, and we'd row all the way back
home. We'd get blisters on our hands from rowing. We'd use the
gull eggs to make cakes.

We'd get up at five o'clock every morning and do our chores.
I had to bring in the wood, and get the water from a well down
below the hill. I'd carry five gallons on each side up the hill. I used
to go into the woods where we had old-growth fir trees with
thick bark—I'd go and peel the bark. I learned how to put a harness on the team horses and drag a wagon, and used it to go and
gather all that bark. We had a fifty-gallon oil stove, and the bark
burned real good and heated the whole house.

There were just women in the house—Grandpa had died—so
we learned to hunt. I used to carry a gun and shoot ducks in the
ponds. We saved all the feathers, and made feather beds. That
kept us warm during the cold winters.

Grandmother trusted us, she let us do what we wanted to
do—like she'd let me go for a walk around that whole island.
When I went back over there and the old house was gone, I cried.
I remembered how we used to sit right up on the top of the hill,
and look out and see everything—boats, birds—one time we
looked out and there were about fourteen eagles landing on the
island. There were no cars going by, we had clean, fresh air, nobody smokin'. We never even used to lock our door. Young people didn't cause trouble then. We were all busy fishing, digging

clams or whatever. We used to take time to go and visit the elders. People cared about one another.

There was a whole bunch of kids on the island where we lived, and my dad used to come in a little boat, and ferry us across to the mainland because we had to get to school. Up where the Northwest Indian College is now we had a little school with two rooms, and eight grades. In a storm, we would just hit the beach, we'd jump out, and it was so rough, the boat'd fill up with water, so we'd go to school soaking wet. The janitor at the school would fill up the coal bin in the basement, and he'd make us stand there and dry our clothes.

I didn't finish school. I did poorly in the studies. I think I learned more at home than I did in school. I used to think my grandmother was mean when she'd say, "Do this and do that," but after she was gone, I thought, "My gosh, I should have paid more attention."

Sometimes I'd go and stay with this other grandmother down by the river [on the mainland]. Her house was a tiny shack with no floor way back in the woods. Oh, the woods used to smell so good. She had a straw bed built of two-by-fours, and I'd sleep with her.

She did a different kind of weaving. This is a storage basket she made of yellow cedar sapling. We used to make big baskets to store dried salmon in. After the fish was brought in, you'd soak it in salt rind all night, then you'd hang it up and smoke it, and that would preserve it. You'd never let the fire go out in the smoke-house. When we were hungry, we'd just cut off a slice and eat it. You call that "Indian bacon." If we were going to the beach for a whole day, we'd carry a slice in our pockets. So that's how we survived.

There were some ceremonies then, but I don't remember much because I was away so much. I had tuberculosis, and I went to the Cushman Hospital [for Northwest Coast tribes]. I was there for two years. I used to have to drink sauerkraut juice and cod-liver oil. When I was cured, I went to Chemawa, a boarding school down by Eugene, Oregon. It was a good school. We raised our own garden, we picked 'tatoes and onions, we worked in the laundry. All the boys from here—I used to do their shirts. But I did a lot of crying down there. It was far away from home.

I came home from school when my dad drowned. It was a year before the war broke up—1940 or '41. I must have been seventeen or eighteen. Anyhow, my dad was a fisherman, and there was a really bad storm. He was a good swimmer, but I think his heart might have given out. So I came home for the funeral. We were poor, and nobody had money to send me back.

I stayed on at home, and I got married. My husband—well, let me see. His dada was the chief and the policeman. We went to school together. He used to come across to the island to visit me in an old leaky boat. On Saturday, he'd go fishing, and then we'd go to the movies in town—it used to be 'bout ten cents or so—and we'd hold hands. [Laughs.]

Anyhow, we ended up getting married, and we were married for forty-seven years. We had a little house down at the Indian village on the island, and that's where my son was raised. [She shows me a photograph.] This is the little shack we used to have. My father-in-law was a commercial fish buyer, and he sold his business to my husband. It was a twenty-four-hour job, really too much, and my husband got diabetes, kidney failure, he had heart trouble and cancer. He was sick for a long time. We went to the Indian health service. But mostly he tried to heal himself. He died a few years ago.

Taking me into the room where she does her weaving, Fran James showed me the spindle whorf her grandfather carved out of cedar and the loom she uses today. She still obtains her wool from mountain goats and sheep—she trades baskets for it. She showed me a dress she is making out of cedar-bark strips and, after some coax-

ing, agreed to put it on. It is meticulously crafted, woven in the old way.

A lady came here and said she wants to get married in a cedar-bark dress, but she doesn't have the faintest idea how to make one so I'm showing her how. I took her in the woods and showed her how to gather the material, then I brought her here, and showed her how to make it. You know, the bark comes in layers, and you have to thin it down, and make it paper thin to work it. It will have a wide cedar-bark belt.

I teach weaving classes [at the local school and at the community college]. I try to teach the younger generation to take time to visit the elders: "Just stop and say hello." This tiny little guy, he calls me up when he's going to town: "Do you want anything?" See, he lost his grandmother and he doesn't have anyone, so he calls me up: "Can I come and visit?" I say, "Anytime." I got these toys so he can play with them when he's here.

In this day and age, young people just get in the fast lane and keep on goin'. The boob tube takes up too much of their time. Or they go into the city, and forget to come back. They don't have time for their traditions.

I'm trying to teach them the basics of life, 'cause we all have to live here.

From an interview with the author, September 20, 1991.

NOTES

1. The Lummi are sometimes called Coast Salish; they speak a dialect of the Salish language family.

2. In three years of negotiations over the proposed development of Madrona Point on Orcas Island in the San Juan Islands, testimony of Lummi tribal elders that this was their ancestral burial ground was given little credence by most non-Natives, in part because it was oral. The Lummi sought the support of church leaders who, in 1987, had issued an "Apology" to Washington State tribes for their churches' "complicity in the destruction of indigenous religions," and a settlement was reached. See *Christian Century*, March 15, 1989, pp. 276–277, and March 21, 1990, pp. 297–298.

3. For information on Coast Salish fiber arts and the environment that produced them, see Priscilla A. Gibson, *Salish Indian Sweaters* (St. Paul: Minn.: Roberts Fiber Arts Publications, 1989), pp. 3–12.

4

In My Family,
the Women Ran Everything

———

E̲MMI W̲HITEHORSE
NAVAJO[1]

T̲he Santa Fe studio of painter Emmi Whitehorse is a comfortable
place. The patio is home to plants, two cats, and a large black rabbit.
Inside the converted warehouse, a skylight illuminates Whitehorse's
treasures—an abstract "chief's blanket," Navajo fetishes standing
like sentinels beside hand-woven baskets, Pueblo pots, and high-tech
stereo speakers. The walls are alive with her canvases, which blend
European influences with her personal visual language. Figures
from her childhood on the Navajo Reservation float in seas of color.
Emmi Whitehorse took me on a tour of her work, then we drank tea
and she reflected on her passage from shepherdess to "postmodern
painter."

M̲Y WORK ISN'T SOMETHING MYSTICAL THAT HAS TO BE
pondered. See this funny little bird? Birds represent different
things in different cultures, so when I first showed the painting,
everybody thought it was an allusion to some Native American
ritual. I said, "Well, if that's what you want to believe, fine. But I
just saw it on a beer label, and I'm painting it." [Laughs.]

I incorporate common, everyday things in my work. I play
with images. In these canvases, there are childlike forms. There's a
comb, like the one we used to use to beat down the wool and

55

tighten the weaving. I like the shape. There's a little house and an upside-down fork floating in space over denuded trees.

There are female body parts in the works, but they're ambiguous. This big figure started out looking like a bowling pin—you know, elongated head and long body. Then the head disappeared, and the bust came in. In this other painting, there's a woman with a head, but she's armless. [Laughs.] You can see the hips and waist, she has this big strapless ruffly dress on, the kind girls wear to the prom. This upside-down thing here, that's the same female form—I flipped it around—only she doesn't have the ruffly dress on; she's become a chalice.

I don't want to be too literal in the work. I'm ambiguous. I'm interested in the presence of the woman. I'm intrigued by the femininity of the female form.

In my family, the female owned everything, the women ran everything. They owned the land and the sheep. They nurtured and carried the family. The woman was responsible for the survival of the people. So in my work, the female is always very big, she is imposing, she is like this big Goliath in the work. The male image is tiny.

In this other canvas, there's a woman shaped like a vase, like the older Navajo women. Even in old age, I think the women still retain a grace that is unequaled.

My grandmother is like that. She's very giving, and she instilled a lot of traditional values in us without having to preach. She was a weaver. She learned how to weave from her mother. Her work is elegant. She is very finicky, very concerned with what she wears in public. She won't go out on a short trip to the store without putting on her best clothes: a traditional Navajo velveteen top and three-tiered cotton skirt down to her ankles. She used to make her clothes, but now she has trouble seeing, so she has someone make them to her specifications. She's eighty-two, and she's pretty healthy, except for arthritis.

I was born in 1957. I lived with my family in a hogan in a

place called Whitehorse Lake on the edge of the Navajo Reservation. It's near Chaco Canyon, New Mexico. Each family lives on a plot of land divided into sections or squares so that each of the relatives can have a section for his or her family. There was my grandmother (I never saw my grandfather), my parents, and five children. Most of the family is still living there.

In olden times, Navajo women would scheme to arrange a marriage for their children to someone from a wealthy family. Wealth meant having cows and horses, or a car. A lot of tribal people were material-oriented, and still are. The mother and grandmother would pick the mate for a girl, but they wouldn't force you. They'd ask you if it was okay first. Our tradition was that the man came to live with his wife's family.

What if a woman was unhappy with her husband? In earlier times, it was easy. She just picked up all his stuff and put it outside the door of the hogan, and that was it. He couldn't contest it. He had to go.

The man joined his wife's family basically to ensure the survival of that family. In other words, he sort of became the workhorse. He would haul the wood, and chop the firewood; he'd take care of the sheep too. He'd make sure there was water for the animals. Older men and medicine men were highly regarded. But that was back then.

Our system worked well until the missionaries came and said that we were "living in sin." How can living with nature be a sin? They said that men are supposed to run everything. That threw everything asunder. My generation of young men was greatly affected by the fact that they had to constantly straddle the fence between traditional teachings and western ideals. Unfortunately, many turned to alcohol and destroyed their well-being.

My father worked in California for Amtrak when I was very young, so we children became the caretakers of our animals. We had over two hundred head of sheep. We had to take them out every day to graze. Every spring, Grandmother marked the ears—

EMMI WHITEHORSE   *Photo by Dirk De Bruycker*

it was the same as branding. We would help castrate lambs. When little ones were abandoned, we had to bottle-feed them, to be mother to all those motherless lambs. We'd shear the sheep in the spring. We had to use huge shears, and cut each sheep's wool by hand. This would take days. Afterwards, we'd take the wool to market, about fifteen to twenty tremendous burlap sacks. We'd get something like five dollars per pound totaling around five thousand dollars, a substantial amount of money that we would live on for a year. Grandmother also had goats that produced mohair which she used for her weaving.

We'd help Grandmother card the wool after it had been washed. It was a nasty business because wool from the sheep is very dirty and oily. We'd sit and pick all the burrs and twigs out. Using a flat wooden brushlike comb, we'd comb it clean and make little long, flat bundles of wool. While we worked, my grandmother told us creation stories like this one, but only in the wintertime.

> Changing Woman was the first woman, born through a sort of immaculate conception. She gave birth to twin boys; the Sun was their father. But because the Sun didn't want children, Changing Woman had to hide their birth, and she raised them in secrecy. When they grew up, they asked who their father was. When Changing Woman could no longer put them off, she told them it was the Sun, and they wanted to go and see him. Changing Woman prepared the boys for the journey. She plucked stars and lightning bolts out of which she fashioned a bow and arrow for each boy. She warned them that their father would try to kill them.
>
> Along their journey, the boys met a gopher who befriended them, and offered to help them outsmart the Sun. When they arrived at the home of the Sun, they announced, "We are the sons of Changing Woman. We know you are our father." The Sun was very angry, and decided to do away with the boys right away. He prepared a sweat for them; he put oversize rocks inside so it would overheat. But the gopher was wise to the Sun; he went inside without being seen, he dug a large tunnel in the middle of the floor that led deep down and to the outside. When the Sun turned up the heat, the boys crawled into this tunnel. Each time the Sun turned up the heat, he would call out to the boys, "How are you doing?" Each time they would answer, "Fine." This went on until the Sun was tired out, and finally the Sun called out to the boys to come out. They emerged unhurt, and the Sun gave in and accepted the boys as his sons.[2]

I asked Emmi Whitehorse if her story affirms her image of woman as a positive force.

Yes. By defying the Sun and having the Twins, Changing Woman liberated her people who had been suppressed by the greedy Sun. She released her people from the underworld where the Sun wanted them to stay; she moved them forward. At one point, I incorporated that story into my painting. See these two figures? They are the Twins.

I was the baby of the family. My siblings had gone off to school, not by their own choice. I wanted to be with them, so I begged my mom to let me go to school. I thought I would play on the swings and merry-go-round all day. She said, "Fine." She enrolled me the very next day! (My mother and my grandmother don't speak English. They never went to school.)

So at a very early age, I went to a Bureau of Indian Affairs boarding school near my home in Whitehorse Lake. I hated it. We were marched around like little cadets: girls were herded around in one area, boys in another. It was very lonely. In the dining room, we were required to sit boy-girl, boy-girl, and that was torture. [Laughs.] All you could do was numb yourself to the whole ordeal.

I wasn't interested in any of the subjects, except art. When we had drawing time, I came alive. That was the only thing I excelled in. That kept me going.

Some of the teachers were very demeaning and made us feel ashamed of our culture. We were forced to wear uncomfortable dresses and hose, with a tight girdle. Boy did we hate it! We couldn't wear our hair loose; it had to be curled, or braided, or piled up on top of our heads to fulfill the school's idea of the "ideal girl."

At Christmas, if we got lucky, we would get gifts, and one year, we all got Barbie dolls. Barbie had a size D bust and a nineteen-inch waist, long legs and blond hair. We all thought we were supposed to look like her. Well, we found out that no matter how we manipulated our bodies, we could never look like Barbie. We had tanned skin and dark hair. When I got older, I realized we had wasted so much time agonizing over something that could never be, and that didn't need changing! I started drawing the female figure with this pinched-in waist and a big top—I was poking fun at the "ideal figure."

We were only allowed to go home in the summer. At home, mother never pushed us hard; she never made important decisions for us. She never encouraged us to be lawyers or physicians. She let us do what we wanted to do.

During the summer months, I got to participate in some ceremonies. We had a Blessing ceremony when we finished our new home.[3] Once when my mother was sick, she hired a medicine man to come and sing over her, but the medicine man considered us too young to witness it, and sent us away. Did she get well? She must have. [Laughs.]

I didn't have a puberty ceremony because I was away at school, and also I was uncomfortable with the idea of having one. This was the sixties. I thought it was too old-fashioned. Miniskirts were in, puberty rites were not! Now, I think it's such a wonderful ceremony, I should have had it. If I have a daughter I will want her to have one.

In this painting there's a long bundle of sticks used in the girl's puberty ceremony. Your grandmother gives them to you; you use them to stir the blue cornmeal during the ceremony, and you keep them for the rest of your life.

I went to a puberty ceremony when I was around eight years old. The girl who was being initiated into womanhood was about twelve or thirteen. We camped out at the girl's home for a week with all our relatives, men, women and children. Now, I guess you'd drive over every day. With the girl, we spent a whole day grinding the blue corn for the "Navajo cake." When there was enough corn piled up, they would pour it into a big metal container, pour in hot water, add raisins, sweeten it with sprouted wheat (a natural sugar), and it was like a thick pudding. The men would do their part by hauling in water and firewood.

Every morning before sunup, the girl would race out toward the East. We would all line up behind her, grandmothers, mothers and children, as if we were going to run the New York Marathon. Someone would say "Go" and she'd race off. You'd never overtake her, even if you were the fastest runner, because the saying was if you ran past her, you would age quicker than she would. [Laughs.] She would race as far as she could to the East, then she would turn around and run back. It was just a wonderful event.

For the ceremony, the girl was decked out in her best traditional dress and jewelry. Her hair was done up and wrapped with yarn, and a piece of parrot feather with turquoise was tied to her hair.

There were specific songs. I remember the medicine man singing and conducting the ceremony. He was sitting in front of us in the hogan with his legs crossed. My sister and I noticed that he had a hole in the toe of his moccasin. We started giggling hysterically, and my grandmother got angry and chased us out of the hogan. We were put to work gathering firewood and grinding corn. We weren't allowed back in, so we never heard the rest of the ceremony.

Recently, my sister's daughter got married in a traditional ceremony at my mother's home. We all went to help with the wedding preparations. We prepared food for the feast. We butchered a sheep and made mutton stew soup. We cooked various other dishes and of course fried bread.

The bride and groom were dressed in their traditional clothes. He wore a velveteen shirt and blue jeans. The bride wore a purple velveteen blouse and a purple satin skirt with see-through white lace overlayed on the skirt. She had her hair done up Navajo fashion. The couple both wore moccasins.

The bride and groom sat in a corner of the hogan on blankets. The groom's family sat on one side of the hogan, the bride's family on the other side. The groom's mother was a medicine woman, so she conducted the ceremony and said the prayers. It was wonderful to have a woman do that.

The medicine woman poured water over the couple's hands—they had to wash before starting the ceremony. A little basket of corn mush was brought in; the couple dipped into the mush with their fingers, marking the four corners as they worked around the lip of the basket, then they ate some.

Next, they opened the floor so that anyone could talk. It all had to do with maintaining a good home and family relationships. Elders counseled the couple on how to be diplomatic. The girl's grandmother told her how to be caring, the boy's father told him how to be giving, financially and emotionally, to his wife. This went on for hours, it seemed, until everybody had run out of things to say and was out of breath.

Finally the food was brought in. The lamb's ribs were given to the groom's family—these are considered a delicacy. The rest of us got to eat mutton stew and fry bread. Everyone ate in a circle around the food.

After the meal, it shifted gears to modern life. Someone from my family had ordered this wonderful three-tiered cake decorated with the plastic image of a couple—a white couple—standing on the very top. [Laughs.] They cut it and passed it out to the guests. There were gifts: a toaster, glasses, a Cuisinart. You didn't get that in the old days. It was bizarre because the first part of the ceremony had been so traditional. But they were young, in fact, they played their favorite music at the end—heavy metal! It was accepted. Everyone went away happy.

After the guests had all left, the bride gathered all the gifts and carried them out to a 1992 Ford Escort, and we watched them drive off.

I thought, well, if I ever decide to get married, I'll have a traditional wedding at night, on my grandmother's land.

In high school, I entered an art contest with a small abstract painting; it won an award, and I got a small scholarship to the University of New Mexico in Albuquerque. The school was male-dominated, and I was very disappointed. When I arrived at my first art history class, I didn't know who Picasso was, I had no idea what modern art was about. I took all the art classes I could, and became a bit more comfortable. I took courses in modern dance, music history and creative writing. I was fascinated. I started showing my work while I was an undergraduate.

I was so happy the day I got my master's degree in fine arts. I sent invitations to all my family and relatives, but my dad was the only one who showed up for the graduation. My sisters were in town, but guess where they went instead. [Laughs.] To a Jimmy Swaggert revival meeting! After the graduation ceremony was over, they came and congratulated me and we all went out for dinner. It was sad that they weren't interested in what I had done, but later I forgave them. The evangelist meeting was more important to them at that time in their lives.

At one point in my life, I suffered from low self-esteem pretty badly. I was trying very hard not to look ethnic. I thought my nose was too big. I guess I was trying to eliminate every trace of who I was. Then a close friend said, "Look at all the things the Navajo are famous for: the weavings, the silversmithing, baskets. These are just as valid as what the Europeans have come up with." It dawned on me that there was this wealth of aesthetic objects my people were creating. Why not be proud of it?

I began looking at the stories my grandmother told me when I was a child, and started incorporating the images into my work. The work became more centered. In some of the paintings you'll see the arc from the bottom of the Navajo wedding basket, or the shape of the cradle board my mother made for me using boards from an orange crate. In another painting, there is a brush made out of dried grass, which Navajo women used to use to brush their hair.

Everything my grandmother stood for I now hold sacred: her love for animals, her limitless compassion for humanity. I would like to be like her when I get older. I will probably trade in my LizWear for a velveteen blouse and a traditional long skirt when I'm sixty years old. [Laughs.]

From an interview with the author, July 15, 1992.

NOTES

1. The alternate spelling is Navaho. In their own language, they call themselves *diné*, which is usually translated as "The People."

2. There are various retellings of the rich origin stories of the Navajos. See *Navajo Creation Stories* told by Teri Keams, Parabola Storytime Series (audio), 1993; Larry Evers, ed., *Between Sacred Mountains: Navajo Stories and Lessons from the Land* (Tucson: Sun Tracks and the University of Arizona Press, 1984).

3. The hogan, or home, occupies a central place in the Navajo sacred world.

II

DAUGHTERS
OF THE
DISPOSSESSED

*"Who would believe
the fantastic and terrible story of all our survival
those who were never meant
to survive?"* ▽

              JOY HARJO
               CREEK

5

From My Grandmother
I Learned About Sadness

ROSE BLUESTONE
WAHPEKUTE DAKOTA[1]/
MDEWAKANTON DAKOTA

In December 1862, "the moon when the deer shed their horns," thirty-eight Dakota men sang their death songs, mounted a huge scaffold, and were hanged. They were buried without rites, in a shallow, communal grave.

This execution culminated years of conflict between the Dakota and whites in southern Minnesota. The Indians were hunters and gatherers. In two misleading treaties, they had ceded all their lands east of the Mississippi in return for annuities, then found themselves pushed off their hunting grounds. They resented their dependence on government payments and on credit from sometimes unscrupulous traders. Disgruntled warriors attacked settlers and traders in the Minnesota valley.[2] White soldiers retaliated against Indians in their path. In the wake of the hanging, the U.S. "justice system" expelled the Dakota from their homeland. Eventually, some returned and their descendants live today on small Minnesota reservations, one of which is in Shakopee, twenty miles southwest of Minneapolis.

The winding Minnesota River snakes through green fields where the Dakota used to camp and pray for deer to feed their families. A parade of cars leads the way to the town of the Mdewakanton, where approximately 150 tribal members[3] live in expanding housing developments and mobile homes, with a clinic, community center, and smoke shops. Billboards tower over the terrain, luring visitors to the *tribally owned Mystic Lake gaming complex with two casinos—one tipi-shaped and one with a stone façade and laser lights. Gaming has brought extensive revenues to this once impoverished reservation and to the surrounding area. Profits have enabled the tribe to update water systems, pave roads, finance health care and latchkey programs, and offer college scholarships to Native students.[4]*

On an unmarked street I located Rose Bluestone's hilltop home, a well-kept rambler. A genial woman in her late seventies with a deeply lined face, she told her story slowly, measuring her words, revealing little emotion. But at times she paused, unable to continue, as if the retelling of painful events had opened old wounds.

MY GRANDMOTHER WITNESSED THE HANGING OF HER father in Mankato when she was thirteen years old. The families were there to watch. It was a tragedy.

The people weren't able to talk about the execution for many years, they were so ashamed of the fact that Indians had killed all those white people. But before my grandmother died, she told me about it. She wanted me to know my history. She told me of her grief. And of her fear. All during that year when there was so much fighting, the family felt their lives were at stake. From my grandmother I learned about sadness. It made me feel so bad, what they went through. But you have to go on living as best you can.

We have just two hundred acres in this little community, the Mdewakanton Sioux community. The big Sioux reservations in North and South Dakota have many hundreds of acres of land. I come from a band that lived in the southwestern part of the state, the Wahpekute. Our ancestors were in different parts of the state for many hundreds of years. See, when the white people came west and wanted land, the government bought up a whole strip of land to the tune of twenty-one million acres. Then they gathered up all the Indians and resettled them there in 1851. They had to live on ten acres on each side of the Minnesota River from Red-

ROSE BLUESTONE   *Photo by Marc Katz*

wood County up to Lake Travis. They were to stay there and
farm like white men. Whites wanted them to be in one place, not
to roam around.

Our people were not farmers. By 1861, they were restless.
They could not get out and hunt, they couldn't go fishing and ric-

ing on the old sites. It was getting harder to find fruits and berries. That was their staple, their subsistence, their survival.

The government had promised the Sioux so many millions of dollars to sign this treaty back in 1851. They were to get annuity payments—the interest off the bulk of the money. But the money wasn't coming to them. I think the government sent some of the money to the trader, John Myrick. Myrick said he'd give them credit at the store, but the Indians knew very little English, and they didn't understand credit. Finally, he said, "Your bill is overdue. You can't have any more food." Well, the people were hungry. They were angry. They felt they had been cheated by the government; they felt they were being cheated by the trader.

The government agent tried to intercede. He said to Myrick, "You know that money's coming." The trader answered, "Well, if they're hungry, let them eat grass or their own dung."

My grandmother remembered how her father and other men went out to fight. Within a span of two hours, the Indians burned down forts, food warehouses and trading posts. They killed John Myrick and they stuffed his mouth with grass. They went to the homes and farms of the white people and killed about five hundred of them. Then the reports came back of who was killed, who was wounded.

The Sixth Minnesota Regiment counterattacked, tracking down and incarcerating Native people throughout the Minnesota Valley. Over two thousand Indian men, women, and children were marched to a prison camp, the men chained together in pairs.

They say President Lincoln got the report that the Indians had done away with a lot of settlers, and had burned down their farms. Lincoln was busy down south trying to free the slaves. What I heard was that when he got this report, he said, "Exterminate the savages."

They imprisoned the Indians in a big, open pen at Fort

Snelling. Some they kept under guard in tipis. The missionary Bishop Whipple had befriended our people, saying, "If you follow the Christian way of life, that will be your salvation." Then, when the Indians he had baptized were imprisoned, he went to Washington and interceded for them. He said that not all the men were guilty. He said that women and children should be spared.

A military court acting without any defense counsel for Indians (they had no legal rights) condemned 303 of the prisoners to death. President Lincoln reviewed the trial records, including testimony that some of those imprisoned had not been involved in the rebellion, and authorized the hanging of thirty-eight Dakota at the fort in Mankato. Later, newspapers reported that two of the Indians had been hanged by mistake.

They had witnesses who testified that some of the Indians had not taken part in the killings. There was an interpreter who spoke for the Indians. After the trial, the way they chose the men for execution was arbitrary. The soldiers lined up two or three hundred of them. They counted them, and went down the rows, and every tenth man, they said, "You step out!" Those were the ones they marched to Mankato to be executed.

My grandmother and her family marched along with the prisoners to be with their father when he was executed. The men were stripped of whatever they had—their clothing, their blankets, their peace pipes. They left their pipes to their families.

My grandmother's family lived on near the fort in Mankato for three years. They had my great-grandfather's sacred pipe. I have it now. It's up there, on the wall. They prayed to God. They didn't need a church. They always knew there was a God.

Old people and some women and children were left behind in the Minnesota Valley. They stayed all winter in their tipis, hungry and sick. Then in May 1863 they were driven from their homes, and the settlers took over the land they left behind. The Indians were put on steamboats and flatboats. They were taken down the Mississippi River to St. Louis, then they were switched to another kind of boat and brought up the Missouri River to Fort Thompson. Sixteen hundred Indians were in that stockade. They lived in tipis, surrounded by the fort. Food rations were limited. There were three hundred deaths of malnutrition, illness, neglect. Many of the elders froze to death, and the little children.

The men were prisoners in Fort Dodge, Iowa, and other prisons for three years. The government didn't know what to do with them, I guess. Then the government issued land in Nebraska to the survivors. They released the men from their prisons, and they tried to find their families. My grandmother told me how there was crying and wailing and grieving because some of the men had died in prison.

In Nebraska, the Indians built houses and farmed, but they never felt at home there. They were supposed to be farmers, but they had no preparation. When my grandfather needed money for materials for a house or for food, he sold some of his land.

Known as the Santee Agency, this Nebraska reservation had an arid climate, contaminated water, and infertile soil. Hunger and disease took their toll during that first winter of 1863. Of the 1,300 Indians brought there, fewer than a thousand survived to pray for the dead.

My grandmother told me she tried to keep up the old Indian ways. She smoked and prayed with her father's pipe. All the people believed in the Way of the Pipe. They prayed to God on top of the hill, on top of the highest rocks they prayed. They tried to keep up their ceremonies, but then they were told to forget all that. White people said our religion was pagan and we were savages.

When the U.S. government comes down and steps on you, there's not much you can do.

The missionaries were sent out to the reservations. They came along and they said, "Go to church. You have to do this, you have to do that"—so much stuff the people were taught. "You should be baptized. Embrace the son of God. Follow the Christian way of life. That's your only salvation." What choice did the people have? They were patient people and didn't want any more fighting, so they obeyed. My parents' generation was forced to embrace Christianity; I was brought up as a Christian. Still, I always had my pipe.

Now, when you go to the Dakotas, you should see the churches standing empty. Weeds are growing over them. The people are all turning back to the Way of the Pipe.

My father grew up in Nebraska. He got a scholarship to go to the Indian school in Carlisle, Pennsylvania. When he returned, it was the 1880s, many of the Sioux were moving back to Minnesota, and so he settled in Morton [now the Lower Sioux Agency]. We had family there. The government had abrogated all its treaties with the Sioux. There was no government support.

My father and mother got married, and they had four children. One died of stomach illness at the age of eight—there wasn't much medical care for Indians then. One boy died of tuberculosis at nineteen. When I was two years old, Mother died of a blood sickness. They drained all the blood out of her body, and then they couldn't do anything for her. My father couldn't take care of us, so he took us back to the reservation in Nebraska, and we were raised by our grandparents.

I don't remember much about that time, but I do remember I walked a mile to school. The other kids treated me okay, maybe because I was the only Indian kid in the school. At seventeen, I quit school. It was the Depression, and I couldn't afford the clothes. The kids would make fun of you if you didn't dress right. I started doing day work for white families.

I was twenty-one when I got married to my husband. He was Sioux. We moved to the Sioux community on Prairie Island, and then we moved to St. Paul. I worked in a hospital laboratory. I had three pregnancies, but I lost two of my children because of complications. We were married forty-two years.

After my husband's death, my daughter received tribal land here in Shakopee, she built this home and invited me to live with her. My daughter's name is Sacred Path Woman. We had a naming ceremony for her during one of the memorial powwows for the Sioux who died in Mankato. There were songs, and she danced. She can predict the future. She could be a medicine woman. When I developed a hiatal hernia, she did a Sun Dance for me at Eagle Butte, South Dakota, and I felt much better.

The Sun Dances are coming back. We don't call it religion. It's our way of worshiping God. It calls for sacrifice, fasting and prayer. The Sun Dancers usually fast for four days—no food, but they drink tea made of sage. [She points to a wreath hanging on the wall.] This is a crown of sage worn by the dancer. See those sticks up there? Those are placed around and inside the Sun Dance ring. Only the dancer can step inside the ring, and cannot step outside it.

The men do the Sun Dance for four years. Then in the fifth year, they attach leather thongs to their chest and tie them to the sacred tree and they dance. The thongs pull out flesh. There's less asked of a woman than of a man because the woman gives life—that's her sacrifice. Some women do offer flesh, but it's not required.

When I was in South Dakota one time, I came down with Bell's palsy—an infection settled in my ear and my nerve went haywire. The doctor didn't know what to do. My eye got numb and I couldn't control my mouth. Well, my daughter took me to Eagle Butte during the time of the Sun Dance. We knew this healer, Stanley Lookinghorse. I participated in the Sun Dance. I went up to the prayer tree, and they prayed for me. After it was all over, we went back up to his house, he built up his sweat lodge, and put medicine on the rocks—it was extremely hot. He told me to sit right by the fire and rub my face and pray. I did that, and within two weeks, I was over the illness. I see a lot of people who don't come out of it, but he healed me.

Another time, I had a lump on my breast and after the biopsy, the doctor called and said it was cancer, and I would have to have the breast removed. He said if I didn't, I'd die. Well, I didn't go in for surgery, I prayed, and I've been well ever since.

I go to our senior center for activities every day. I still drive—it's not a long trip. I'm healthy. If you have a good attitude toward life, the healing substance comes to the fore and you'll be well.

I pray every morning with my pipe. I smudge sage. You take the sage and set it afire. When it catches, then you smother the flame and you use the smoke in your pipe. I pray to the Grandfather, to the God of the Four Directions. I ask for good health, I ask for the health of those I love.

Out here in Shakopee, there's plenty of trouble with the younger people. There's just not much for them to do at night on a reservation. Some people are trying to develop programs for them. Many of the Indians work for the tribe. There's bingo and the casino, and that has meant jobs.

Are our lives improving? If you're thinking of assimilation, no—that's not what we want. We're Indian. We live our lives in our own way. We know how to laugh at ourselves. That's what keeps us going.

From interviews with the author, March 3, 1988, and November 16, 1989.

Editor's note: After a prolonged illness, Rose Bluestone died in May 1993.

NOTES

1. The Dakota (sometimes called Santee Sioux) make up the easternmost flank of the Sioux Nation. The Mdewakantons and Wahpekutes are bands of the Dakota. While they were originally woodland peoples, the Dakota have close ties to the Western Sioux (Lakota). See Royal B. Hassrick, *The Sioux* (Norman, Okla: 1964, reprint 1989, p. 6).

2. Dakota Chief Little Crow warned the warriors against what he perceived to be a losing battle with whites, but militant voices prevailed; some formerly disparate bands united in an attempt to drive whites from the region. See Gary Clayton Anderson, ed., *Through Dakota Eyes: Narrative Accounts of the Minnesota Indian War of 1862* (Minneapolis: Minnesota Historical Press, 1988).

3. Rules specifying eligibility for membership in the Mdewakanton Dakota Tribe are in dispute.

4. In 1990 a tribal official announced that grants totaling hundreds of thousands of dollars were being made to community food shelves, chemical dependency, and cultural programs for Indians. "We would like to become the McKnight Foundation of the Indian community," he said (*Minneapolis Tribune*, September 24, 1990). In the spring of 1994, the same official announced that dividends of approximately $450,000 from gaming had been paid to individual tribal members the previous year. The U.S. Gaming Commission began investigating the fiscal management of this lucrative enterprise, fueling speculation that the war for control of Dakota resources had resumed.

6

Still Grieving over the Loss of the Land

ELAINE SALINAS
WHITE EARTH OJIBWAY[1]/CHIPPEWA

T*hey call themselves the Anishinabe, "the original people." The elders of Minnesota's White Earth Reservation remember the days when their small cabins were set deep in tall stands of birch and scrub oak trees. They fished, hunted, logged with horses, and harvested wild rice. Despite treaties decreeing that the land would be theirs "in perpetuity," they witnessed a land grab of massive proportions. Today only an estimated 6 percent of the 830,000 acres originally promised to them is in Ojibway hands, the reservation's leading product seems to be not lumber but poverty, and tribal members are in negotiations with the state, federal government, and private corporations to reclaim the land.[2] Through gaming and other enterprises, the tribe seeks to improve its economic status, and reassert its sovereignty.*

Uprooted from her childhood home at White Earth, Elaine Salinas experienced the dislocation that afflicted her generation, then went to work helping other Native Americans put the pieces of their lives back together. We met in her office at the Urban Coalition in St. Paul, where she works for increased educational opportunities for people of color. Elaine Salinas has served on the Governor's Task Force on Prejudice and Violence. Her lobbying efforts have resulted in passage of legislation calling for the teaching of Indian languages and culture in the public schools. Tall and lithe with brown shoulder-length hair, she's warm and outspoken.

I WAS BORN IN 1949 ON THE WHITE EARTH RESERVA-
tion, a member of the Pembina Band. When I was seven, my
family moved to Wahpeton, North Dakota. My parents went to
work at the Wahpeton Indian School, a Bureau of Indian Affairs
boarding school. My father was a carpenter, my mother worked
in the dormitories. Because I was the child of staff, I could not
attend that school, but we lived on the campus so I saw what
went on.

Since the late 1800s, Indian boarding schools have existed in
various parts of the country. Initially the thinking was that if you
left Indian children on reservations, they'd remain "savages," so
representatives of the Bureau of Indian Affairs virtually kidnapped children from tribes all over the country and bussed them
to military-style boarding schools to "civilize" them.

I'd stand in front of the school at the beginning of the year
and watch the buses arrive: children from six to eighteen looked
lonely and scared. School personnel herded them like cattle into
showers and treated them for lice. The youngsters slept in large,
cold dormitory rooms. At night, I heard little children and even
older ones crying for their parents.

Some of the children spoke their Native languages; some did
not. But all had been isolated from families and traditions. In this
period, they were not allowed to speak their languages or practice
their ceremonies at the school.

The system was dehumanizing. If a girl disobeyed a rule
she'd have to wear a long, green dress as a signal to others that
she had misbehaved, or she'd have her beautiful long hair cut
short. A boy who disobeyed had to scrub the basement floor
with toothbrushes; if he was defiant, he was sprayed with a fire
hose. If he tried to run away, the police would track him down,
the school superintendent would pick him up and make him run
beside the car.

The most severe punishment I witnessed was "the hot line."

An eighteen-year-old boy had been allowed to attend a movie downtown and had come back late. The staff made the male students form two lines and gave them belts; the boy had to run the gauntlet and be whipped by his peers. That created a lot of hostility within the student body, which I think is what the staff intended. There was a divide-and-conquer mentality.

I witnessed a gradual reduction in abusive practices at the school and eventually, they were outlawed. But I was becoming aware of a policy of cultural genocide implemented in the boarding schools.[3]

I attended a Catholic elementary school. I had to defend myself against racial slurs. I played the system, I did what I had to do to win approval from the nuns. But I always reserved a part of myself. In high school, the prejudice of the white students was more subtle. By then, I hated school, but I knew I could not fail—that would hurt my parents. My grandfather spoke several languages. My grandmother was the first Indian teacher in Minnesota and wrote music.

After graduating from college, I got a job as community services director for a school on my reservation. Returning to White Earth cured my sense of separation, and it brought back memories of what it was like growing up there. We used to live in a house on a little dirt road running through the village. Nearby were aunts, uncles and grandparents. A whole gang of us kids hung around together. We hardly had any toys, but the outdoors was there for us. We'd ice-skate and play ball, we'd invent stories and games. We'd collect live frogs, and dare each other to bite off their legs—we were awful kids. [Laughs.]

I had a Raggedy Ann doll that I loved. Once, my dad was leaving town in his old pickup truck to work on a construction job. I ran to him to say good-bye, and when he was gone, I realized I'd lost my doll. It hurt, because I had only one doll.

As part of my job, I visited elderly people in their homes.

Some of them didn't speak English, and I didn't know Ojibway, but we communicated. Grandma Ellis, a ninety-eight-year-old woman, was out chopping wood in the middle of winter. She lived to be 104. Fred Weaver made kinnikinnick out of red willow, and he told marvelous stories.

I found out that in the nineteenth century, White Earth had been a thriving town with a hotel and a number of stores. Ojibway worked in the fur trade and the logging industry. My grandfather owned a livery stable. The Allotment Act passed in 1887 divided tribal land into small plots. Indians were supposed to become farmers, "productive citizens." They had been used to moving with the seasons in search of wild game, fish and rice, sharing what nature provided. The idea of dividing the land into individual plots and planting seeds was totally alien to them. People sold acreage just to buy food for their families. In desperation, they accepted the low prices whites offered for the land. A lot of land was also lost through illegal tax forfeitures. That's how we lost most of the White Earth Reservation.

When the Relocation Act was passed in 1956, the government told the Indians, "You move off the reservations, come to the city, we'll find you a job." But the people weren't trained for the few jobs open to them. They crowded together in small, overpriced flats.[4] To this day, many Indians don't like living in places where there is so much congestion and traffic, where the pace is so much faster than on the reservation. Those who have settled in the city have sometimes had to relinquish close ties to family and community, and a chance to practice their religion on ancestral land. A lot of Indians feel like foreigners in the city. They are still grieving over the loss of the land.

Relocation was hardest on the men. Historically, the man was the provider. Indians who had some status within their tribe as religious leaders, chiefs, hunters and warriors came to the city to find themselves viewed by the larger society as extinct. When you're faced with racism and unemployment, how do you express your anger and frustration? Do you strike out at the community's business leaders? That wouldn't be tolerated. A man's anger often surfaces as self-destructive behavior and violence against others.[5]

There were so many losses for the women. There were cases in South Dakota where contaminated water caused abortions and premature births. A number of Indian women were sterilized—it happened in hospitals across the country. Children were taken away from their mothers.[6] Collectively, we lost so much.

There's a theory that Indian people have never been allowed to go through a grieving period for the world we lost. So, this theory goes, the problem is depression, which often leads to chemical dependency. Every Indian is touched by that. I have it in my family. Studies show that many hard-core street alcoholics were brought up as traditional Indians. They could not adjust to the loss of land and culture. I think Indian people need to find a way to live in the world as it is, and still remain Indian.

Life in the Indian community has changed. Today most of our Indian parents are single women, and for them, the job of supporting and holding the family together is overwhelming. In tribal communities, women's lives were difficult; they often did backbreaking labor. But you had a group of people who operated in sync with each other toward a common goal. Today, there are so many forces undermining what we do, it's amazing we survive at all.

Walk down Franklin Avenue, the hub of our community, and you'll see people without homes or medical care lining up for free meals. The poor become poorer as the rich become richer, and there's anger. Recently, an Indian boy was killed in the crossfire between rival gangs. A baby caught in the middle of a fight was hit by a chair and killed. These are innocent victims! But in our communities, it's old news. It's as if the community is turning on itself.

The police often turn their backs on violence in our community, or they perpetrate it. When they don't respond to calls for help, Indians feel that as long as we're killing each other, the police don't care. Hate crimes are on the rise. We have mobilized to protect ourselves. The American Indian Movement patrol has had some success in dealing with crime, but it's hard to get Indians to believe that they can make a difference. There's a sense that what you do won't change anything.

It's hard for young people to feel good about themselves in a hostile environment. Look at what happened to the Cherokee after they were removed from their homeland and brought to Oklahoma. Within a span of about forty years, they became "civilized" by every definition the white man had. I mean, they became literate in English, they had a newspaper, they made tremendous economic gains, but still they were not accepted. The Cherokee experience suggests that education is not "the great equalizer."

Inherent in this country is a real sense of white supremacy. You can go to college and get a doctorate, but if you're a minority, especially if you're a woman, you have to prove yourself all the time.

Sure, education can help to change this negative climate. But when white people talk about education, they're talking about more math, more science—they want their kids to graduate and fit into the cogs white people have created, so they will serve this market-based economy. Fewer kids fit that mold today. More and more of them come from low-income backgrounds where the market economy has never worked. You have families on AFDC for generations, so the public school system becomes less and less relevant.

Indians today are obtaining college degrees and becoming social workers, architects, computer programmers, managers of businesses, so there are more role models. Still, in our community as a whole, life has not improved significantly. We have the highest rate of poverty, unemployment, infant mortality, diabetes, alcoholism and suicide of any group in the country.

What hope is there? We are looking at traditional programs that worked within tribal societies. People in the mental health field are using the "talking circle" for healing. Our Indian-run school programs work for many of our kids because in them, being Indian is an asset.[7] We are trying to convince those who have the resources that they should be investing money in our communities, but there are often issues about who "owns" the program.

I think that young people are our hope. Tribal societies nurtured the young, and prepared them for adult roles. As children aged, their responsibilities within the family and tribe increased. We need to give our young men a voice in decision making, we need to build their self-esteem and leadership skills. Another thing we can do is to reconnect young people with elders who transmit an appreciation of life; kids often find them more accepting, less judgmental than their parents. To join the young and the old—that is a healthy alliance.

I talk to schoolchildren about careers. I urge them to develop their skills so they will have choices. I talk to my son about using his strength to give back to the people. In order for Indian people to survive, we all have to contribute.

I don't value money or position. What really matters is that Native people will continue to be distinguishable as a people by virtue of our sovereignty,[8] our value system, our worldview, and our respect for unborn generations. They are our future, our hope.

From interviews with the author, June 7, 1988, and September 2, 1994.

NOTES

1. The alternate spellings are Ojibwe and Ojibwa.

2. See Louise Erdrich and Michael Dorris, "Who Owns the Land?" *New York Times Magazine*, September 4, 1988.

3. The 1934 Indian Reorganization Act encouraged placement of Native children closer to homes and on reservations, and gradually many of the boarding schools were phased out. See Margaret Szasz, *Education and the American Indian: The Road to Self-Determination, 1928–1973* (Albuquerque: University of New Mexico Press, 1974).

4. Annette Jaimes writes of the Relocation Act that "it was coupled to a denial of funds for similar programs and economic development on the reservations themselves. Those who availed themselves of the 'opportunity' for jobs ... were usually required to sign agreements that they would not return to their respective reservations to live. The result, by 1980, was a diaspora of Native Americans, with more than half of the 1.6 million Indians in the U.S. having been scattered to cities across the country." See M. Annette Jaimes, *The State of Native America* (Boston: South End Press, 1992), p. 16.

5. See Winona LaDuke, "Domestic Violence in a Native Community: The Ontario Native Women's Association Report and Response," *Indigenous Woman*, vol. 1, no. 1 (Spring 1991), pp. 38–41.

6. In response to growing concern over the high numbers of Native children removed from their families and communities, Congress enacted the Indian Child Welfare Act in 1978, giving adoption preference to Indian families.

7. A reference to "survival schools" started by the American Indian Movement in response to the high dropout rate of Indian youngsters. See Laura Wittstock and Cassandra Holmes on this subject in their interviews in this book. Some urban districts serving large Indian populations have established Indian-run schools or programs within the public school system.

8. Asked for clarification, Ms. Salinas said: "We are citizens of sovereign tribal nations, as well as of the U.S.; we have dual citizenship. White people begin to see us as distinct from other people of color when they have to interact with us politically."

7

The Power
Comes from Within

INGRID WASHINAWATOK
MENOMINEE

I n December 1992 delegates representing Native communities the world over addressed the United Nations General Assembly, inaugurating the International Year of the World's Indigenous People. Noeli Uliana of the Wayuu people of Venezuela proclaimed: "What would humanity be like without aboriginal peoples, without blood linkages with Mother Earth, without forests, without rivers, without . . . butterflies?"[1] Grassroots indigenous leaders deplored depredations by government and industry worldwide that threaten their very existence, and pledged to work for self-determination.

One of those delegates was Ingrid Washinawatok, chair of the Committee on the International Decade of the World's Indigenous Peoples. A writer and filmmaker, she is program associate for the Fund of the Four Directions in New York City. While in Minneapolis for a meeting of the Indigenous Women's Network, which she cochairs, a tireless Ingrid Washinawatok talked with me about the upheavals experienced by the Menominee, and Native American community life in the nation's crossroads.[2]

ORIGINALLY, MY PEOPLE INHABITED NINE AND A HALF million acres in Wisconsin. We hunted, fished and harvested wild rice. The name Menominee means "the wild rice people." Parts

INGRID WASHINAWATOK   *Photo courtesy of Ingrid Washinawatok*

of our reservation are hilly; we have unusual rock formations, and eighty-two natural lakes. We have one of the best stands of pine in the northern hemisphere. I think people from Germany settled there because it reminded them of the Black Forest. When I was in Switzerland, I remember walking in the woods, and thinking it was a little like home.

Our ancestors understood the value of our resources. The

elders told us, "If you harness the forest from west to east, you'll always have a forest, you'll always have food on the table for your kids." It's no big complicated plan. It's very simple. When we took timber from one area, we replanted, and moved on to the next section. Somehow, through the years, land was sold, or stolen, and we lost much of that resource.

We had a traditional form of government, a general council, with decisions arrived at by consensus. But the Indian Reorganization Act of 1934 changed our government into a corporate structure. In some tribes, dynamic leaders like Wilma Mankiller are trying to make it work. But the system also produced bureaucrats in tribes all over the country who abuse their authority, and take care of their own families exclusively.

Both my parents are Menominee. In the early 1950s, they were living on the Rez where they had grown up. My mom had completed a nursing degree, and worked as an RN at the tribal hospital. I think that in those days our reservation still had a sense of community. You'd take care of Grandma Jones down the street if she didn't have anyone to bring her meat. You'd get a basket, and bring her some food.

In 1954 the federal policy of Termination went into effect, ending the federal trust responsibility to certain tribes, so that meant that those of us born after 1954 were no longer eligible to be on the tribal rolls. We no longer had a relationship with the Bureau of Indian Affairs.[3]

Termination was a disaster for the Menominee. We had had our own electric department, our own telephone company, we had schools, we had a hospital. Ours was supposedly a model reservation. But when Termination went into effect, they closed down our phone company, our electric department, and a lot of people lost their jobs. The hospital closed—it wasn't up to state codes. When people were sick, they had to go twenty miles or more to the nearest clinic, and few people had cars.

Our kids used to be able to look to adults for safety. There were people who cared enough about a child to look out for him, to say, "Hey, don't do that. You're gonna hurt yourself." But after Termination, a lot of people had to go on welfare just to survive. By the 1960s, our annual per capita income on the reservation was down to just around sixteen hundred bucks. So people thought, "How am I gonna feed my kids? I can't pay my bills." When that happens, you stop worrying about the little kid down the street who has no shoes. Your whole existence is wrapped up in survival.

People felt so helpless because they couldn't provide for their families, and that's when a lot of them started drinking. Some of the Menominee were relocated in cities. One of the first lessons they learned is that in order to make it in American society, you have to promote yourself. In order to climb up the corporate ladder, you have to step on everyone. In our culture, and I've seen it in the black and Hispanic cultures too, that goes against the grain.

We get asked, "Why can't you get a fast-food job and work your way up the way a lot of immigrants have done?" Some Indians have done that, but you have to look at the reality of who we are. This is our land, and we don't have control over it anymore. We feel for those who have come over here from other countries. We can't imagine life being so horrendous that people would leave their homeland and ancestors behind to come here. Ironically, immigrants have a better chance of making it than we have. It's not because we lack industriousness.

It's because historically, we've been herded from one side of the country to the other by the U.S. Army. It's because we see toxic waste being poured into our rivers. We see our land base diminish. Our reservations have been battered. With each trauma that occurs, a piece of your heart is taken away.

My dad didn't finish high school. He was one of twelve children; he couldn't afford to go to college. He joined the navy at seventeen. We have a long tradition of service in the military. The Menominee have fought in every war since the Revolution. My dad only talks about his experience in the service in bits and pieces. He was in the invasion of Normandy. I gather he saw a lot of ugliness in the war. Years later he told me, "You know, they said I was going overseas to fight for my rights. Then after I came home, I became aware of the gross violations of the human rights of Indian people. I realized I was fighting for somebody else's rights."

I think it was in the navy that my dad really started drinking. I've heard from many men how hard it is to deal with the boredom of life in the service, and the killing. If you're Indian, you're brought up to care about all life; it's not okay to bomb towns and blow people to smithereens. But if you question it, then you're told, "You're not a man." You're told, "That person is the enemy; you are there to kill." I think that people drink out of shame—to dull the pain.

It's been very hard for Indian men to discuss this. Some of our communities pride themselves on having kids who have served in the army or the marines. Some of our boys go into the service to get an education. As the mother of a boy, I'm concerned about it, because today if you go into the military, there's a good chance you'll be mobilized to fight in foreign countries where you'll be face-to-face with indigenous peoples, pointing your gun at them.

Also, I heard an estimate that eighty percent of the resources of this country are on Indian land: water, timber, gas, coal, silver, gold, uranium. The mentality hasn't changed since they chased us down at Wounded Knee.[4] In Wisconsin, they throw rocks and beer bottles at Indians spearing on nonreservation lakes. I feel that at any point, if those resources are needed, the guns will be pointed back at us.

My dad went to Michigan State University on the GI Bill, the first in his family to go to college. He got a degree in police administration and political science, but ended up working as an insurance adjuster in Chicago, so that's where I grew up. Compared to a lot of Indians, we had a comfortable "middle-class" life, but it was hard to make ends meet, and my parents struggled.

In school, I was on the outer fringes; nobody wanted to play with me 'cause I didn't look like everybody else. Then I started making friends. I was supposed to know everything about Indians. Well, you get an American education, schools try to turn you into little white kids, but still you're supposed to know everything about Indians. It made me feel dumb. Like "the real Indians" live on the reservation, the real Indians ride horses.

As I got older I found that people expect the Indian woman either to be a backwoods person or a wise woman who knows the secrets of the earth. In old cartoons and movies being shown on cable television, they see an Indian guy with a knife in his teeth swooping down on a poor white family. They don't see real Indian men who come home and laugh and hug their families and say, "I missed you."

My son and I were watching the cartoon "Tom and Jerry." All of a sudden, Jerry has a bow and arrow in his hand, and is shooting arrows at Tom. And my little boy turned to me and said, "Mom, is that supposed to be us?" Last Halloween, on the cover of a parents' magazine, there was a picture of this little kid with flaming red hair—he had three lines of paint on his face, he wore fake buckskin and a fake headdress. For some people, being Indian is comical; they don't see us as human.

So many Indians are really lost. Some don't know they're Indian. I've seen people try to make a better life for themselves. I have friends who have gone to law school; they find out how negotiation has been used to legally swindle Native people out of their land and water rights. Some of them rationalize what they're doing. Some find a balance between their own needs and those of the community. Others go back to ceremony—that's one way of dealing with all the pressures.

What about Indians who go into corporations? I don't know very many who do because when we do, we find there's an emptiness. There's the danger of letting go of who you are as an Indian person to try to grasp for that American dream which is individualistic, not community-oriented. You might feel sorry for the guy on the corner, you might give him your token quarter, but that's not being a part of your community. And it's an ethical dilemma: how can you be comfortable working for corporations that you know are making a profit by taking our resources and poisoning the earth?

I went to the University of Wisconsin but I left because what I was learning didn't have much to do with the lives of Indian people. I wanted to learn things from the elders. I went to work for the national Federation of Native Controlled Survival Schools.

In 1984 a group of women active in the Indian rights movement formed the Indigenous Women's Network. There were two hundred women at our first gathering on Janet McCloud's land in 1985. We had sweats, we had talking circles—women talking about battering, about alcoholism, about sexual abuse of children, about feeding your children on food stamps. We asked, "What's the point in working to defend the land if our families and communities are deteriorating?" We formed a board, we started a magazine. Since that time, so much healing has gone on. I have seen women go back to school, become professionals, get Ph.D.'s, and the majority of them return to work in Indian communities; they bring their talents home to their people. The changes in the last ten years have been phenomenal.

I moved to New York City to work for the International Indian Treaty Council, translating documents from Spanish to English, and eventually moved to my present job. At first, I missed my reservation. But I was lucky to be welcomed by Shinnecock families who have a reservation on Eastern Long Island. They were there before the first settlers came. Originally, they were a sea people, whalers and clammers. We go out there to visit friends, we go there for powwows.

Everyone thinks there aren't any Indians in New York City, or if there are, they aren't "real Indians." What they don't know is that there's a very long history of Indians in the city. The Mohawk people have worked as ironworkers for generations; they built New York's buildings and bridges, and some of them settled here. I know Indians whose parents originally came to the city with Buffalo Bill's Wild West Show, and stayed on. There are Indian people who come to New York to go to school, to work in banks, the stock market, industry, police administration, some are computer whizzes. So we have a pretty diverse population. Many of us live in Brooklyn.

You can create community wherever you are. I'm on the board of directors of the American Indian Community House in the NoHo district in downtown New York City. We have a whole conglomeration of Indian folks: Hopi, Cree, Winnebago, Mohawk, Lakota, Kunas, Quechuas. There's this one couple that just had a beautiful little baby who's the apple of everyone's eye because it's the new life, the continuation of this beautiful community.

We have an elders' luncheon. People come from Brooklyn, the Bronx, Queens. We can't have them riding trains, so we pick them up. They come and eat, and learn about health issues. We have a day care center. We have a dance group that performs tribal dances, and dance clubs for the kids. Spider Women's Theater[5] performs plays on contemporary issues. Writers come in from all over the country to give readings of their work.

There was a conference a few years ago for Adult Children of Alcoholics. We sat in a circle holding hands, we talked and we listened to each other. I remember sitting next to one of the guys who had recently quit drinking. He was so nervous, he was shaking. All these years, you've flung responsibility to the wind. Then, when you feel responsible for having to maintain your sobriety, it's scary. Recently, I met that guy on the street, he told me he has stayed sober for four years, and we just hugged.

I travel a lot, and in communities across the country, I see women in leadership roles. There's a recognition that women are powerful, but it's not authority in western terms. There's a balance between young and old, between men and women. There's a recognition that power comes from within. It comes from having knowledge, and vision.

The sun has power. The wind has power. We have the power to bring forth and nurture new life. That's the power Mother Earth has. There's the power of love.

If you raise your children to be good people, then the future is theirs. That's more important than being president of a corporation. How can you not be fulfilled if you teach your children to be loving, honest, thinking people?

I remember how we used to go to Grandfather's house on the Rez. He lived on the Wolf River. I'd sit in the backyard and just look up at the pines and evergreens against the blueness of the August sky. Now, whenever I get homesick for my reservation, I close my eyes and think about that.

From an interview with the author, January 23, 1994.

Notes

1. Cited in Winona LaDuke, "Words from the Indigenous Women's Network Meeting," *Akwesasne Notes* (Winter 1985), pp. 8–10.

2. Ms. Washinawatok estimates that more than thirty thousand individuals from more than fifty nations make up New York City's diverse Native American population.

3. Following a determination by the Bureau of Indian Affairs to withdraw federal services from certain tribes, Congress passed the Termination Act in August 1953. This led to enactment of statutes ending federal

support for schools, hospitals, and other vital services within the Menominee, the Klamath, and other nations. Over one hundred tribes were affected in some way. Some suffered spiraling unemployment and a drastic decline in their standard of living. Termination contributed to the move of impoverished Indians to cities in search of jobs. The Menominee and a few other terminated tribes won restoration of services in the 1970s.

4. Seeking reform of tribal governments, in 1973 members of the American Indian Movement and their supporters occupied the town of Wounded Knee on the Pine Ridge Reservation, site of the 1890 massacre of more than three hundred Lakota by the U.S. Cavalry, declaring it the Independent Oglala Nation. The federal government surrounded the village with a blockade of federal marshals and FBI agents armed with high-powered machine guns and armored personnel carriers. In a seventy-one-day siege, an FBI agent was wounded, and two Indian men were killed. Following an eight-month trial of occupation leaders Dennis Banks and Russell Means, Judge Fred Nichol dismissed federal charges against them, citing the government's illegal use of force.

5. Founded by three Native American women at the American Indian Community House, this nationally known theater collective performs original satirical plays drawn from Native American experience.

III

Mending the Tears, Weaving the Strands

*"In the silence of recovery we hold
the rituals of the dawn
now as then."* ▽
Paula Gunn Allen
Laguna
Pueblo/Sioux

8

The Cottonwood Tree
Talks to Me

JUANITA ESPINOSA
TURTLE MOUNTAIN OJIBWAY/
DEVIL'S LAKE SIOUX

From earliest times, indigenous peoples have used materials found in their environment to create art forms conveying their way of looking at the world. Today, from the powwow circuit to the stage, from street mural to urban art gallery, Native arts flourish. First Nations artists use traditional forms, motifs, and materials in new ways, incorporating a variety of media from paint to video to computer to tell us who they are and how they relate to earth and sky.

Creativity drives Juanita Espinosa. While she doesn't call herself an arts administrator, she is the founder and prime mover of the Native Arts Circle, which promotes the work of six hundred Native American artists in Minnesota. She organizes school workshops and art exhibits, as well as film and video festivals that draw nationally recognized Native artists to the Twin Cities. In her office in an Indian-owned "enterprize zone," speaking in a musical voice and vivid images, Juanita Espinosa retraced some of the detours she has taken in her life, all leading to the path she follows now. "To live is to be an artist, to be creative," she says.

I OFTEN THINK ABOUT WHERE I CAME FROM, AND WHY I am here. I was born on the Pine Ridge Reservation in the Black Hills. I first stepped into the sunshine on September of 1956.

JUANITA ESPINOSA   *Photo by Marc Katz*

My mom is Turtle Mountain Ojibway. My dad was from the Devil's Lake Sioux Reservation in North Dakota, and we lived there when I was growing up. It's a prairie community with rolling hills and trees, little streams and creeks, rocks I could climb on and sand I could dig my feet in. There were berries growing wild. There were tall grasslands where my friends and I could hide from everyone and tell stories. My parents gave me free rein to explore. I had a sense of space, a sense of being connected to the land.

We traveled a lot in the Black Hills. There is an agelessness there. I remember thinking the hills were so old, they knew so much. You could just sit there and listen to the breeze, you could hear the trees rustling, and talking to you.

We lived in a little log cabin, without electricity or running water. As the oldest of eight kids, I was responsible for hauling water from the stream. I helped bring in wood, I helped Mom bake bread, I filled the kerosene lanterns, I did laundry in the outdoor, wringer washing machine. I took care of my brothers and sisters. We used to listen to songs on a battery-operated radio. At the time, it seemed like a hard life, but my mother taught us to appreciate what we had, she taught us humility. In some ways, it was a very rich life. Now, if I could go back to that time, I'd go in a second.

My dad had been in the service, he was a travel bug, and we didn't see him much; my parents separated when I was around six, but still I was a daddy's girl. When he came to see us, he'd go out and buy me fancy dresses. He encouraged me, he wanted me to shine. When Dad left, we went on welfare, but Mom began volunteering at the school, and then got a job there so she was very involved in our education.

In the summers, we'd travel to my grandmother's home in Rapid City. She'd take us in her car to powwows on different reservations. Those were special powwows. We did round dancing, social dancing and fancy dancing. I made my own dance outfits. I had a jingle dance dress—we'd sew little circular snuffbox covers onto the dress, and they'd make music when you danced.

We'd set up our little white canvas army tents with tons of blankets—it was like a little village. We had our campfire, Grandma would cook soup and we'd invite people over to eat with us. I ran around with the other kids, and made lots of friends. After the dancing, we'd come back to our campfire, have something to eat and go to bed. Grandma would fold blankets all around me so I couldn't get out, but sometimes I'd sneak out.

When I was twelve I had a falling-out with my mother, I was unhappy in school, and I told my friends I was going to go and live with my father in Chicago. They didn't want me to travel alone, so this big farm boy came with me. I said, "Okay, but you better behave!" We hitched rides, we slept in haystacks on the side of the highway, it took us four days to get to Rapid City. When we got there, I found out my dad had been stabbed on the streets of Chicago, so I never got to see him. We buried him in the Black Hills. I stopped dancing after my dad died. I decided to go back home and resolve my conflict with my mom.

Our community had a little theater. They were doing Shakespeare, I auditioned and got the part of Juliet, and I got hooked on theater. It was very exciting. I learned to get up and express myself on stage in front of hundreds of people; my family was real proud of me.

I had always been sort of a wild child, unused to structure, and in school, I'd question and challenge the system. I guess I felt like I was the voice of Dakota people in our little community. There were few course options for students in our school, so we formed a student council. We asked the school board to let us plan our curriculum, and they did.

I went to live with my grandmother in Rapid City when I was around seventeen. She was college-educated, and a worldly woman. She adored me, and always challenged me to be better than I was. In the summer, we traveled the powwow circuit. I made beaded jewelry and sold it, along with fry bread and hot dogs, at a friend's refreshment stand. But living with Grandmother, there were so many rules, so I moved in with some friends. I worked in a restaurant to support myself, and I finished high school. I really wanted to show my family I could graduate. I saw that if I wanted to do something, I could make it happen.

I had a boyfriend. I was going to start college, but I found out I was pregnant. My family was very supportive. They put things together for me: pots, pans, dishes. We got married, we lived in New Mexico, and when my little boy came, I was ecstatic. We had two sons. I was doing Northern Plains-style beadwork, and I learned how to weave quilts. People started giving me orders, so I developed a little business. I went to a vocational school in Albuquerque and became a computer programmer. But I realized I'd be working with these big corporations that were building bombs, and I couldn't do that.

My husband was Pueblo and Chicano. He didn't want me to go to school, but I had to spread my wings. When we divorced, he took off with our two boys and hid them from me for years. In the next fourteen years, I saw them only once.

I moved back to the Rez in South Dakota. In 1983 I received my Indian name on my Rez. It is Tatewakanwin, which means Holy Wind Woman. That was my great-grandmother's name. The name comes from the place where my great-grandma was born in Canada. It's where two mountains meet, some kind of magical place where the winds actually go in two different directions. I could see that she was a unique person brought here at that time for some reason, and I began to wonder if I was born in the Black Hills for some reason.

They had a public ceremony for me. One of my grandmothers spoke for the family; she told me how hard it is to be an Indian. She tied this eagle feather on my head, she walked me around the arena, and they sang a song for me. It made me aware of the responsibility of being Indian: you have to go beyond the human realm and do things that will elevate your people. Now I have an eight-year-old daughter whose name is Wastewi, which means Good Woman. I think through our names, we rebirth our family history.

Because there were so few jobs on the Rez, I moved to Minneapolis. I got my degree in humanities and political science. I went to work for the Indian Health Board, going door-to-door doing a study of diabetes in the Indian population. That connected me to Indian people here.

I began organizing events for the Indian community. We'd have social events to honor the elders. One friend donated pies, another donated flowers or little plants we could give them. We had a day care center for the children and programs for the teenagers. I helped organize a resident's association for the people of Little Earth, a housing development for Indian people. Native women who had had no power began learning how they were being manipulated by management into accepting substandard housing. They learned their legal rights, and began to make changes.

I think it was in 1986 that I was in the Four Corners area of Arizona for an International Treaty Council gathering, and I met Roberta Blackgoat and some of the other Navajo elders who were fighting to hold on to their land. The strength they brought to that work, their commitment, brought tears to my eyes. Roberta had the energy of a teenager. She was rich in laughter. I remember she was supposed to get on a plane to fly to Washington State for a gathering. Well, she missed the plane, but somehow, this grand-mother in her seventies got on the highway and hitchhiked a ride all the way to Washington. Those women see change evolving, and they move with it comfortably.

Espinosa's community organizing gained momentum. She ran a gallery for women's handmade art, she edited The Circle *newspaper, she sat on an arts panel that decided which artists to fund. When a board member suggested limiting funding for Native artists, she was enraged and challenged the group's "tokenism," a smothering kind of racism. She began raising funds for an independent arts agency, and it was her drive and energy that brought it to fruition.*

Anger gives you energy. Sometimes, it is the juice that makes a person strive to keep doing his or her art. Art is healing. It is a way of perpetuating your family's lifeways, and your own vision. Whether the art reflects beauty or pain or struggle, it allows other people to experience our culture, and to see the similarities be-tween people.

My work with artists is a sort of networking. Wherever I go, I have that feeling of family. It's a way of "making relatives," we say. I think that's been a part of our cultural survival as a people. Our way is to share what we have, what we create.

Society wants to pigeonhole everybody. I grew up on welfare. There was alcoholism in my family. There were all those messages about "dirty Indians." I haven't had a chosen life. I've had to struggle. But I learned to value the struggle.

There are so many walls around Indian people, so many limits society places on us. At the same time, we set up our own blocks. Our thoughts are powerful; words are powerful. Our belief system can have a lot of impact on how we live, so I've always tried to have good thoughts. When people see me, I want them to remember that I'm not a lost and confused soul; I am consciously taking each step with all my people. I'm not any better or any less than others. I have only the rights the Grandfathers gave me to be here, to fulfill the path they set out for me when I was born.

I rely on my Grandmothers in this world; it is the women who are my teachers. But it is the Grandfathers who are most often listening to me as I go off and make my prayers and offerings. So I walk with both my male and female parts. Sometimes I feel as if I'm in charge of my direction; sometimes I feel as if I'm being pushed, or dragged, or flying.

I've made mistakes. We all take wrong turns. I've had to learn a lot of lessons, and I'm still learning. My boys came to live with me two years ago; I'm getting to know them. My daughter goes to an Indian school. She sings, she dances in powwows, she knows who she is. How do I make sure that my children and their children have respect for their culture, and hear the rustling of the trees?

Some people think of us as locked up in the past. Society still wants us to eat hay on our reservations; they still want us to disappear. We've dealt with the federal government for so long—the federal government defines who can be tribal members. It reinforces the conflict between full bloods and mixed bloods. That's one way of keeping us on the path of nonexistence. In our history of dealing with the Feds, we find it hard to trust people. We've been hurt and ripped off and blamed and accused and lied about for so many generations, so we don't have a trust level even among ourselves.

If you do wrong, there's the belief that something will happen to stop you. But if people want you to succeed, they give you support. And so change is a slow, deliberate process.

I've been fortunate: when I found out what my path was, I followed it. I think that happens to a lot of Indian people. We believe our culture is in our blood, it's a root for us to hold on to, and we must perpetuate it. That idea still exists. There's the rebirth of the powwow, of Indian kids wanting to sing and dance. There's still ricing, there's still sugar bushing, people are still traveling and "making relatives," there are ceremonies. Young people go off to college, but they come home and still want to know the old stories. Our understanding of the world is circular. There's no beginning, no end; there's a continual energy flow. Whatever it is you learn from your life, you carry with you all the time. Whatever you choose to do, there are consequences. So we have to continually raise questions: Why are we here, what is our responsibility to the earth and to the people?

Our ancestors prayed for the seventh generation.[1] I am of the seventh generation since the colonization of this land. I have to believe that the Grandfathers who put me here wanted me to survive, to perpetuate the children, and a lifestyle for them. Otherwise, why would I be here? We are the epitome of our ancestors. They are always right here; I sit at the table with them regularly. Whatever I do, I have to do it the right way because they're watching me, guiding me, reminding me that I am a Dakota/Ojibway woman of my people.

My rootedness to the land is my identity; it is the food they fed me. Right here in the Twin Cities, I have a big cottonwood tree in my backyard. Not all trees talk, but this one does.

In the summer, I sit in a rocking chair on my back porch

every day and listen to the tree talking to me, and I listen to the wind telling secrets.

From an interview with the author, March 1, 1994.

NOTES

1. See Carole Anne Heart Looking Horse on this subject, chapter twenty-five, page 291 and note #3.

9

We Are All Members of a Family

LAURA WITTSTOCK
HODENOSAUNEE[1]/SENECA

Ｉn the shadow of their "great tree of peace," in a huge, ceremonial longhouse, the Seneca Indians gather annually to recite the Great Law of the Iroquois Nations passed down through the centuries. The law proclaims that a woman shall be "custodian of the Good Tidings of Peace and Power" so the nations will live in harmony, so "the human race may live in peace."[2]

One of those working to safeguard the peace and order of her community is Laura Wittstock. She directs MIGIZI, a national Native news network, and trains young Indians for the field of journalism. Working quietly behind the scenes, she provides crisis intervention for community groups. In her Minneapolis office, phones were ringing, she had deadlines to meet, but still she took time out for lunch, a few laughs, and this inside look at her environment. Laura Wittstock returns frequently to the Seneca Reservation where she lived for many years because, she says, "The homeland is the center of our universe. No matter how long you've been away, you feel that connectedness. It's a gift."

I WAS BORN ON THE CATTARAUGUS SENECA RESERVA-tion in upstate New York. We've been there for many hundreds of years, in permanent agricultural villages. Our tribe has stability, and a broad base. We call ourselves the Hodenosaunee, which means the Longhouse People. We are part of the Iroquois Confederacy, a political alliance which was set up many centuries ago to unify and protect the Six Nations.[3]

We have the Great Law, originally recorded on wampum belts—the symbols are geometric shapes formed with shells, conveying complicated messages widely understood by the people. We are a multilingual people. I learned the Seneca language from my grandmother. I was part of a large extended family. I remember attending ceremonies. I remember funerals.

I'm from the Heron Clan. The clan is a sort of sisterhood. Clan members used to live together in a huge longhouse under the authority of the clan mother. A woman derived her clan name and status from her mother. A son brought his wife home to his mother's house. The clan mother knew the menstrual cycles of all the young women, and she determined when they could participate in ceremonies.[4]

Women "owned" the fields, but actually it was a communal system, a sort of profit sharing based on the belief that the earth belongs to all. Everyone worked. The only time they sat around was in the deep winter when they told stories. They had a sugar-gathering industry—they marinated beans in maple sugar—that's the origin of baked beans. The business of agriculture was scientific. Men developed the best ways of raising and storing corn, and new strains of plants. Women did most of the cultivation. There are stories about how the women went out and danced around the corn.

There was cooperation, diversification of roles. The men hunted. The hides were urinated on. (Urine is an ammonia solution that breaks down the hair bond with the tissue.) The women helped with the scraping of hides.

There was a certain toughness in the women, who had a tremendous amount of power. Women selected the chiefs, and were consulted in political matters. Women elders were considered special people, with visionary powers. Those most knowl-edgeable about our history and traditions were called "faithkeep-ers" and taught the young.

Men and women were equals. Most marriages were long-term relationships. But the women were not dependent on the men—the same yoke was on both their necks. If they separated, it wasn't such a big deal. The woman remained with her clan, the man re-turned to his mother's home.

There were special societies for healing. There was a bond be-tween doctor and patient, who was treated as a whole person—Indians always combined psychiatry with traditional healing methods, using herbs and teas, as well as prayers to spirits, ritual incantations. There was the belief that body and spirit were con-nected; there was an awareness of the link between the individual and the universe.

My great-grandmother Eliza Mohawk was a member of a medicine society. She made calls to patients in a little one-horse buggy; she cured illness; she delivered babies. My father told me that when he was nine months old—around 1899—he contracted pneumonia. The local doctor said there was no hope for him. When Great-grandmother heard that, she took him to her home; she doctored him; and, he got well. Some people thought it was a miracle; some thought she used witchcraft. (I think that was the European influence.) She was sworn to keep her procedures secret, but she was allowed to teach them to her daughter, my grandmother, who delivered babies until she was eighty-three years old.

Our False Face Societies have a role in healing. I'm not a member so I can speak only in general terms. My grandparents were members and to this day, men and women are involved. The societies embody the ideals of the Iroquois Nation. We are taught that we must live an exemplary life, that we have a responsibility to all living creation. The false face mask worn by society mem-bers during healing ceremonies symbolizes that unity. It is cut from a living tree, then finished in fine detail; it's an art form founded in spirituality. While it's in use, the mask is considered to be alive and it is fed, an expression of our responsibility to one another. In time of sickness, you can be comforted knowing that the members of your society are there to support you, for you are all part of the same organism, one being.[5]

Through the generations, we experienced setbacks and devastations. Our institutions, developed over many thousands of years, were challenged. The formal parts of government are the ones that get kicked in the teeth. Europeans came to our territory, they'd find out who the head guy was, they'd bargain and make deals, there was corruption, and this weakened us. Treaties were broken, we lost much of the land, many Iroquois were removed to western reservations.

The Bureau of Indian Affairs made the people on our reservation jump through hoops. Schools tried to extinguish our languages. The churches were looking for souls, land and an economic base. My grandmother remembered that during periods of economic depression, missionaries would entice Indian people into the church with promises of clothing and food—but they'd have to be baptized first. So my grandma's family was baptized— it was survival. They continued with the Longhouse Religion, and that duality continues today.

After construction of the Saint Lawrence Seaway, there were great waves of immigration of white people into Iroquois territory in New York. The settlers drove out our animals, and this forced us to look for other means of subsistence. Iroquois men provided cheap labor for the surrounding white society, and were willing to do hazardous jobs. They built roads, bridges, skyscrapers. They drove long distances to work in the cities, then back to the reservation for the weekend. They were devoted to home and place. My brother worked in the steel mills and drove forty miles each day. Another brother was engineer on a road crew, and he'd be gone for weeks traveling hundreds of miles. When he returned, there was a celebration. All this traveling took its toll on family and community life. There were many displaced people.

The women took on men's roles. They did house repairs, some began doing construction. Did they do the housework too? Oh yeah, that doesn't change. [Laughs.]

After World War II, returning Indian servicemen brought home non-Indian wives from overseas, and many moved into cities in search of economic prosperity. So that continued the separation from the Longhouse Religion.

Despite the threat to this ancient religion, it has survived, miraculously. We have held on to the practice of verbalizing the wrongs we have done. It's like the Judaic idea of Atonement. In January or February during the first moon of the year, the time of our midwinter ceremonies, the fire in the ceremonial longhouse is extinguished, fires are lit in individual homes, and that's when you atone for whatever wrongs you have done. Historically, the declaration of the Great Law took ten days: there were predictions, songs, dances, feasts with special foods. (The clan mothers served the chiefs first.) Today, people still come for days to take part in the recital of the law and the festivities.

After World War II, when I was eight, my parents moved into the city of Buffalo to work, then they separated. My mother went to San Francisco, and I was sent to live with my brother's family in Hawaii.

That was a dark time for Indians. The BIA was enticing Native people into cities with promises of jobs and education. You could be trained as a welder, a cosmetologist, a janitor—jobs considered suitable for Indians. If you did get a job, there was no chance to advance, no retraining for another field. People felt cheated. To break out of that rut, they felt they had to integrate. Thousands of Indians did go into the general society, and lost their identity. Thousands didn't, and they had nothing. You can still see them and their children in the cities, living on the streets.

Mother worked as a maid, cleaning hospitals and hotels. She

hated the work—she had talents beyond emptying bedpans. But she worked hard, and saved up money so she could afford to have me live with her. She knew what it was like to be a displaced person. She became a beacon for Indians coming into the city. They'd say, "Let's go stay with Cleo Waterman." She'd feed them, give them clothing. She became an advocate for Indians—she was outspoken, seemingly unafraid. Later, I learned that was all an act to make it in the big city.

Mother and her friends founded the San Francisco Indian Center. They had a sewing circle. They made dolls, quilts, potholders, bedspreads, anything white people would buy. With the money, they were able to send the bodies of the dead back home to the reservations. The center brought people of different tribes together.

I moved to San Francisco from Hawaii when I was seventeen. Mother and I lived in a little efficiency apartment in a battered flat in a ghetto area. It was cheap rent, a good place to live. I remember seeing Mother leave for work in her white uniform, white stockings and shoes. She was small, but to me she seemed strong and independent.

Coming from Hawaii, I found the city very big and cold; people would look through you as if you weren't there. There were a lot of poor people in our neighborhood, but there was no sense of community. I was very shy. I had dark skin. I wasn't slender. I didn't feel attractive. My clothes had flowers on them, I was used to going barefoot on the beach, and felt clumsy in high heels. I suppose I was depressed. I became a hermit, retreating to my room, reading. I used to lie on the bed looking at the plastic angels on the ceiling. You build a barrier which helps you deal with the ugly, insensitive world. You remain inside your shell, protected.

In high school, I made friends. We were concerned about apartheid in South Africa, and vowed to never own diamonds— I've kept my word. I began getting attention for my writing. To earn money for college, I applied for a job at the *San Francisco*

Examiner. On the phone, the editor had been really cordial, but when I showed up with my mother and he saw I was Indian, he lost interest.

My mother believed the annihilation of Indians was part of the national agenda. She collected clippings of Indians from all over the country who were being persecuted, their homelands were flooded, they were dying. She said if we were not vigilant, we'd disappear.

Events occurred in the fifties and sixties which led to formation of the American Indian Movement. AIM says that it was always there; some of the things that happened were inevitable; there had always been resistance to government policy.

In the 1950s, the National Red Power Movement was building its organization.[6] In the 1960s, AIM grew out of the move of Indians to cities. In Minneapolis, there was police brutality, so AIM organized first to protect Indians from the police. Next it moved to establish claims against the U.S. government, then it designed programs to serve Indians. Within a few years, separate groups working in different parts of the country coalesced into AIM.

Mother worked with one on the West Coast called National Urban Indians United. They'd bring in buckets of rotting fish and dump them onto the desk of some mayor to demonstrate that our lakes and rivers were being polluted by industry. They'd say, "Look, you're killing the fish. Next you'll be killing the Indians."

My mother was active in the AIM occupation of Alcatraz.[7] She raised money, she brought clothing and food to the people on the island. But at age sixty-nine, there was a crisis in her life. She was about to get into a boat to go out to Alcatraz and some young, rude Indian said, "We don't want any old people out there." So Mother got out of the boat, she never went back to the island, and was very hurt. That young man had forgotten that elders are revered in Indian life. He was a lost soul epitomizing the loss of culture and the turmoil that had occurred during relocation. When mother told me about this, I realized her vulnerability. She became less active, and, eventually, went back home to the reservation to die.

I studied journalism in college. I married at nineteen, a non-Indian from California, and we had five children. After I put the kids to bed, I wrote articles for journals and magazines. Were they published? No. I went to a support group for writers—some of them hadn't been published either. [Laughs.] My husband and I divorced after thirteen years, and I worked at different jobs to support my family. After I remarried, we moved to Washington, and I got a job writing for the *Legislative Review*, an Indian publication. I went to legislative sessions, I asked questions, I deciphered the language of bills. I joined the Indian Press Association; I felt I had "come home" to my field.

It was the early seventies, there was an "Indian renaissance," and we were optimistic. Peter McDonald was elected chairman of the Navajo Nation on the basis of competence. LaDonna Harris was building Americans for Indian Opportunity, a think tank. At the same time, there was corruption in some of the Indian political movements. There were fights for seniority, some of the leaders drank, media attention was seductive and they became "stars"— that clouded their thinking.

There was also the potential for corruption within tribal governments. They'd had new governmental systems imposed on them, based on the white model. A great deal of power was invested in one elected individual. This was counter to the traditional tribal system in which power was shared. The temptation to abuse this power was overwhelming.

These were tumultuous times. As journalists, we reported as objectively as we could on events in Indian Country. I joined AIM in 1971 because I saw it as a force for change. Its basis was spiritual. There were elders and spiritual leaders at meetings; they always started with a prayer. Just as there were societies within the Iroquois Confederacy which helped us understand our place in the universe and our responsibilities, AIM did that for all tribes.

The whole idea was solidarity, the sense that everyone Indian belonged to AIM.

We'd meet in a smoke-filled room to talk about what our mandate from the people was. We agreed that we wanted to improve the quality of education for Native people; we wanted to take control of our communities and protect our land and resources. We talked strategy—should we march? Should we take over buildings in order to influence legislation?

In 1972 AIM members organized "The Trail of Broken Treaties." Indians from all over the country converged on Washington, D.C. Arriving on the eve of the U.S. presidential election, they demanded that the new Nixon administration negotiate with them before taking office. They called on the government to deal with the tribes as sovereign nations and to provide relief from treaty violations by state and federal governments. Trail participants occupied headquarters of the Bureau of Indian Affairs for a few days, leaving only when the new president assured them he was "open to discussion."[8]

AIM delivered a 20 Point Program which called for formation of a commission to review treaty commitments and violations, restoration of 110 million acres of land, restoration of the rights of terminated tribes, abolition of the BIA and so on. AIM recast the relationship between the U.S. and Indian nations. In the past, the government had always set the agenda.

Trail participants occupied the Bureau of Indian Affairs for a few days. I was working as a reporter for the Indian Press Association. I went over to the bureau and I noticed the disorganization. I was doing my best to maintain my reporter's distance, but some things going on I found appalling. AIM members were talking about blowing up the building, but that would mean the destruction of some valuable records such as those in the water rights office. I noticed open containers, some containing gasoline, some water. A reporter threw her cigarette into one of them. I remember standing there watching the cigarette butt arc through the air into the container, wondering if it contained gas or water, wondering if we were going to be blown up. Luckily, it was water. The building was not blown up.

AIM leaders couldn't agree on strategy. I offered to help with communications, then found out somebody had poured glue in the copy machines—that made it difficult to communicate with the White House.

In meetings at the White House, we protested the system of colonial government blocking change on many reservations. We made it clear that this grassroots hoi polloi group known as AIM was a legitimate voice of Native people. We had a groundswell of support from Indians all over the United States, and we were heard.

AIM created the ferment which led to change. Congress passed the Indian Education Act in 1972, the American Indian Religious Freedom Act in 1978, an act which has no teeth; a new law has broad support in Congress.[9] The Bureau of Indian Affairs was reorganized, the tribes gained increasing autonomy in spending their resources and operating their own schools. The 20 Point Program is still there for AIM to accomplish.

Clyde Bellecourt came out of prison (he had been convicted of drug dealing), went through a spiritual conversion, and dedicated the rest of his life to young people and families. He and other activists founded the AIM survival schools to promote traditional tribal values and spiritual ways, and the AIM Patrol to reduce drug use and street crime. AIM took over management of a housing development; it founded a legal rights center for Indians and other poor people.

I think of AIM as a phalanx, plowing new ground in order to meet the needs of our community. Its strength is that it has been able to change with the times. Today, AIM is active in bringing the generations together. We have a Peacemakers Center with a council of elders which mediates community disputes. Instead of going to court, a juvenile offender may go before elders trained by tribal judges. The Peacemaker Center has sports teams and leadership training programs; it sponsors communal gardens where kids raise produce for their families. It just sent a group of Indian kids to the headwaters of the Mississippi to collect water samples so they can help in the cleanup of the river.

Our goals today are to protect the elders and the children, to educate our young people, and to get out of poverty while holding on to our culture. How are we going to get through the next few years? We're finding that we can't rely on politicians to finance our domestic programs, so in the old tribal way, we are sharing limited resources in order to survive. Last night, I was at a meeting; someone said, "We need a vehicle. Can we use yours?"

If I have any spiritual belief, it is connected to the Longhouse Religion. Spiritually, we Iroquois are all members of a family. We have a strong link with our homeland. I can understand why "The Trail of Tears" was so painful for the Cherokee.[10] They had to leave behind the graves of their ancestors. That was sacrilege. It tore them apart.

Despite the battering of our traditions through the centuries, we have been strong enough to avoid extermination, to continue as a nation, to continue our government and salvage our identity. We still aspire to the ideals of the Iroquois Nation. It's hard for me to see Bingo, the sale of cigarettes and other profit-making ventures on tribal land benefiting just one person or a small group. That sort of entrepreneurial activity tears at the fabric of the Iroquois Confederacy.

We believe that all living things are linked; death is a transition from one form of matter to another, a return to the earth you came from. It is not our purpose in life to question why things die, but rather to do well while we have the opportunity to do so.

I hold all of life sacred. Ideas are sacred, the collective wisdom that we poor humans, with our limited understanding of the universe, can leave as a legacy to our children. The essence of that legacy is to live a good life, while fulfilling our responsibility to our community. This is a universal theme that has survived many generations.

From interviews with the author, November 3, 1988;
July 24, 1990; and January 22, 1992.

NOTES

1. The alternate spelling is Haudenosaunee.

2. Kristin Herzog, "Women, Religion and Peace in an American Indian Ritual," *Explorations in Ethnic Studies* (January 1984), pp. 16–38.

3. The term Six Nations refers to the original members of the Confederacy that provided security and unity for its members.

4. Wittstock has written that while clan mothers were the keepers of family histories and conferred names on children, it was a basic principle of Iroquois society that "parents do not possess their children." She explains that "individual identity is . . . important within the context of an extensive kinship with up to hundreds of other living individuals, countless thousands of ancestors, and millions more of those yet to be born." For more on family lineage among the Hodenosaunee, see Laura Wittstock, in "The Power of Names," *Colors* (January 1994), pp. 18–21.

5. Traditionally, the false face masks of the Iroquois were carved in response to a vision and were worn by their makers in public and private curing ceremonies. The carver roughed out the form of the mask in the trunk of a basswood tree, then split it from the tree and finished it at home. Painted red or black, the masks had distorted facial features and horsehair simulating human hair. The masked figure represented formless beings dwelling in the forests whose aid was invoked for curing. See

William N. Fenton, *False Faces of the Iroquois* (Lincoln: University of Oklahoma Press, 1987).

6. Under the leadership of Tuscarora "Mad Bear" Anderson, this movement attempted to unite Indians in a drive for sovereignty.

7. In 1969–1970, a coalition called Indians of All Tribes took over the abandoned federal prison on Alcatraz Island, hoping to turn it into a spiritual and cultural center for Native people. Despite the inadequate food, medicine, and sanitation, the occupation lasted two winters. The Indians' demands were not met; they were evicted by federal agents in June 1971. See Peter Blue Cloud, *Alcatraz Is Not an Island* (Wingbow Press, Berkeley, CA:1972).

8. See Vine Deloria, Jr., *Behind the Trail of Broken Treaties*, 2nd ed. (Austin, Tex.: University of Texas Press, 1984), pp. 48–52; and *BIA, I'm Not Your Indian Anymore* (Mohawk Nation via Rooseveltown, N.Y.: *Akwesasne Notes*, 1973).

9. The Religious Freedom Restoration Act was passed in 1993. See chapter nineteen, interview with Cheryl Mann, note [3].

10. The forced march of the Cherokee in the 1820s from their homeland in the Carolinas west to Indian Territory.

I See an Incredible Force within Native People

FAITH SMITH
LAC COURTE OREILLES OJIBWAY/CHIPPEWA

An elderly woman listens to Dakota language tapes while her daughter programs a computer. A class analyzes river water samples for a course in ecology. They are all involved in lifelong learning at NAES College in Chicago, which began as a small grassroots operation and has evolved into NAES,[1] a national Indian-oriented college system.

An estimated seventeen thousand Native Americans live in the Chicago area. I went there to meet Faith Smith, the woman Chicago Indians refer to as "our college president." She has been a delegate to the White House Conference on Indian Education and serves on a variety of boards, including the Ms. Foundation, the Funding Exchange, and Common Cause.[2] She prods "the system" to respond to the special needs of Indians. Faith Smith is dignified, soft-spoken, direct. She believes in people power. In her office in the small gray and white building that is NAES headquarters, she told me: "A recent fire destroyed much of our college building, but so many people came in to help us clean up, they came with their shovels and bags of food, they shared our struggle, and we rebuilt."

MY FAMILY MOVED TO CHICAGO FROM OUR RESERVA-
tion in Wisconsin, and after college, I became a caseworker at the

Indian Center. Over thirteen thousand Native American families had been relocated to Chicago from 1955 to 1970. I met Indians from Little Alaskan villages, from California rancheros and New Mexican pueblos. The trust status of some of their tribes had been terminated. The Bureau of Indian Affairs usually helped them for six months, then they were on their own. Jobs were hard to get. Most didn't feel comfortable going to welfare—they'd rather do without.

Two or three Native families would live in one apartment. Landlords would raise the rent if the bureau was paying. There were cockroaches. The people didn't know about subways or elevators, they didn't know that the streets were dangerous at night. I remember, there was this man from Arizona who had just been in the city a few months—they found him dead in an alley, with all his teeth knocked out. The police told us it was an accident, they said he had run into a wall.

Some Indians came apart. Some went home in a box. Some of them went back to their home communities—I'd have to make the arrangements for them. Those who stayed often came to the Chicago Indian Center because they needed bus fare or a ride to the doctor. We treated them with the same respect we showed members of the board of directors. No matter how somebody was dressed, no matter what their lifestyle was, we wanted them to know they belonged there.

People came to the Indian Center to obtain child care. They'd come to eat fry bread, attend a powwow, a wedding, a ceremony after a death—the things that bind people together. Over the years, they obtained schooling, they prospered and became part of stable communities, but they still came back to the Indian Center to work with youth and elders.

The Chicago Indian center was the first in the country to involve urban Indians in decision making. It was exciting. Still, as a woman you have to deal with the stress of working, continuing your education, going home and making dinner for the family.

The challenges and the failures force you to stand back and take a look at what is really important. That helps you keep your sanity.

In 1971, I found myself in the midst of a terrible political battle. Some staff members wanted to back away from social service. Some of us felt our job was to provide social service, and we spoke out. We were attacked in the Indian community and in the papers. I had seen that happen to others. In Indian communities, you grow up being political.

I went to Purdue University in the 1960s. Because of affirmative action, colleges were vacuuming Indian communities across the country, finding the brightest Indians, but after college, a lot of them couldn't make the transition back home. They had changed. Their communities had changed. They didn't fit in anymore. I know a lot of people today in my age group who are really lost. They've lost their relationship to tribe and community. They don't fit into white society.

I majored in education, and looked at the education of Native people. There were Indian kids who wouldn't question a teacher in a classroom, wouldn't look a teacher in the face, their parents wouldn't come to school. Families were alienated from the classroom and the system, and the children would drop out.

Faith Smith was a cofounder of NAES in 1974. This innovative program gives Native people some grounding in their history and culture while they work toward a Bachelor of Arts degree in community studies. An estimated 70 percent of NAES students graduate, and many go on to further education.

We began NAES in order to make higher education meaningful to Native people. We volunteered a lot of our time; we sold arts and crafts to raise funds. We got some support from an Indian health project I was working for. We linked for a while with Antioch College which had pioneered the work-study model and nongraded classes.

We began in a small space we shared with another organization. We had eleven students in a class in community health, mostly adults working in the human services field. We looked at programs involving people in their own healing. That concept was new to whites, but it was what Indian people did all the time. We got a grant which enabled us to bring people in from other parts of the country: someone who ran an effective alcohol-abuse treatment program, a Navajo healer. For their ceremonies, Navajos call singers, notify clan members, get food together, and collect money to pay the healer. He talked about healing as a community process.

People came to our classes. Even if they worked all day and had families, they came to class two nights a week. Once a student disappeared, so some of the students went to find her; she was undergoing a crisis and they gave her support. A few years later, she came back and said, "I left something undone." She completed her degree and now she's in graduate school.

People brought their life experiences into the classroom. My mother had lost most of her Ojibway language in boarding school, but she began volunteering here, and coming to language class. Pretty soon, she was studying traditional child-rearing practices of the Ojibway, and sharing what she remembered. So there's a sense of continuity. What you know is part of the wholeness of who you are.

One of our classes dealt with racism. The students who had grown up on reservations remembered being called "dirty, lazy Indians." It was spring and the fishing rights protest in northern Wisconsin was warming up. Students came into class and said, "We were down at the boat docks, and they called us timber niggers." Well, I grew up with that. It destroys your self-esteem. But in that class, people who had always accepted racism as "the way it is" began to talk about how to change attitudes.

One student was an alcoholic relocated here from South Dakota. He did a research project on the skid-row society that developed among Chicago Indians. Had some non-Indian done that study, it would have dealt with "oppressed peoples," but he wrote and talked not about the people's pathologies but their strengths. He said that when he became involved with Native people at the Indian Center, he stopped drinking. "You know, there were bad things about that life," he said, "but we supported each other." Now he's counseling other alcoholics in a way that allows them to be people. He's over sixty, and he's going to graduate school.

Over the years, we've had students dealing with the issues of chemical dependency, suicide prevention, treaty and land claims issues, child welfare. A student on the Fort Peck campus in Montana did a study of Head Start programs on reservations that influenced federal and state policy.

Most of our students come from families where nobody has a college degree, so when you see them working for several years to meet all the requirements, then graduating and taking what they've learned back to their communities, it's thrilling. We do not all come to the table equally endowed. People of color have to work hard to break through the barriers of poverty and racism. And they are doing it.

It took years to obtain accreditation. We'd go to a meeting of college presidents—mostly white, middle-class men in suits, and we'd have to explain what the baseline knowledge was for our program, and how we would put it into practice. Without a standard curriculum, it was hard to convey in a meeting. We'd say: "We're not isolated from the rest of the world. We're not separate little enclaves preserving our culture. We are acting out who we are at this time. We interact with different peoples and with government. We have to be the ones to define our needs."

It's important for us to verbalize our needs, but non-Indians sometimes wear blinders. I remember sitting in a seminar at the Newberry Library. A white scholar was complaining about an Indian "informant" he had talked to about the history of a tribe. The Indian had told him all kinds of crazy stories about what went on on the reservation. I'm sure that Indian man thought it was a stitch to put on this white man who sat there with his notebook and tape recorder. The scholar was angry—he'd used up an eight-month fellowship—but the Indians in the audience knew that the scholar would organize a theoretical construct about tribal life that might have nothing to do with reality. We knew that whatever he wrote, our lives would be the same.

Over the last two hundred years, our own governments and the legal system have been defined for us. Indian voices have rarely been heard, women's voices have rarely been heard. Many of these systems have not worked.

I'm impatient for things to change. I'm probably the orneriest person in the city. [Laughs.] That allows you to survive. I know that progress will come only when Indian people decide to change. There's incredible strength within our communities. Women are gaining power.

I joined Common Cause because I feel we need to have impact on institutions which influence public policy. Without access to power, Indian people will continue to remain at the bottom of the economic ladder. The way the economy is structured causes gross inequities. While Indian people have developed individual entrepreneurial skills, community-based economic development is needed to impact on the lives of Native people as a whole.

I'm a single parent with a twenty-one-year-old son. I want to make sure he will feel part of and contribute to Indian communities. I took him back to my reservation in Hayward, Wisconsin. We went into a restaurant, and all the white people got up and left. We went into a store, and the woman wouldn't put our groceries in a bag. She shoved them at me. We saw other Indians just put their food in their arms and walk out of the store, but I insisted that she put the food in the bag.

I told my son, "You can walk out, you can stand there and scream, or you can find a way to deal with it head-on." Anger is a compelling force that makes you take on issues directly. You just can't view "the others" as powerful. Recently people on our reservation boycotted that store.

My son's generation has had to face racism, but not the same barriers I faced growing up, so the young people are more positive. They know who they are. Part of that comes from the longtime existence of Indian organizations in Chicago. They've grown up with Indian canoe clubs, girls' cheerleaders, baseball teams, powwows, activities which re-create a sense of tribe and community.

In 1990, a fellowship enabled me to travel, and I went to Africa to see firsthand the struggles of other indigenous peoples trying to break colonial ties. In Zimbabwe, although they won independence from Britain in 1980, school tests are still sent to Cambridge to be graded. I attended a celebration in Namibia, which finally won its independence from South Africa, but only after thousands of Native people were killed. I went to New Zealand where the Maori women are seeking recognition of their cultural traditions and a national voice, just as we are.

We need to form coalitions, to cross boundaries, to understand how the same issues impact on communities of poor people, and on women all over the world. There are common concerns that transcend race and national boundaries.

I see an incredible force that exists within tribal peoples across the world, and within Native peoples here in this country, which allows us to flourish in our tribalness, in the face of tremendous adversity.

From an interview with the author, August 26, 1991.

NOTES

1. Native American Educational Services, a national network that operates colleges in four states.

2. Washington, D.C.–based citizen's lobby.

11

I Give You
Seeds of a New Way

CHRYSTOS
MENOMINEE/LITHUANIAN

hrystos grew up on the streets of San Francisco, "a war-swollen city." Active in Indian political movements, she supports herself by working as a maid and giving poetry readings. She has lived, and has done some of her writing, on the land of the Suquamish and Quileute nations. Her first book, Not Vanishing, *which appeared in 1988, conveyed her way of looking at the world in powerful, iconoclastic poetry. Her second,* Dream On, *was published in 1991 and dedicated to ". . . the Crows, Wrens & Swallows who arc by my window & keep my mind moving."[1]*

From her island home near Seattle, Chrystos took the ferry into the city to meet me. Wearing long, beaded earrings, she carried a bunch of daffodils from her garden and a brand-new poem. I was struck by her huge, dark eyes and jet-black hair, her honesty, her laughter. We ate salmon steaks looking out over Lake Washington, and Chrystos spoke about growing up outside the tribal circle.

MY MOTHER IS WHITE. MY YOUNGER SISTER GREW UP being my mother's favorite child, and I grew up hating my sister, and beating her up whenever I thought I could get away with it. My sister was born with blue eyes, lighter skin color than mine, and dark hair that she dyes blond.

My mother was affectionate with my sister, spent time with her, and it's a pattern that holds to this day. She'll call my sister every day, and me once every six months. I felt she didn't like me. I felt she was ashamed of the part of me that was Indian. We still have trouble communicating respectfully:

> Better Homes & Gardens says daughter is supposed to
> show up smiling   Pretend it's not old cans
> bottles   yellow newspapers
> I come to your vacant lot   put a teacup on my knee
> watch you try to drape my queerness in ruffles.[2]

My mother wasn't prepared to be a mother. I think she resented the fact that she didn't have the choices women have today, and that my father wasn't a very good husband. She resented some of the choices I made. She used to throw up her hands and say to me, "I just want you to be happy," which was a way of dismissing me and not listening to what I was saying. And she could be violent. So I escaped from Mother by going to the library and reading voraciously. Even as a little kid, I hated children's books—I thought they were boring, so I'd read books in the adult section, and the librarians would kick me out and send me home.

My father was born on the Menominee Reservation in Wisconsin in the 1920s. His father was Menominee, his mother was Lithuanian. There were problems with alcohol on that reservation; life there was one trauma after another. When he was nine, his mother died, his father was locked up, possibly for severe alcoholism, and my father ran off. He doesn't like to talk about that period in his life.

My father ended up in boarding school, where there was sexual and physical abuse. (Those who were abused often abuse their own children today.) I think that in traditional, intact cultures, that kind of abuse was rare. But the elders were not able to protect the generation of Indians who grew up in boarding school.

CHRYSTOS   *Photo by Ana Kissed*

For my father, learning English was painful. His letters show the effect of that—it's still hard for him to write in English. His handwriting has a beaten quality.

My father was not able to be a good parent because he had no experience of parenting. But he was an interesting man. He used to tell us stories, probably from his Menominee heritage, which showed us the right way to behave. He never went to college, but he had a big library, and he read to us from the Greek and Roman myths.

My father believed that if you assimilated, you would be safe. He lives his life in the white urban world, and that world shaped him, as mine has shaped me.

I went to a Catholic school—it was my mother's idea. I think I was looking to the nuns for mothering, but that was the wrong place to look. The nuns were vicious—they beat kids. I had quite a fascination with Jesus. [Laughs.] You know, kids are literal-minded, and when they told me I had Jesus in my body, I thought I did, so I spent a lot of time communicating with Jesus—that is, with myself.

I was a prude. That was all right with the nuns, but not with the other kids. I read and read, because none of the kids would talk to me. In San Francisco, there weren't many Indians at that time. The black kids beat me up, the Latino kids beat me up, the white kids beat me up, and I developed a lasting fondness for Asian people because they never beat me up. [Laughs.]

I started writing at the age of nine. The first things I wrote were awful—they all rhymed. They were hymns of praise to the Blessed Mary.

From the time I was twelve until I was twenty-one, I was sexually abused by an uncle, a Frenchman who was married to my mother's sister. I lived at home until I was seventeen. Then I hit the streets. I got into drugs and alcohol. I think that what was happening was that I was in agony because of what had happened to me in my family—the violence, the sexual abuse—and there was nobody to talk to about it. I was self-destructive. I continued to struggle with alcoholism. I didn't get published until I was older, partly because of the alcoholism, partly because I was so busy getting into trouble.

Alcoholism is hard to overcome because our lives are so filled with despair. It's hard to find a good way to live. A number of my close women friends also suffered from neglect, alcohol abuse, sexual abuse. It's our legacy. We're all trying to heal. There's a certain comfort in knowing people who have been through that hell, and survived.

It seems to me that the reservation system destroyed the ways in which we related to each other in the past. Alcohol was used to control Indians—by whites trying to acquire our land, by the fur traders. You could send an Indian out to bring back fifty beaver pelts, for instance, and when he showed up, if you got him drunk, you didn't have to pay him very much money.

It's easy to become ensnared, to believe that alcohol will solve your problems, or at least dull them. I've been sober since 1988. When I started seeing writing as essential to my survival, it was easier to give up alcohol. Now I devote a lot of my energy to encouraging others to write as a way of surviving, and staying sober.

Other writers have encouraged me. I was fortunate to meet the poet Kate Millett at Berkeley in 1975. I had just gotten out of the nuthouse, and still thought of myself as a crazy person. In the mental hospital, what I wrote was confiscated. But I took Kate Millett's class, and she praised my writing. She was the first person who saw me as a writer.

One of the things which influenced my writing was the Beat poets. In my teens, I used to stay up in coffeehouses all night listening to them ranting and raving about sex, about everything that was going on in their lives. What I wrote seemed mild by comparison. I had also developed a pretty strong political conscience. Having grown up during the sexual revolution and other liberation struggles, political resistance became a theme in my life. I worked against war and the abuse of women. I supported Native prisoners.

We've dead relatives & friends with no common burial place
Scattered   they say we are vanishing . . .
The only part of us they can't steal
is what we know[3]

I began to feel that words were the way I could argue the case for change in society. Through words, I could express my understanding of the world, which is that we're all profoundly connected. What I do every minute affects what happens to you, to others, to the planet. And so that theme echoes throughout my writing.

I'm still in the process of change, struggling with things I don't like in myself. Recently, someone sent me a really nasty letter which hurt my feelings. Instead of answering with a nasty letter, which continues the whole cycle, I wrote two loving letters to two other friends. That process of changing pain into something beautiful, or startling, so others will hear what you're trying to say, is what writing is all about.

I've never lived a traditional life. I'm not looking for a traditional life. There is no accurate record of what our lives were really like in the past. Most of those who described us saw us filtered through the crazy lens of Christianity. The church had an atrocious record with Natives. The men who came with Columbus had no concept of brotherly love. They were murderous, abusive of women. For the last five hundred years, Native people have been viewed through that Columbus binocular, rather than through our own words.

It's exciting to me that in the last fifty years, there has been a renaissance of Native writers from all different tribes claiming literacy, demanding that First Nations people be the ones to describe their lives and tell their stories. It's uplifting to be alive at this time.

We Indian writers are all profoundly shaped by our worldview. We don't believe that we are the center of the universe. We have a sense of mystery. We have a tolerance of divergent lifestyles. We use teasing to correct behavior. It's like if you really screw up as a Native person, people will say, "Well, it's human to screw up, no one does well all the time . . ."

In our writing we incorporate different voices, we play with the idea that we are not the center of the universe. We take the stand that "well, this may not be reality; it's my version."

I just returned from a conference of Native writers from all over the Americas held at the University of Oklahoma, called "Returning the Gift." It was really moving and powerful. We stayed up till dawn every night talking, we read our poems outside, our books were for sale. An Alaskan writer brought sealskin dolls she had made, with little tattoos on their chins. An Ojibway poet was there selling winnowing baskets. It was like an Indian market. It was wonderful.

A playwright named Bill Yellow Robe, Jr., staged a play he wrote about recovering from alcoholism. He was walking around looking for something he'd set down just a minute before, and did all the things you do when you have problems with alcohol. The audience was roaring, and at the same time weeping.

I think Native writing walks on the edge of the razor of joy and pain. You can read it and cry, or you can read it and laugh.

To be a writer is to stand outside of your culture, and reflect on it. And when you're Indian and already an outsider, it's sort of like being on Mars. I think the most interesting writing today is coming from those not accepted in the mainstream. That was true for generations of Russian artists—they were the outcasts of their society. And it's still true for many Central American writers not recognized in their own countries. We stand in that same place outside mainstream culture. To be an Indian writer is to be a dissident.

I have many mixed-blood Indian friends, and we all love to watch "Star Trek." It's one of the few places on TV where aliens who don't belong anywhere have a voice. Last night, they had this episode about "gorgons"—creatures with huge foreheads and ruffled faces—and I was laughing hysterically. It's set in this fantasy-land future where everybody gets along.

Some Indian nations have been able to maintain aspects of their traditional culture, others of us had to deal with invasion in an early period, and had our reservations tromped through the middle. We can long for a traditional life, we can see remnants of traditional ways our parents have taught us, but actual tradition has been gone for a long time. What we have in its place is an amalgam of different cultures and ways of doing things. At a pow-wow, you'll see women doing a traditional dance, but the "traditional" contest dress, with its beadwork, calico and silk ribbons, comes from European culture. So I think the word *tradition* is a misnomer. It's not tradition that holds us together, but our history and language, our common values, a sense of what makes the world right.

I'm a nomad. I'll be traveling to poetry readings all autumn. I'll just come home to do my laundry and repack. I've got my performance attire down to an art—just T-shirts and leggings—they pack easily. I love reading, and talking with audiences. I feel blessed to be able to do this work.

I live in a little apartment house on Bainbridge Island, close to Puget Sound. I walk along the water. There's driftwood, you can see blue heron, eagles, crows and gulls. Sometimes you see seals going through. This poem I just had printed on brown paper really captures what the place has been for me: "Before me the land and the water open. . . ." I've done a lot of healing there; that's where I became sober. I pray down by the water.

I attended a Native woman's sobriety group last year in British Columbia, and I'm going back in November. It ends with a Cedar Circle ceremony. It's one of the most moving things I've ever been involved with.

This is a give away poem . . .
. . . In this circle I pass each of you
a shell from our mother sea   Hold it in your
spirit   Hear the stories she'll tell you . . .

I give you blankets woven of flowers & roots . . .
I give you seeds of a new way

I give you the moon shining on a fire of singing women
When my hands are empty
I will be full[4]

From interviews with the author, September 9, 1992,
and September 22, 1993. Poetry segments used by permission.

NOTES

1. *Dream On* (Vancouver, B.C.: Press Gang Publishers, © 1991), acknowledgments page.

2. "Mama Wants Me to Come," *Not Vanishing* (Vancouver, B.C.: Press Gang Publishers, © 1988), p. 25.

3. "Vision: Bundle," *Not Vanishing*, p. 21.

4. "Ceremony for Completing a Poetry Reading," *Not Vanishing*, p. 100.

12

The Pipe Ceremony
Is Really Cool

CASSANDRA HOLMES
LAC COURTE OREILLES OJIBWAY/CHIPPEWA[1]

At Heart of the Earth Survival School in Minneapolis,[2] more than one hundred students, ages four to eighteen, gather with their teachers for circle time. The little ones sit on the floor around a huge drum. Three older boys and an elder beat the drum, singing in Ojibway—the drumbeats are soft at first, then the volume builds. A young woman lights a fire in a bowl of sage, then carries the burning sage to all parts of the room, using a feather to waft the smoke over the students. All are silent while an elder with long braids lights a pipe, then points it to the Four Directions and skyward, praying softly. As the drumming and singing resume, girls dance around the drum.

One of the participants was fifteen-year-old student Cassandra Holmes. After school, we sat in a classroom filled with the latest computer equipment. Her large eyes shining, Cassandra talked about what this ceremony means to her.

THE PIPE CEREMONY IS REALLY COOL BECAUSE RECENTLY, boys and girls have been holding it together. The boys play the drum, and we girls dance. I just heard that in the old days, women were the ones who taught men how to sing around the drum; they taught the men all the songs. Nowadays, women usually stand in the background. We can sing on the drum if we want to, if we're not on our moon, but none of the girls want to. When a woman is on her moon, she has a lot of power.[3] There is a special drum women can play at that time.

The pipe helps us. When somebody is in the hospital or there is a death, we all pray. Those of us who are older try to be role models, and show the younger kids that being Native American is okay, studying your traditions is okay. Some of the kids will goof off, but then an elder will tell them, "Have respect for the pipe because it's important in the lives of Native Americans."

I'm involved in lots of activities. I love sports. I'm reading lawbooks with my grandfather—I don't know if I'll be a lawyer. I was part of the AIDS Task Force. We went into schools and put on plays trying to get kids to take precautions.

I'm on the National Youth Leadership Council. We have camps for kids of all colors, to help them be in a good way and build leadership skills. I went to a NYLC conference in Albuquerque called Undoing Racism. There were speeches and games that made us aware of how class differences and stereotyping affect people. Then we did a workshop for the younger kids; we let them speak up and give their opinions, we listened, and afterwards, they clapped. That was the first time I ever heard anyone clap after a workshop.

We just had an Earth Day conference. We were sitting and watching students from our school singing and dancing, and this white guy sitting behind us said, "I hate Indians." We told him, "Earth Day isn't just for Indians; it's for everybody, because we're all affected by what happens to the earth." Then he said he was sorry; he said he was drunk.

We experience things like that every day. Like you go to a shopping mall, and they chase you out. Or if you go in and have money, the floorwalker is on you right away, asking: "Are you looking for anything in particular?" [Laughs.] Then they follow you around like you're gonna steal something.

Recently, I was out at sugar bush making maple sugar. There were students from various schools, and two elders who taught us

CASSANDRA HOLMES   *Photo by Jane Katz*

how to do things in the old way. They spoke to us in Ojibway;
I'm learning the language. We camped there for four days. We
went for water, we gathered wood, I even sawed wood; we tapped
the trees so the syrup could come out, we cooked it over the fire—
it's hard work, you need lots of wood to keep the fire burning
overnight. We all worked together from early morning to late at
night, and it was really fun. We put the syrup in bottles, then we
gave it away.

Since I was five years old, I've been a fancy shawl dancer.
Then my grandma passed away in 1991. Usually when someone
you know dies, you give up something for a year, or you may cut
off all your hair. My friend did that when her grandma died: she
put her hair in a braid, and put it in her grandma's hand when she

was lying in her coffin. That's something people have always done, out of respect. I loved and respected my grandma a lot, and I decided to quit dancing for a year. Now I'm dancing again; I'm making my own outfit. It has leather leggings and beaded moccasins, there's a yoke that goes over the head. My mom is helping me with the beading.

I've been doing community work since I was thirteen. They were having lots of problems in our neighborhood, so the American Indian Movement put together the Peacemakers. They have a center where kids come and play pool, listen to music, watch TV, movies, they have sports teams and other activities. I coach a basketball team there. The kids know if they want to go to the activities, they have to be respectful. They're interested in the activities; they behave.

I'm part of the AIM Patrol. You have to be at least fifteen, you have to be drug- and alcohol-free, and you can't be a troublemaker. Four of us, boys and girls, go out at night in a car with a CB radio, we drive around and see if there's trouble in the neighborhood. One time, we saw a guy who had just robbed a house rolling a big TV down the street. We caught up with him: he took off, but we got the TV back for the people. On Friday nights, after people are paid, they have parties, there are gang fights. One time, we were driving down the street, there was a big party and a fight outside, these dudes had ripped each other's clothes off, we didn't know if anybody had been stabbed or shot, so we called the AIM office, and they called the police.

I like being a part of the AIM Patrol. I like helping people.

I like expressing my opinions, not only about Native Americans, about racism and about every kind of "ism" there is. In our community, people of all colors and different backgrounds manage to live together and, for the most part, get along. I dream of a world in which young people will stand up and express their opinions, and people will listen. I would also like everybody to try to help the earth, to clean it up a little.

I live my life, I do what I want to do. I want to learn about my traditions. That's why I'm here. People will say, "Oh, it's so cool to be Native American 'cause you have this tradition." I just think, "Everybody's special."

From an interview with the author, April 25, 1994.

NOTES

1. Her father is from the Lac Courte Oreilles Reservation in Wisconsin. Her mother is White Earth Ojibway.

2. Founded by the American Indian movement in the 1970s as part of the "survival school movement," the school continues to be Indian-run but has an affiliation with the Minneapolis Public School system.

3. Much has been written about menstrual taboos that have to do with women's power, not contamination. Many Indians think that "women who are at the peak of their fecundity are believed to possess power that throws male power totally out of kilter. They emit such force that, in their presence, any male-owned or -dominated ritual or sacred object cannot do its usual task. . . . Women may be segregated . . . on certain occasions, but on certain occasions men are also segregated. In short, each ritual depends on a certain balance of power." From Paula Gunn Allen, *The Sacred Hoop: Recovering the Feminine in American Indian Traditions* (Boston: Beacon Press, 1986), p. 47.

IV

THEY ALWAYS COME BACK TO THE REZ

"People didn't have jobs, and the HUD houses* were falling apart. My husband and I went back home to the Rez and started a construction company. We build homes, schools, office buildings . . . on reservations. We help Indians form their own plumbing, electrical and framing companies. . . . Economic development makes our people self-sufficient. It strengthens our reservations. It strengthens the people." ▽

SUZANNE SMALL TRUSLER
NORTHERN CHEYENNE▽▽

13

The Puyallup Tribe
Rose from the Ashes

RAMONA BENNETT
PUYALLUP

I*n the 1970s, Ramona Bennett served as chairwoman of her tribe. Cited by the* Congressional Record *as "one of the nine most militant Indians" in the country, she frequently found herself in the center of a storm. Forced out of office after eight years by an internal power struggle, she moved to the sidelines but remained active in tribal affairs. I found Bennett somewhat mellowed in contrast to the fireball I had read about for years, more willing to accept the slow process of change. Calling herself "the little red hen," she founded and directs the Rainbow Youth and Family Service.*

We talked in her office on the Puyallup Reservation in East Tacoma, Washington, where rural terrain meets urban devastation. A thin, wiry woman around fifty, with brown hair and bright eyes, Bennett is a quick thinker, a rapid-fire talker, a graphic storyteller. She works hard, rarely taking time out to eat, seeming to exist on pop and cigarettes. She speaks out with a passion for truth-telling, sparing no one.

I'M FROM THE TOWN OF RAINIER, WASHINGTON. WHEN white people came here, they pointed up at the Mother Mountain and said, "Who owns that?" And the Indians cracked up—what a funny idea, to own a mountain! For us, the Mother Mountain is for everyone. It brings fresh water, it's where our river comes

RAMONA BENNETT AND AH-BEAD-SOOT   *Photo by Jane Katz*

from, it's forever. Then the white people wrote up title to the mountain, and changed its name to that of a beer baron, Rainier. They cut roads on it, they put ski slopes on it. It's an atrocity. This mountain is sacred to us. It would be like putting a recreation center on the Virgin Mary's breast.

The Puyallup have always lived on the sea, harvesting and smoking fish, and trading it to the interior. The Puyallup are a little like the newspaper. We're curious and outgoing because of our location on everybody's trading and traveling routes.

There really is only one Nation of Indians. You can find evidence of this from Alaska down to the tip of South America: there are similarities in the art forms, culture and languages of the tribes. We are one people with different dialects.

White people have always looked at us as though we were transients, lost people who wandered across an ice bridge from Asia. But according to our religious beliefs, Grandfather Great Spirit created us, which is a miracle, he created us right here on the Turtle Continent [North America]. He created us right here on the Puyallup River to protect the finned ones, our brothers and sisters.

My mother is Puyallup, and her family band lived at Wollotchud, known as McNeil Island, on Puget Sound. These were Longhouse People, and in a longhouse, you have security and protection for people of all ages. You have the old people who know all the rules necessary for social order, and the best methods of making and doing things. The old people don't get thrown out like garbage because they have wisdom and can teach the little ones. Children want to please, they've got strong legs and bright little eyes, and they're quick and helpful. In their middle years, people are stronger and able to do the hunting and fishing, and the heavy work. So you have a very good team.

That was what was really good about Indian societies. Everybody knew the rules for social conduct, so there was no confusion. Everybody was useful and part of the future, so there was no need for unemployment insurance or welfare, juvenile detention centers, prisons or nursing homes. These Indians had extended families—the finest form of social security there is.

In the mid-1800s, white men came from Boston to negotiate treaties; some tribes negotiated for wild rice or pine nuts, for others it was hunting and fishing rights—whatever was basic to their economy. The Indians didn't trust whites because they came without their families. To Indians, if you traveled without your family, that meant you'd been banished because you were a bad person. Furthermore, the white people never bathed so they stank, whereas our people here had sweat lodges, they bathed in the river, and knew that chlorophyll from vegetation will keep you smelling good.

The men from Boston went to our Longhouse People and said, "Send out your leaders." Since these were matrilineal societies, the old women went out. The white men said, "No, no, we want your leaders." So then the old men went out. "No, no, we want your leaders," they said again. The Indians said, "Golly, what do they want?" And they sent out the young men. So right from the beginning, whites imposed on us methods of choosing our representatives; our traditional way of identifying leaders had to be set aside to accommodate the sexism of white people.

Under the provisions of the Treaty of Medicine Creek signed in 1854, the Puyallup ceded their territory in western Washington to the United States and agreed to move to land set aside for them on Puget Sound, near Commencement Bay.

The treaty "reserved forever" for the Puyallup twenty-three thousand acres, and they moved the Indians here. This whole area, from the top of the hill down to the delta, is our reservation. But "reserved forever" just means until somebody needs it. When they did their first survey they included only eighteen thousand acres, so right away we lost five thousand acres. Then we were hit with three major epidemics—smallpox, measles and influenza (they don't count tb, but tb really broke up the tribes) so illness decimated ninety percent of our population. By allotment time, there wasn't much left of the tribe.

Whites divided the reservation into separate parcels. Then they tell these Indians, "You gotta use it, you gotta improve it, or you lose it." For white people, improve means cut off everything that lives, plow it up, doze it under, put asphalt and concrete on it. Rip it up, flatten it. You know, like white people train their grass to be just this tall, so it doesn't resemble what it was. Anyway, the allotments were parceled out and they were undersized compared to the original mandate from the federal government. The allotment system broke up our longhouse security systems.

Whites said we should be free to make our own decisions about selling our land because we were generally more ambitious and industrious than other Indians they'd encountered. But then they'd assign us guardians because we couldn't read, write or speak English. They treated us like children. The guardians, mostly crooked lawyers and businessmen who had full authority over us, would ask for permission to sell our land. There was some correspondence that said, "I have sold this Indian's land. I went out to give him the money and he refused it, saying, 'My land is not for sale.' Now what do I do?" And the government's response was, "Well, the reason he was assigned a guardian was because he's not competent to manage his own affairs. Keep the money for probate fees, and get the sheriff to remove him."

So these Indians were taken off the allotments at gunpoint. Remember, this was reservation land with trust status—it's off the tax rolls, it was owned by the government "in beneficial interest" of the Indians. Counties put the land back on the tax rolls—all illegally in violation of the treaty. But the U.S. government wouldn't come forward to protect the tribe or individual, and the sheriff had the gun.

My grandfather, John McKinney, lived here during this period, and he was one of the few Indians who was educated. He was a contractor, he ran logging crews and played the fiddle. And these Indians were coming to him with pieces of paper, tax assessments. He'd say, "You need to pay money for taxes." And the Indians would say, "What's money?" They were still in a bartering economy.

There were murders on the reservation. The white men would go out drinking, then they'd go down to the fishermen's cabins, they'd kick in the door, rape the woman, murder the husband, and put his body on the railroad tracks. Years later when I was on the council, I found the death certificates of these "railroad accidents." They'd take the homes of the murdered men, and put "no heir" on the deeds. They'd kidnap the children, and send them to orphanages on the East Coast.

My grandfather made funeral arrangements for the Indians. All the abuse broke his heart; he died of stress on this reservation. My grandmother moved to another reservation and started a new life. My mother was sent off to boarding schools and that's where she grew up, traumatized by isolation and racism. Her alcoholism was related to that.

Mother married a machinist employed by Boeing, and our family relocated to Seattle. I attended Franklin High School, where I gained a solid, basic education and work skills. But my values were different from those of the dominant society; I felt like the odd duck. I was depressed, and I got heavily involved in alcoholism. After high school, I had a job, a nice home and friends, but I was living at the edge of society, without any real direction. My heart wasn't full. Then a friend invited me to a cultural program at the Seattle Indian Center. I went, and became involved in the American Indian Service League. For the first time, I really belonged. The Indian Service League gave me opportunities to socialize and volunteer, and the healing began.

You know, there's a big difference between surviving and living. I began learning how to give. When people need something, you give it—you don't wait to be asked. What you put out comes back to you. If you put out anger, you get back anger. If you put out love, you get back love.

It used to break my heart when I'd see a little Indian girl all beaded up in a beautiful buckskin dress, and she had rickets really bad. I'd set up a placement for her with an Indian family, and then I'd go to her white foster home, and the black and Latino children in that home would want to come too. It was sad leaving these minority children in homes where there were language barriers and nobody could understand them.

It made me think of the Indian boarding schools—five generations of Puyallup children were rounded up and taken off to government schools. Things our children needed to know didn't get taught. In an institution you learn to wash sheets for three hundred people, but you don't get a chance to know human beings, to see them laugh as well as cry. In a family unit, you see your parents tending babies and old ones, you see them sitting down and talking about making out a budget and solving family problems. It's important to children of any age to see that their people can be productive.

In the 1950s, I moved to this reservation, and it was the frontier. The government had simply folded its carpetbag and moved off, leaving the Indians owning everything morally, but with no clear undisputed title to anything except a few parcels of land. When they took Indians off other reservations for job training, they brought them here, but there was nothing. Indians were excluded from the community, they remained reserved, if you'll pardon the pun. In the shipping industry, which is big business here, they were the last hired and the first fired, and it's still true. All day you see trucks driven by white men hauling out timber, and the Indians are there by the side of the road watching.

When the men do not work, they feel guilty and angry, they feel they have disappointed us. Alcohol is self-medication.

In the 1960s, I became a member of the tribal council. I had a background in human services delivery in Seattle, I had experience writing grants, I had taken part in the struggles for justice. I wasn't inhibited, and if I needed to know something, I'd ask. I had children, but because I was a student and wasn't tied down to a job, the council sent me to Washington to the Department of the Interior to work on legislation. I'd go in on a one-way ticket on a red-eye flight, and hit the ground running. I'd go around to various government offices to get the documents I needed. I'd find a typewriter and at night I'd type out a position paper and write letters to whoever it was I was approaching. I'd put through calls to tribal members to fill them in and get consensus to act, then the next morning I'd be running through the halls of Congress.

If I couldn't get an appointment with a congressman, I'd wait outside his door for the bell to ring calling him into chambers to vote. I'd have my papers ready, and when he came out, I'd run with him. Some of them were physical fitness freaks, and here I was smoking a couple of packs of cigarettes a day, but I'd run with them, tellin' them the whole story and handing them the papers and lobbying them on the run. This other Indian woman, Ada Deer from the Menominee Tribe, was doing the same thing.

One year, I went to Washington thirty times. I'd sleep on people's floors, and they'd feed me. If there was money, I'd fly home the next day. If not, I'd go to the Presbyterians or Episcopalians who supported us and they'd find money for an airline ticket, or I'd hitchhike home.

Our tribe lacked recognition, we had a very high rate of infant mortality and suicide, we were losing our children through adoption. Families were living in condemned housing, and there were fires. We needed protection, law enforcement, education, job programs. It was a matter of life and death.

There were stumbling blocks. There were people who didn't want us to succeed. You develop what we call a Puyallup paranoia—anticipate anything that might go wrong, because it probably will. But we kept on working.

While Bennett served on the tribal council in the late 1960s, the fishing rights struggle, long brewing, erupted.

Our fishing rights had been guaranteed in the 1854 treaty. Our Puyallup River meandered freely, and sometimes overflowed its banks. We set up traps and wheels so we could corral the fish. The runs were plentiful. Indians would come to harvest with their wives and children, they'd have naming ceremonies, giveaways and pony races with feasting and dancing.

But white people were using traps and wheels, and they were so greedy, they were wiping out the runs. So the state outlawed traps and wheels in the name of conservation, only they failed to assign any time for Indians to do subsistence fishing. This was devastating. If you can't afford to take care of your family, you can't live with dignity.

In 1970, the state was on the river preventing our men from fishing. Law enforcement agents came out with the tactical squad, and just ran right over our people with high-powered boats. They pushed people around, arrested them, then confiscated their gear. Our people had every right in the world to be there. We were on federal trust land. If anyone should be protecting resources on that river, it was the Indians—they lived there for thirty-five thousand years, and the fish always came back.

We set up a security camp in the city of Tacoma. At first we had no arms, but then we had to arm ourselves to protect our fishermen from three hundred law enforcement agents and the vigilantes. If we'd given up our arms, they'd have lost interest in us.

In our camp there were thirty men and women, there were teenagers and children. We put the babies in secure places. One woman was so scared, her knees were knocking, so she sat down on this box. Well, the police looked at the box, they opened it, and in it were Molotov cocktails. She was nursing a nine-month-old baby, but she got locked up, she went down big time.

I was spokesperson for the tribe. I called up Seattle asking for first aid supplies. Mostly what I wanted was bullet-removal kits and Kotex to use for pressure packs to resist bullets. Well, this truck came down from Seattle and they had a case of Tampax. I said, "Tampax? What we need is Kotex for pressure packs and wounds." And these people looked at each other and laughed, and they said, "We didn't know you asked for anything. These are the fuses for your Molotov cocktails."

The state bulldozed our tipis, took our typewriters and clothes. I was physically assaulted, gassed and arrested along with about fifty-nine other people, and I went to jail for several days until bail could be raised. The bails were set really high.

The international media picked up the story. People would be sitting and eating dinner watching television, and they saw Indians being thrown to the ground, they saw government agents beating an Indian man or woman, and they thought they were watching John Wayne theater. Then it dawned on them that this was real, and they began calling from all over the world, and writing to the Department of the Interior and the Justice Department asking, "What are you doing to those Indians?" People contacted their government officials, and insisted on knowing why such brutality was being used against the First Americans.

I was in the second round of trials, and I was looking at a thirty-five-year conviction. The morning of the trial, a solicitor's report came in that stated that we owned the land, we owned the river we were on, the government had violated its jurisdiction and was therefore trespassing. I had been saying that, but they totally ignored what I was saying until the report came out. The case was thrown out of court. But there never was any compensation to the fishermen who had suffered illegal arrest, or to their families.

The Puyallup won the right to keep 50 percent of the fish caught in their coastal waters under the terms of the 1974 Boldt Decision. But the tribes continue to protest the depletion of the resource by non-Indians, the construction of hydroelectric dams that block the salmon runs, and the industrial pollution that Indians say turned their rivers into "toxic soup."

We lost half our fish to commercial and sports fishermen. The fishing runs have been diminished by industry, and we've never been compensated. But the Boldt Decision forced the state to stop abusing us, and recognized our right to regulate our own fisheries. I met with these white commercial fishermen. They were yelling, "You f—ing Indians, you think you own everything." They said we wiped out the run. I told them that the fish were crowded, they were blind, sick and dead. Nothing will return if it's dead. I said, "Grandfather Great Spirit knows exactly what these fish need—fresh water, clean gravel, no crowding—and then the fish will reproduce because they will come back to the spawning grounds. You can't improve on what Grandfather has put here."

Our council worked very hard to take care of the watershed, to make sure there was a place for our salmon to return to. We undertook stream cleaning, pulling car bodies and bedsprings and barbed wire fences out of the creeks so the returning fish wouldn't have to go through this debris.

We got after the farmers for their use of large quantities of pesticides—that stuff washes down into the rivers; it kills the salmon, it poisons the bugs, and the birds that eat the bugs. The hawks were laying eggs that were soft, that wouldn't hatch. The food chains were disrupted.

We went to court, we got organizations like St. Leo's Church, the Anti-Defamation League, the Quakers to support our struggle. White people were beginning to understand that it wasn't the Indian that was the enemy. Some of these practices began turning around. The tribes developed independent management systems for the rivers, and they worked at restoring them. Now the sports and commercial fishermen are seeing more substantial runs.

I was elected tribal chairperson in 1972. My tribe sent me to the National Tribal Chairman's Association meeting in Denver or someplace. I bring my ID and our tribe's resolution to the credentials committee, and they tell me my tribe's been terminated. I say, "It's not terminated, it's been neglected." They say, "I'm sorry, we can't recognize you. You should have designated your vice chairman (he's a man) to represent the tribe."

I said, "My council delegated me to attend this meeting as their representative. This is an insult to my tribe. I'm here to represent the children and the elders and all the members of my tribe, and I insist that you recognize their right to determine their own leadership." They recommended that I sit in the lobby with the chairmen's wives. I told them, "I am not a chairman's wife. I am a chairwoman of a federally recognized tribe."

Well, they let me into the meeting, and I didn't even notice I was the only woman. They're talking about fishing, housing, so many topics. They're listing natural resources they need to protect: timber, minerals, land, water, fish, and I step forward and say, "I'm Ramona Bennett, I'm here representing the Puyallup Tribe, and I'd like to make a motion that you add our Indian children to that list of endangered resources. They're being alienated from their tribes through interracial adoptions, they have such a hard time finding their way back, they never belong anywhere."

This Indian man near me says, "Somebody tell that skinny little bitch to sit down." Then this other man says to me, "Can I buy you a drink?" Another man says, "We're not losing children in my area." Well, I can read his nametag, and I know where he's from, and I tell him, "I live in a tiny little town called Rainier, Washington, and within three hundred feet of where I live is a little boy from your tribe who's been adopted outside the tribe. I can tell you his birth name." "Really?" he said. Everybody was tense.

Then a man says, "You need to listen to this woman. It's true," and he came over and stood with me. Another man from Mississippi got up and stood with me. Then Joe DeLaCruz of the Quinault Tribe said, "She always does her research, and if she says it's a problem, it is," and he stood with me. So they voted children onto the list of endangered natural resources. Eventually, Congress passed the Indian Child Welfare Act in 1978, which gives jurisdiction over minor children to the tribes so the adopted ones can access information about their heritage.

After that meeting, I saw Ada Deer sitting out in the lobby, and she was really upset because they'd made her sit with the chairmen's wives. And I thought, "If I'd known they could intimidate you, I probably would have backed out." I still didn't realize I was the first woman who'd made it through the door. Sexism. I mean, it's one thing to have to deal with racism and sexism when you're talking to a senator or a governor, a white man; it's another thing when it's your brother.

We're in the same struggle. Those Indian men did not learn sexism from their traditional teachings. They learned it from women teachers who were subservient to male principals, they learned it from a white boss on the job, so I don't blame the Indian men. I blame every woman who put up with it, and the organizations for not being more responsive.

Traditionally, our men were builders, hunters, and shaman, but when they moved into cities, they were without work, they were isolated and filled with self-hate. I saw it in my family. As long as our men are drunk and are dying in doorways, as long as our children are kidnapped and adopted out of our communities, we will remain an "endangered species."

If something's wrong, you've got to keep working to change it. It says in the 1854 treaty, "A teacher will live among you, a physician will live among you." We had traded hundreds of thousands of acres of land in exchange for a few services, and then these were almost totally cut off. We worked our asses off to get everything we were entitled to.

We wanted to improve the level of health care. In the thirties, forties and fifties, Indians had been almost wiped out by tb. The Indian Health Service came on the reservation, killed dogs and cows, bulldozed homes and sent Indians to sanitariums far from home, which disrupted family life. Then the government phased out the IHS Hospital for Northwest and Alaskan tribes, the Cushman Indian Hospital, and turned the property over to the state for a juvenile detention center known as Cascadia.

With supporters from all over the country, we occupied the facility in 1976, demanding its return to its rightful owners, the tribes. We're in negotiations, the state and the Feds are threatening to blow us up, and we're saying we're not gonna leave the building because it's ours. We're all carrying on. Scotty Calloway yells, "We'll never leave this building. We'll blow it up before we give it back to the state." I start laughing, and I said to the officials, "I bet you think this guy is a radical." They nodded their heads. And I said, "No, he's the director of our clinic, and he's got three master's degrees. This other guy, Sid Mills, he's a radical, and he hasn't said a word."

Dennis Ickes from the Department of Justice,[1] was there, and he went over to Freeman Ladderout, this little old Indian man in his nineties who was sitting in his chair with his eyes closed just rocking, and Dennis says, "Do you know why you're here?" Dennis thought we'd just brought the old man in for show. And Freeman opens up his eyes and says. "Of course. This was supposed to be a regional hospital." That was a good one.

So we booted the state out of Cascadia. All the people who stood up with us were wonderful. I remember how Freeman Ladderout used to say he was from the Broken Arrow Tribe in Montana. He used to say his grandfather was one of Custer's scouts, but he was on his coffee break when all the excitement took place. I remember the time these guys on food stamps went out and bought strawberries for all the people working with us.

Indians have to have something to give. So you feel you've gotta be there for them. We're brothers and sisters.

Our tribe went from no recognized rights to an annual budget of nine million dollars, with three hundred employees and a recognized enrollment of over one thousand members. A few of us stood together and fought for what we needed, and the Puyallup Tribe rose from the ashes. And we did it without chemicals. We were the first tribal council to be completely sober. We proved that it could be done.

The Puyallups won praise for their alcohol and drug abuse and drug prevention program but, as Bennett says, "The damage it took generations to do will not be undone in one generation." Tribal officials estimate that 50 percent of the Puyallups are alcoholic or drug-dependent and fetal alcohol syndrome affects one in one hundred babies. Throughout the afternoon I spent with Bennett in her office, she was distracted by the presence of drug dealers on the street just outside her window. She jotted down license numbers and called them in to the tribal police. She locked the outside door saying, "They'll try to come inside to do their dealing away from the eyes of the police." As it grew dark, the action on the street intensified, and we conversed to the accompaniment of racing motors, screeching tires, and police sirens. On our way out to tour the reservation, Bennett mentioned that just a few weeks before, gang members had burglarized the tribal office and raped the computer operator. I declined the nighttime tour, rescheduling it for the next day. Instead, we visited Bennett's reservation home, a sprawling, comfortable place decorated with Indian baskets, blankets and her intricate beadwork. A long-eared shaggy dog named Lord greeted us, and I met members of Bennett's extended family. How many children does she have? "Six or seven, depending on whether or not you count the children of relatives and others who come to live with us from time to time. Will you have dinner with us? You're welcome to stay here tonight. We always make room for people. You know, Indians buy a couch not because of the way it looks but according to how many people it can sleep," she said. The next day, we drove through the reservation and Bennett pointed out tribal buildings.

We have our own school. This is our elders' center. Over here is our mental health facility. The government made us crazy, so we had to have it. [Laughs.]

On this hillside is our cemetery. When I first asked for a clinic, they did a three-year feasibility study to find out if the money would end up in my pocket. I took the officials out here and showed them baby graves, I showed them the graves of teenagers from alcohol-related suicides, and I said this was the only feasibility study we needed.

We established the first clinic that had medical care, mental health, nutrition and dentistry, serving nine thousand Indians. We built it with CETA and community block grant money. This clinic saved my mother's life. She was a patient in a terminal ward in a hospital in Seattle. She wasn't receiving proper care, she'd been physically assaulted by one of the doctors, and she was giving up hope. A doctor from our Indian clinic had an ambulance pick her up. She told people in the hospital, "My daughter is having me picked up," and they just laughed at her, but out she went with her flowers. Once she started receiving care from a surgeon here who cared about her, she recovered completely.

People started to return to the reservation. Freeman Ladderout was one of them. He was close to ninety years old when he got into a cab and said, "Take me home to my tribe." He came to see me. I had just moved into a trailer with my family, somebody had just come by and cleaned fish in my bathtub, but I told him he could move in with us. He stayed with us until he needed congregate care.

In August 1988 Puyallup tribal members voted to relinquish their claim to thousands of acres in Pierce County in exchange for a $162 million package including land, payments to individuals, and money for social programs and business development.[2]

I voted against the Puyallup settlement because I felt what was offered was just a pittance. But I went to the meetings to make sure certain things were included—like control of navigational routes so boats going in and out don't bother our fishermen. I made sure that the settlement included compensation for our fishermen when they are injured. This will impact on families for a long time.

I used to believe if we can't get justice, we'll take revenge. But now I know if you walk around looking backwards, you'll constantly slam into things. Now that our tribe is intact, we have the potential to heal.

Children have literally saved my life. Virtually everything constructive I've done has been because children might need it. I started Rainbow Youth and Family Service to help children of color resist adoption so they can remain within their communities. They need advocates. We got a small grant from the state but we haven't received a nickel, so my assistant and I are working without pay. We're trying to obtain art supplies, sports equipment and musical instruments for poor children. They need activities to relieve depression. I'd love to do theater projects, writers' workshops.

These programs are like your babies. You conceive them, you breathe life into them, and then expect them to behave in a certain way. Some of the programs don't make progress for years; others save lives over and over again. You never know the impact something you do will have.

We're trying to reverse the high dropout rate of Indians from public schools. Schools used to be the heart of the community; now most are boarded up at night. A lot of our children live in overcrowded homes without privacy, without proper nutrition. If you're hungry and sick, how can you keep a thought in your head?

The Spokane school district invited me to talk to their students about Indian history. I asked them who had the first baby born west of the Mississippi. Well, the kids were racking their brains trying to think of the name in their textbook, then some of the Indian kids started saying, "It must have been an Indian." [Laughs.] I asked, "Who discovered America?" They said, "We were never lost." I asked, "Were there any survivors of the Battle of the Little Bighorn?" Well, everybody's been taught the only survivor was a white man's horse. But the kids answered, "There were Sioux and Northern Cheyenne, and most of their horses."

I tell young people that there would not be a United States of America if it were not for Indians. When England and America were at war, the Americans were outgunned, and they turned to their true-blue best buddies who stood with them and said, "Will you Indians help us?" And the Indians said, "What do you want us to do?" The whites said, "Okay, this is what we do. We line up in straight lines, we have these fifes and drums, and we march directly into the mouths of their cannons." And the Indians said, "Bullshit. That's what you do? No wonder you're losing your asses. This is what you need to do. You need to travel by night and hide behind rocks and trees, and you need to head them off at the pass." And the white Americans said, "Really, that's a good idea. Will you show us how to do that?"

So the Indians went out and showed the white people how to fight a war, as we have in each and every war thereafter. Indians have always stood with their white brothers.

Did you know that white people invented buffalo? They just discovered that buffalo is low in cholesterol, has to be grain-fed, and is very immune to diseases. Oh, these white people are still discovering medicines that our medicine people have used for thousands of years.

White people just discovered co-op housing. Different generations live together and share a huge living room and recreation center and a big common kitchen, and each family has its own sleeping and bath areas. This promotes a sense of security, mutual protection, as well as emotional support. It cuts down on excessive use of heat, utilities and space, and is thus efficient and economical. You know what we used to call that? A longhouse.

We have some important messages to convey. We believe we're here to protect the continent. We're in a race against time. The issue is clean up this environment before we're living in a cesspool.

I went to a service at the Native American Church. I sat in the tipi and heard the prayers: "Grandfather, help our brothers and sisters with wings, our brothers and sisters that have roots and live in the earth, those that crawl on the ground, those that live on the beach, and the nations of fish. Help the brothers and sisters with white skins. Help them, Grandfather, take care of this planet and stop hurting the earth."

The reason white people can go from continent to continent destroying everything is because they believe they're going to heaven and it doesn't matter. But we know this is paradise. The spirit world is right here; the ones who aren't born yet and those who have passed on are with us every day. They teach us things. The young ones depend on us to leave something for them.

I always think about my little boy, Lah-huh-bate-soot. I was driving, taking a shortcut across the port, and he started crying. He said, "I never seen the cedar trees, I never seen the deer." He was five years old. All of these Indian people are magical; they know about these things without being taught. He knew in his Indian-boy head that there was something he'd missed, that he'd been robbed of his heritage.

The level of spiritual communication is very strong. Lah-huh-bate-soot sang a song in our language, and he whistled, and I thought, "Oh, isn't that wonderful, they're teaching him something new at school." Then I talked to his teacher, a Puyallup woman, and she said, "I thought you taught it to him at home." I asked him, "Who taught you that song?" And he said, "The hawk taught me that song."

It's a new day, with new opportunities. Despite all the things that have happened to my tribe, I believe there is hope. Our children are our bright and shining stars. With each child, the promise is reborn.

From an interview with the author, November 1–2, 1989.

Notes

1. R. Dennis Ickes was director of the Office of Indian Rights, U.S. Department of Justice, from 1975–76.

2. See Kate Shutzkin, "A New Future?" *Seattle Times*, Pacific section, February 25, 1990, pp. 8–30.

14

I Dream a Lot

AH-BEAD-SOOT
PUYALLUP

"You *should hear what our kids have to say," said Ramona Bennett, taking me to the Chief Leschi School on the Puyallup Reservation, where her daughter, age ten, was a student. Ah-bead-soot got permission to leave her class to talk with me. I found her disarmingly candid and self-assured. She spoke of her dreams, her fears, and her goals. I asked what it was like to attend a reservation school.*

YOU LEARN A LOT ABOUT YOUR CULTURE. WE HAVE A circle every morning, and I'm one of the drummers, and we get to play and sing and stuff. Some kids are embarrassed to come up, but I think it's really fun. I'm proud to be Indian.

As an Indian, I have responsibilities. One time, I didn't want to get up for a parade, and I wished I were white so I wouldn't have to get up. But then I found out how much fun it is to take part.

My teacher is white, and I think she's learning more about Indians than we're learning about whites. We're learning some of our old language, and our history. If you don't learn history, you'll make the same mistakes. Like if people keep on cutting the trees down the way they did in the past, there'll be no more trees. Whites do that. Indians do it too, for money.

The best thing about being in an Indian school is people don't tease you for being Indian. When we go into the white community, kids sometimes put their hands over their mouths and go "Wawawawaw."

I'm in a drama group which meets at the public school. Once we put on a play, and my dad came to a performance. He's Indian, he's a scientist. And this one white girl who I thought was my friend took one look at him and said to the other kids, giggling, "Look at that Indian with long hair!" Then, one of the girls I didn't like before because I thought she didn't like Indians, she stuck up for me saying, "Shut up! Just 'cause he has long hair, doesn't mean he's ugly." It was funny—I saw a different side of that girl.

My neighborhood is mostly Indian, but I have a couple of black friends. There was a little white girl who lived across the street from us—her name was Amber—and whenever I saw her, she'd pick a fight. Once, she started throwing rocks at me. Her mom came out and *she* started throwing rocks at me, then my sister came out to help me. We hit the mom in the head with a rock. I was going to apologize, but Amber pushed me down, and pulled my hair. My sister beat her up. Her parents never let her play with me again.

There are gangs here, and they're getting bigger and bigger. They sell drugs right near here on Portland Avenue. They're taking control. So many children are druggies—it's like peer pressure. When I was seven or eight, one of my brothers took an overdose of LSD and died, but the doctors brought him back to life. Another one of my brothers was hallucinating—he was walking on snakes. Now he's in jail for stealing car radios.

There was a crack house right next to the home of this tiny little girl who rides on my school bus. Things got so bad, she couldn't go outside. Finally, the police closed down the crack house. Now it's for sale, all the windows are fixed, the yard looks pretty. So people are trying to do something about the drugs.

You have to care about what happens. If you care only about

yourself, it will just go on and on, and will affect future generations. Pretty soon everybody will be taking drugs. Drugs and alcohol, once you start you can't stop. There are all these relatives that my parents won't let me see because they use chemicals. My cousin is alcoholic. We don't have any alcohol in our house, but once he brought over three cans of beer—we found them in the backyard. Another time, his family, they got drunk and had a big fight and punched a hole in the wall of their house, and the police had to take them away.

There are homes I can't go to because they know I'll tell about the drinking. It's a secret. The parents drink because they're messed up, and they give alcohol to their children. The children who have parents who are drunks are the quietest. Sometimes they come to school with a black eye.

There are a lot of broken homes, with one parent gone, or both parents, and some of the kids have been taken from their families, and adopted. Sometimes kids drink because they miss somebody in their family who was part of their life. If chunks of your life are missing, you have to fill it with something.

My brother, Lah-huh-bate-soot, he's always in trouble with chemicals or the law, and that makes me sad. But then I just lie down and go to sleep. I dream a lot. I dream about how it would be if my cousin weren't here—he pushes me around. [Laughs.]

I dream about having everybody speak their tribal language. Your language is your way of life. Pretty soon even the grandparents will all talk English, and they will forget about the past, and then we won't hear the good stuff about when they were young.

We believe that when you die, you go to the other side of the world, and it's really pretty. It's all green, and the trees are green, and all the people who died are there in the spirit world. Grandpa is there, and I talk to him sometimes. He tells me how much he misses us.

I dream about being an actress some day, in theater and films.

I know there aren't a lot of roles for Native Americans. But I think if you're really confident and have talent, you can get opportunities. Some people are snobs and meet one Indian and think all Indians are the same. But some people will take the time to get to know you and find out that you have ability.

I'm a fancy dancer. I go to powwows, I take part in dance competitions, and represent my tribe. Sometimes I win, and then I have to speak. Every year we have a big giveaway. You give everybody in the powwow something to show that you're proud of being what you are, and to thank those who helped you out. You give things you collect, like blankets. And you make things—beaded earrings, bracelets, special gifts for special people. My mom does beadwork—she taught me how.

Giving is important. If you don't give, you won't get anything in return. I'm not talking just about things, but about kindness. People have kindness in their hearts, and they share with others.

Family is important to me. My mom stays home a lot, she takes care of us, she feeds us good meals, and she makes us feel loved. I think how you raise your children is important. You have to take care of the child you brought into the world.

From an interview with the author, November 2, 1989.

15

You Take Care of the Land, and It Takes Care of You

VIRGINIA POOLE
SEMINOLE/MICCOSUKEE

Alligators swim in the marshy wetlands of the Florida Everglades, egrets and kingfishers fly over cypress forests. The Miccosukee Tribe lives in relative isolation on its 333-acre reservation in the Everglades National Park, keeping watch over this fragile ecosystem. The ancestors of the Miccosukee fled from whites seeking to drive them west and took refuge deep in the swamps of the Everglades, where they survived by hunting, fishing, and raising corn and pumpkin.[1] Development of nearby cities brought highways, airports, and tourists; flooding and drought choked foliage and destroyed wildlife, forcing the Indians out of their sanctuary. To this day, however, a number of Miccosukee remain aloof from the white man's institutions, retaining their language and traditions.

I toured the contemporary buildings, which provide services for 360 enrolled Miccosukee tribal members, most of whom live in cement-block houses along the Tamiami Trail. I sampled a "Miccosukee burger" at the tribally owned restaurant. Through this and other commercial-ventures shops, a service station, a bingo hall, airboat tours of "the Glades," all promoted by ever-present billboards—the Indians strive for financial self-sufficiency. I sunbathed on the bank of a canal, careful not to donate an arm or a leg to the alligators who make appearances there. Then I drove a few miles along the trail to one of the scattered roadside camps in which two hundred "trail Indians" reside *to meet with Virginia Poole, the only woman in that community who had agreed to talk to me.*

Passing a boarded-up shop, I opened a door in the fence and entered a traditional village where two open-air structures called "chickees" sat beside a cactus garden, and an unassuming alligator lolled in a pen. Four "sleeping chickees" encircled the village. In one of these sat Virginia Poole, gently rocking her grandchild in a cradle. At age forty-five, she was beautiful, at peace with the natural life around her. We sat on a bench and talked while just a few feet away, two of her elderly uncles conversed quietly in their language. Birds chirped and a rooster crowed, their voices blending with the din of traffic on the trail.

You see these two totem poles? My uncles made them to go in the gift shop here—we're fixing it up. They make totem poles for people on special order. These are thunderbirds. My uncles learned how to do the carving from their uncles. I might be a little prejudiced, but I think they do the best woodwork around here. [Laughs.]

We call ourselves traditional Seminoles, but we are not part of the formally recognized Seminole tribes, and we choose not to be. My family is not enrolled in the Miccosukee Tribe either. We just try to make our own way.

This camp is over fifty years old. It was started by my grandfather and grandmother. There used to be over sixty families here. The others left to form their own little camps further down the trail, and we stayed on. There are just four people now: my two uncles, my husband and myself. I brought up my six children here. I have twelve grandchildren.

We have our own clothing and traditions. Our chickees have no walls; they are open-sided. It's cool. You feel the air. You feel free. The roof is made of palmetto fronds. The whole family drives to where they grow near Naples or Lake Okeechobe,² we cut them, then we come back, and the men do the thatching of the roof. The women feed the whole bunch. That's usually our job. [Laughs.]

There is an art to weaving the roof. The men teach their sons. The men carve the poles for the framework. That little platform near the top is for storage. That's my grandchild's backpack hanging up there.

Virginia Poole and her daughters create dolls dressed in elaborate, layered garments. They sew brightly colored costumes for the annual Green Corn Ceremony, which brings members of the Seminole and Miccosukee tribes together every summer in an isolated spot in the Everglades to celebrate their collective life.[3]

We set our [foot-operated] sewing machine up in the display chickee so tourists can see how we make things. We make dolls using red, black, yellow and purple—we tend to be a little loud in our colors. [Laughs.] We do our own patchwork—it's a lot of cutting and stitching—and our own embroidery. Some people think the patterns are specific to a family, but everybody does what they want. We do beadwork too.

The Green Corn Ceremony—that's our big fashion show of the year, when we show off. We do different dances around our main central ceremonial fire. Children and grandchildren, they all get into the act. We sing different songs in our language. It lasts four days. Most of the families stay in the Glades in chickees. All the Indians are welcome.

This camp has electricity, installed by Virginia Poole's brother, who is an electrical contractor. There is a microwave and a refrigerator. The "cooking chickee" has pots and pans stacked from floor to roof. In the center of it sits the traditional Miccosukee cooking fire, with four logs pointing to the four directions of the universe, symbolizing the Miccosukee worldview: "The universe spins slowly in a circle; what was will be, and will cease to be."[4]

VIRGINIA POOLE   *Photo by Jane Katz*

Every family has its cooking fire with the four logs, even if
they live in modern homes. Four is a sacred number to us: four
colors [the Miccosukee flag is yellow, red, black, and white]; four
directions. The logs are laid by the men pointing to the four directions. If you get married and move to your wife's village,
you're expected to do it that way; it shows respect for the village,
and for our traditions.

It's a matriarchal society here. The mother and the uncles
teach the culture and tradition. The father is the breadwinner. He
may do a little disciplining of the younger children, but mostly
that is the responsibility of the uncles. It's always been that way.
The punishment depends on the seriousness of what you've done.

It might be a spanking. But we don't just haul off and spank our kids, we don't beat them. We're taught that you never hit a child with your hand—it passes on ill feeling. If you're going to spank them, you use a little stick or a belt. We tell them why they're being spanked.

For a serious offense, you have to go to your uncle, you tell him what you've done, and he'll say, "We are disciplining you so you'll know what you've done is wrong." You see, it's teaching. Until recently, he would scratch three or four rows on your skin with a needle, usually on the arms and legs. We didn't worry about passing on germs because the area was washed before and after, so you'd hardly ever see any infections.

We don't usually do this now because when the children go to public school, they consider it child abuse. It's not; it's a cultural disciplining tool. I know to outsiders it looks harsh, but everything is done in moderation. It's just part of our way of life.

One of my daughters will sometimes bring her children to me to be disciplined. This is our way of keeping the mother and child relationship peaceful. We're responsible for human beings. We try to teach the children what we were taught, and hope they will pass it on to their children. None of my children have rebelled. They live on the four Seminole reservations in Florida.

Very few people from this community live outside the reservation or the camps. If the children go off to boarding school or college, they come back; most work for the tribe. Even if they get married to a non-Indian, they usually come back. I think it's the family unit that brings them back. I think my family found a firm middle ground in our lives. We were taught our culture in our language. School wasn't mandatory, but my grandfather, the late William McKinley Osceola, saw that the day was coming when we would be forced to deal with the non-Indian world. So he made a decision, which was very unpopular at the time, to enroll us in public schools. Some of us got as far as junior high, we got our GEDs and enrolled in junior college. One of my brothers is a success story. He finished college, he started his own business, and now he's doing construction for the Seminole Tribe.

I was born in 1946, and I started school when I was six. There were other children whose parents had little businesses on the Trail, and the school bus came and picked us up. I didn't want to go. It was scary. But my uncles were there, and they said, "Well, you're enrolled, and you have to go." You didn't dare disobey, because you knew what punishment was waiting for you. They'd start with a spanking. [Laughs.]

At home, we were taught to be soft-spoken; then one day you're in a situation where they're all talking, talking in another language. It was a lot of noise. [Laughs.] I was lucky in that my teacher gave me extra attention until I got used to being in a classroom. I listened, and learned.

I loved to read. I'd get through three books a week; I do to this day. Our family always made sure we did our homework. If we didn't have anything to do, they would find something for us—beadwork, washing clothes, watching little brothers and sisters. I almost always had a baby in my arms.

I got sick, and dropped out of junior high, and just never bothered to go back. When I was twelve, my family arranged my marriage with a boy from another Miccosukee camp a couple of miles down the road. You marry a man outside your clan. I think that what my in-laws perceived as an advantage was that I could read and speak English. His father spoke to my mother about the marriage, and she spoke to my uncles.

I had seen my future husband, I had spoken to him a little bit, but I didn't know that the offer had been made. He started coming around, and we gradually got used to one another. I liked him. If I had not liked him, it wouldn't have made any difference. I would have told my mother, and she would have said, "Tough luck." [Laughs.]

I wouldn't dream of disobeying. I wouldn't *dream* of disobeying. If I had protested, they would have talked to me about duties, responsibilities, probably something more drastic if I had really screamed and hollered, but I didn't say anything. He moved in, and we built a chickee. It used to be back there; it's gone now.

I think I was very lucky. I married a good man. From then on, it was just oh, married life, babies.

You teach your children what you were taught. What was hard was that because my husband didn't speak English—he had not gone to school—he wasn't able to work in town. So we got jobs in Homestead, a farming community; we picked tomatoes, beans, squash, whatever was available. When we had children, we took them to the fields with us. Somebody always had a car, we chipped in for the gas. The children would stay in the car or play in one area. It wasn't scary back then—you could leave a child alone.

We worked for the agricultural companies—the food wasn't ours—so we brought our own food along. We were paid like six dollars a day. It was the early sixties. We never had a lot of money, but things weren't so high then so we always had food on the table, and a little extra. We had secondhand clothes. That's the way we raised our kids. I tell my children not to have a large family. You can't afford to now.

With federal recognition in 1962 came financial assistance, which enabled the Miccosukee to construct homes, schools, and a clinic.

My family had always been independent, so we just broke off from the group that wanted federal recognition. They constructed the tribal complex in 1968. We were eligible for health care through the clinic.

When my youngest child was in school, I went to work as an aide in the Miccosukee school, and then became assistant to the director of the health center. The director had to leave, and I was offered the position. It was a little scary—I had enrolled in junior college, but never finished. I had no medical training. But I decided what the heck, go for it.

I was running the whole health program, and overseeing twenty-one people on the staff. I had to deal with funding and the budget, government regulations, public relations. It takes common sense. [Laughs.] We are taught that you can do anything you set your mind to do. I went back and read all the contracts and needs assessments that had been submitted when they started the clinic. I read medical books. Oh, medical doctors [they were non-Indian] and medical terms!

Communication with the Indian elders was difficult. We'd show them pictures of the human body and ask, "What do you call this?" They'd tell us the Indian word, and we'd tell them the English word, so we were translating back and forth. Some of the Indians went to traditional healers, and we'd provide transportation. There was no conflict. Indian medicine is the same as what the doctor prescribes, but in liquid form—just herbs and teas instead of pills.

I was director of the clinic for twelve years. I felt I was laying the groundwork for other Indians to build on. Our teachings helped me.

I was taught to be healthy and strong. You do things for yourself. Even if you're sick, if there is just one last breath in your body, you get up, take a walk around the camp, visit family members. You don't lie around in bed waiting to die. It's how you go about living that's important. You take care of all your family. If you see somebody in need, you do what you can for them. It might be your worst enemy, but you still do what you can. That's just part of being human. This is what the clan elders taught me. It's our tradition.

Virginia Poole lowered her voice, explaining that she was hesitant to discuss clan matters with her uncles so close, but she agreed to meet me at the tribal office a few days later. There, she ushered me into one of the offices and continued sharing her ideas.

The clan elders told us stories, usually in the evening. My grandmother told us how the world was created. I'd ask her why there are so many different-colored people in the world. I'd ask why we were not supposed to kill a certain species of bird, or a panther. She'd answer if she could. The bear was seen as part human at one time; that's why you don't just randomly kill it. There is a story about the bear that was handed down through the families, but we're not allowed to talk about it. There were chants at the time of killing. It's a form of respect. I can't go into detail about this.

Our stories are almost like fairy tales, but to us, they're true. They teach us that there's a right way and a wrong way of doing things. This one story, it's a little gruesome. A man didn't listen to his friend's advice, and then he changed into an animal. From that we gather that there are spirits to fear; you don't take chances. If somebody warns you, you listen. If you don't, you suffer the consequences.

We believe that in the beginning, creatures had the ability to change shape—from animal to human, from human to animal. Animals talked, but they abused their privilege, and it was taken away from them. So we learned that you had to be careful what you said; you never knew if you were talking to a human or animal. Things are not always what they seem. [Laughs.]

We were taught that there is somebody who watches over things in nature, like thunder. It's all part of the natural order of things. We were taught there is a God. That doesn't mean you pray to Him asking for something. I don't need to pray. I do what I can for myself. But I believe He is there. I get my strength just from believing.

We never attended mission schools. But I've dealt with church people who told me if you don't accept the Bible, you're not a good person. My answer is the Bible was written by a man. It's what he thought God said. I don't need the Bible. I don't need any formal religious organization. I look at the churches, and I see what they do to each other.

Some of our people believe in "the Breathmaker."⁵ Whatever

you call it, to me, it's all the same. We accept the fact that God sent his son Jesus down in human form. He was here; he spoke to the people of Florida. He handed down some of our teachings, our duties and responsibilities to the land, to each other, to Indian people. When he went back, he was murdered.

Everything on this planet was made by God. Everything has a purpose. Chickens and roosters are really important to us. They cluck when there's a snake or fox around or someone comes into the camp—just like a burglar alarm. We've had this alligator for over twenty years. We used to sell the hides and eat the meat; now he's a tourist attraction. We don't play with him or abuse him. He's part of God and the universe. Everything has a spirit—even the lowly caterpillar.

One year later, I returned to the camp and found Virginia Poole in her reopened shop selling jewelry, dolls, and woodwork made by family and community members. She was rocking her grandchild in a cradle she had made out of cloth. Asked how she acquired this skill, she smiled: "When you have twelve grandchildren, you know how to do it." We spoke of the difficulty of retaining cultural practices.

Way back in our history, it was foretold that we would lose the kids to some kind of outside influence. We could try to keep our eyes open, but we couldn't stop the process. Look what alcohol and drugs are doing to our children. We've lost about half of them.

A lot of the parents don't teach the children anything. There's lack of respect, rebellion. But if the young people cause trouble, they're never abandoned or cast out. They may go from one reservation to another, but they always come back. You hope that one day, as they mature, they'll come to realize what they've lost.

My grandchildren have it better than their parents did because now their mothers work for the Florida tribes and they're paid a decent salary. But sometimes the children ask for something and their parents just go out and buy it, so they don't learn to work for things. We were always taught to work for what we wanted. I interact with the elders in the community; we discuss ways of getting the younger people back on track. Now they are bringing elders into the school to teach the language and traditions.

I don't have a voice in the council—I'm not a member of the tribe. I go to meetings just to listen. In the past, it was the men who ran the government; the tribal chair has always been a man.

Many of the men do not graduate from high school. I don't know why not. Traditionally, by the time the men were in their midt~ens, they were expected to have a job and contribute to the family. From there, it was just one step to having a wife and children and working for their support. The man was used to being the authority figure in the family—even though we know it's the woman who really is. [Laughs.] A woman influences her husband; that's the way it's always been. She approaches a problem in a subtle way. You don't just hit your husband over the head with an idea. You get him to agree with you.

But the woman's role in society changed. Women are more adaptable than men. In school, women realized they had choices, they didn't have to stay home, and they started going for higher education. They read newspapers, they realized it takes education to have an effective government. There are female council members now. Women are a little more aggressive. I think the men are threatened by this.

Our prophecies said a different race would come and would vanquish whoever was in power. When white people first landed here, the Indian men wanted to kill them and throw them back in the ocean, but the women said, "Let them live. There might be some purpose in their coming."

Responding to pressures from slave owners and land speculators, the U.S. government fought three wars against the Seminole and Miccosukee, trying to clear them out of Florida. Virginia Poole's great-grandfather fought under war leader Osceola, who led the resistance. Defending their territory, the Indians raided settlements, then faded into the marshes. In 1837 Chief Osceola agreed to come in for peace talks, but instead was imprisoned. His physician decapitated him and displayed his head as a trophy.

I've heard stories about the wars from my relatives. There were atrocities on both sides. War is never a noble cause. The army chased the Indians deep into the Everglades. Our people hid from the scouts in the hammocks.[6] They could live there because of the orange, guava and banana trees.

I think all the survivors of the wars are gone. The old way of life has died out. Nobody lives in that part of the Everglades now.

Whites used to call us Seminoles, which translates as "wild, savage." We never considered ourselves wild. [Laughs.] We were just free. We looked upon them as savages because of their wanton killing and destruction. Look at what they did. They killed off whole species throughout the planet, and they're still doing it. That's civilization!

"Civilization" advanced in southern Florida, swallowing up wetlands to make way for cities, highways, sugar cane plantations. The panther and wading birds were nearly wiped out, fish and alligators were contaminated. The Indians' old canoe trails gave way to drainage canals built by the Army Corps of Engineers. In 1983 the chairman of the Miccosukee Tribe forged an agreement with the state granting the tribe perpetual lease to the land base it still occupies and payment for flood damage. The funds have been used to develop and market tribal businesses.[7]

White people are changing the channels of the rivers. They put roads where rivers used to flow. They dig canals, and put up levees. When Lake Okeechobee is low in one area, people come around and tear down some of the levees so they'll have higher water in another area. So we have high water one year, and a drought the next. To me, it's destructive. You're changing the whole ecological system.

I mean, you're talking about Mother Nature. You can't improve on that. They should have left it alone.

We're taught not to kill anything unless we're going to eat it, or have a use for it. But some people have no respect for different life forms. There was always an abundance of wild animals: deer and wild turkey, fox and other stuff you could eat, but now I hardly ever see wild animals. There used to be little snails—of course they're gonna disappear if you change their habitat. You can't eat the fish in the canals because of the mercury content. It's not like it used to be here.

The airboat makes a lot of noise, but you get around quicker. Where before it took maybe a couple of days to pole into the hammocks in a dugout canoe, now you can get there in a couple of hours, so change can be good. You adapt. You might do all the commercial stuff, but so long as you don't lose your traditions, you'll survive.

We don't own land. We don't buy or sell land. That's always been prohibited. Nobody owns the land. We said we'd watch over it, because that's our responsibility.

You just take care of the land, and it takes care of you.

From interviews with the author, January 30 and February 2, 1990; and February 12, 1991.

NOTES

1. Once part of the Creek Confederacy, the Seminole and Miccosukee lived in agricultural communities in Georgia and Alabama. When the tribes were removed to Indian Territory in Oklahoma, some of the Indians fled southward. The alternate spelling is Mikasuki.

2. A lake in southern Florida considered by the tribes to be sacred.

3. When the Seminoles and Miccosukee were on the move, they held their annual ceremony far from the white man's towns and forts, secretly giving thanks for the corn and other gifts nature provided for the people. The medicine men held on to their "sacred bundles" used in these rites, and in recent years the ceremony has been revived, according to "A History of the Miccosukee Indians," a publication of the Miccosukee Tribe of Florida.

4. "A History of the Miccosukee Indians."

5. A major deity in the Seminole religion is the Master of Breath, who is believed to control life, the universe and humans. See Charles H. Fairbanks, *The Florida Seminole People* (Phoenix, Ariz.: Indian Tribal Series, 1973), p. 80.

6. Areas of high ground deep in the Everglades once concealed by clumps of trees. One of these areas is the site of a traditional Miccosukee village open to the public.

7. The Miccosukee refused to join the Seminole Nation in accepting a cash payment in exchange for dropping claims to a vast expanse of land in southern Florida. See Peter Matthiessen, "No Man's Land," *Miami Herald*, November 8, 1981, and his *Indian Country*. (New York: Penguin Books (reprint), 1992), pp. 17–63.

16

We Give
Energy to Each Other

LOIS STEELE
FORT PECK ASSINIBOINE

O n Arizona's Sonora Desert, the long arms of the saguaro cactus reach out for rain. In the midst of this arid terrain sit six traditional communities that make up the Pascua Yaqui Reservation. The Yaqui Indians fled north from Mexico to escape persecution and now reside on eight hundred acres surrounded by and yet somewhat remote from Tucson's urban development. Their reservation consists of older homes, HUD houses, a Catholic church, tribal offices, community facilities, and a bingo hall, which, says physician Lois Steele, "brings in much needed revenues." There is a tribal landscape business, but no stores—the people sell food and pop from their homes.

Lois Steele taught in public schools and was dean of women at Dawson College in Montana before entering medical school at the age of thirty-four. Since graduation, she has served as director of the INMED[1] program at the University of North Dakota and at the time of this interview was clinical director for the Pascua Yaqui Tribe. An exuberant individual with a sense of the absurd, Lois Steele provided this perspective on the challenges facing a contemporary medicine woman.[2]

WHEN I WAS GROWING UP IN MONTANA, I WAS CURIous about everything. We had dogs and cats—I saw animals being born and dying. I used to go down to the creek and observe the life cycle of frogs and tadpoles. When the men went hunting, I helped gut out a deer and learned about anatomy and about parasites. I learned to put mud on bee stings, to use teas for diarrhea and bitterroot for colds. I wondered why the white kids got polio and no Indian kids did. I decided I would be a biology teacher.

We lived on the Fort Peck Reservation in Montana. It's large, very progressive. We have a government that is relatively stable. Considering how bad things can be in Indian country, our tribe is doing well.

My mom was Indian and Irish Catholic; my dad was Norwegian. My dad worked at a government internment camp for the Japanese in Arizona during World War II. My mom objected to his working there. She saw that the Japanese had to leave everything they had behind when they went to the relocation camps—just like Indians who were relocated to reservations.

Eventually, my parents moved to Chicago, and my mom left my father. His family thought she was crazy for walking out when they had a three-bedroom house near Lakeshore Drive, and then going back to "nothing" on the Rez.

We lived with my grandparents in Poplar, Montana. My grandmother was Assiniboine, her husband was Irish. The Indian women of that generation seemed to me to have a lot more freedom than non-Indian women. They could come and go when they wanted without their men—to a ceremony, to church, to a powwow. Grandma stood up to Grandpa. Once, they were out rounding up horses, he started telling her how to do it, and she just rode off, telling him where to put the horses. I see that independence in a lot of Sioux/Assiniboine[3] women.

I was raised free on the reservation. One girlfriend had horses, and we went riding; we'd go up the river and go swimming. A few times, we played hooky from school. A lot of the elders spoke the language, so I learned some Sioux from them. There were a lot of traditional ceremonies: they did naming ceremonies during powwows, there were giveaways, feasts and wakes.

I didn't have a naming ceremony, but I was called Cha-poonka, which means *mosquito* in Sioux. Why? I was skinny, I never sat still, I organized all the cousins and we'd be off and running. I was named that by an auntie who didn't like me. Mother remarried, and we moved into a one-bedroom shack on the creek bank that didn't have running water, didn't have indoor toilets. My stepfather, who was not Indian, stayed until my mom had her fifth child, then he left. Somehow, we got along with my grandfather's help. We were never on welfare. Mom worked at the post office, and at the BIA after the divorce. I'd come home after school and baby-sit the younger kids, and I learned to cook.

In my teens, I saw our reservation change. It had been dry, but around 1952 a law was passed allowing liquor on the Fort Peck Reservation. They had struck oil there, and outsiders wanted the land. The way to get it was to be sure liquor was legal; then the land would change hands fast. A lot of non-Indian families moved in, many of them transients.

With the oil money and booze, there was chaos on the reservation.

Houses replaced the old shacks, we added onto our house and had indoor plumbing. There were more cars. While the parents were out drinking and driving, children were often neglected, there were car wrecks, deaths, suicides. We lost a generation.

What happened to the ceremonies? The Indians celebrated oil. They thanked the Great Spirit for the oil that relieved some of their dire poverty.

When I was in my teens, kids played chicken. I remember one time we were out all night raising Cain. We drove down an almost perpendicular embankment—I shudder to think about it. We were there to show how brave we were. This car came down with a smashed windshield. We said, "Hey, man, what happened?" We were laughing. And I thought, "My god, this is stupid. He could have been killed!" After that, I'd get out and walk.

Two of my girlfriends didn't get out and walk. They were killed in car wrecks. You didn't cry. You went on laughing.

I married a man from my reservation. He is Sioux and Blackfeet; he was a football player and rodeo rider. He went into the army and was stationed in Colorado, so I got my B.A. degree at Colorado College, and then I taught in reservation public schools. We were married ten years. My husband wasn't controlling. We both did what we wanted to do. When we split, I was finishing my master's degree at the University of Montana.

At twenty-eight, I decided to be a doctor. I wrote to this doctor at the Indian Health Service who wanted to help Indians go to medical school. He replied, and said my grades were "not exceptional." Well, at one time I had had the highest GPA at my college, but he tried to discourage me. I thought, "These guys don't really think an Indian woman can do anything." I'd been up against that before. In high school geometry class, I knew the material well: I could put proofs on, I knew my theorems were correct, and the more I knew the more hostile my teacher became. That made me really study—it was a challenge to beat him intellectually. Sure, competitiveness was counter to my training, but vindictiveness wasn't. [Laughs.]

When I finally got to medical school at the University of Minnesota, Duluth, I didn't understand real one-upmanship. The idea was to beat each other out. It was a dog-eat-dog situation. I found it dehumanizing. If you do well, then they say it's because you're "not a typical Indian." Well, I don't know what a typical Indian is.

My daughters and I moved to the Twin Cities. I was in my last year of medical school, doing a residency at Children's Hospital, when my daughter got pregnant. She shouldn't have, but she did. She was seventeen. It was a nightmare—not because she was pregnant, but because the "professionals" poked their noses into our lives and did more harm than good.

My daughter's pregnancy wasn't all that accidental. They often aren't. She asked for homebound tutoring so she could finish high school. She was in the ninetieth percentile on standardized tests and she could have done it, but the counselor said "No," she'd have to go to classes. When she started showing, the girls in school picked on her, they called her a "dirty Indian slut." At that point, although she was just five-one, she threw one of the girls through a glass mirror. Finally, the school let her go homebound, but the whole experience left emotional scars on all of us.

My daughter wanted to keep her baby, but she kept on getting calls from a social worker who wanted her to have the baby adopted. "Why are you trying to keep this child?" the social worker would ask. "You can't give it anything. You're gonna raise another kid on welfare!" And my daughter would answer, "My mom raised two of us alone, we had what we needed, we've never been on welfare, and we don't intend to be." When I asked the director of my residency for a leave of absence so I could spend some time with my daughter, he refused. I finally took a few weeks off, and made up the rotation later.

My daughter gave birth in the hospital where I was doing my residency in family practice, and I was in the delivery room. Her doctor had to leave to take care of another emergency, and he said, "Lois, take over." So I brought my grandson into the world. It was a thrill when we saw that he was alive and healthy. My mother was there; the doctor returned in time to have her cut the umbilical cord. My daughter didn't cry or scream; she was controlled, like a good Indian woman.

The child had a heart defect, and because I had medical insurance, I adopted him. It's a status symbol to be a grandmother. It implies that you've lived long enough to have some wisdom.

We have a permissive approach to child rearing. We usually don't fight with our children, we don't scream at them, we let them work things out for themselves. My oldest daughter learns her lessons the hard way. I groan, but I try to keep my mouth shut. Life is getting easier for her. My grandson is now nine. In school, his teacher holds him back, but at home, I let him run free. I take him with me when I travel. He's been through the Smithsonian and other museums. He learns more this way than in school.

I was the only Indian staff who had faculty status in the University of North Dakota INMED program, which recruits and trains Indians for health careers. They've graduated over 115 students, over fifty of them physicians. As an associate professor, I used to put in sixty hours a week, but I never got tenure. Minority faculty, especially if they're women, are often kept in "soft money" untenured positions.

I left INMED for a research position in the Indian Health Service in Tucson, and then became clinical director for the Pascua Yaqui Tribe. The work is rewarding. We have some well-trained Indian people in the Indian Health Service. But there have been big budget cuts, and our staff is underpaid. The best and brightest often leave for other jobs. It's pretty scary—the AIDS babies, the cocaine patients, the aging of the population and the rising cost of medical care. Whether you're white, black, pink or green, it's serious!

In Tucson, we're sitting in a hotbed of drug use. Poverty breeds hopelessness; it helps drug dealers thrive. It's like if anybody succeeds, that weakens the drug dealers' hold, so they target kids before they have a chance to succeed. On some reservations, the average income for a family of four is five thousand dollars. Children sometimes see the drug dealers living better than their parents do.

Throughout the state, the spending for drug rehabilitation, mental health programs, the homeless, day care and education is inadequate. The schools are in shambles. We can't meet people's needs. I stay in the Indian Health Service because I feel we can make a difference in people's lives.

With substance abuse, we're starting to see some changes— you have to attack it as a community, from the inside. Here's one example. Alkali Lake is a little town in Canada where ninety percent of the people were drinking. Someone came in and talked to them about changes they could make. Because this person wasn't judgmental, they listened. Then a little girl talked her mother and father into getting sober, and the parents used their leadership abilities to pull the whole community behind them. The community focused on jobs, housing, self-esteem. They involved young and old people. Today, ninety percent of the town is sober.

We're using traditional healing methods. The sing, for example, comes from traditional culture. You can ask the group to pray for you, then afterwards, everybody eats. In Phoenix, Dedee Yazzee runs the Indian Rehabilitation Program. She has a "talking circle" and a sweat lodge. She tries to get people to stop making excuses for drinking and drug use, to believe in themselves. It's like group therapy. There is confidentiality, camaraderie. They pray with sweet grass; they pass around the pipe.

Because of the historic rivalry between different tribes, there's a lot of teasing that goes on on our reservations. The Sioux and Assiniboine didn't get along, so the government in its wisdom put them on the same reservation. [Laughs.] That's not uncommon. The teasing is mostly good-natured joking about other tribes. A Crow Indian will ask, "What's the difference between the Turtle Mountain Chippewa and the Fort Peck Sioux?" And someone will answer, "When they go hunting in the winter, the Chippewa is chasing rabbits through the snow, while the Sioux is whistling."[4] [Laughs.]

Let somebody non-Indian appear, tribal affiliations fade, and you're all Indian.

When people take themselves too seriously. That's when they get teased. Here's what I mean. We eat puppy in a ceremonial situation, and it's a delicacy. The puppy is dead and cooked. There's a prayer before eating. You ask the puppy to forgive you for taking his life.

Well, there was this white VISTA worker-type who was a teacher on our reservation. She lost her puppy, and she walked into a bar and asked if anybody'd seen it. So these Indian guys, of course they're gonna put her on. One points up the hill to a little house and says, "Go ask him." So she goes up the hill to the house, and there's a little old guy who can hardly speak English with a big pot of something on the stove. He thought she was accusing him of killing her puppy, and he joked, "No, I don't think I killed that one yet." Well, she went into a screaming rage and took off. She told a reporter from *Life* magazine that she left because we ate her puppy. She said we were "barbaric."

If you're gonna live on an Indian reservation, you've got to be able to laugh at yourself. It's survival.

Look at the people who take life too seriously. People under constant stress undergo changes in their internal organs, they develop hypertension and heart disease, and some of the research indicates that it makes you prone to diseases like cancer. It's not just the type A personality. People who appear outwardly calm may be under as much or more stress because they never deal with it.

Of course you don't find many type A personalities among American Indians. [Laughs.] Well, if you work with the outside world, you have to at least appear to be type A or they don't want you around. I mean seriously, a lot of it's appearance. This is why woman don't do as well in the job market as some of those more hyper men. Women can be very well organized, but the blustering, aggressive type is what people have learned to look for.

I've missed opportunities because I'm not willing to put on any exterior. [Laughs.] I don't kiss ass properly. Of course, if it's something important—for example, if you're going before Congress to ask for passage of a bill, then you play the game and do the best you can to appear a creditable type A. But you gotta remember it's a game. Those who forget who they are and where they came from get into trouble.

Walking this fine line can make you crazy. I knew an Indian physician who had a difficult time when he went to work in the outside world. He couldn't accept the materialism, the concern with status and schedules, the fact that he didn't have time for relatives, that he couldn't stay all night at a sing, that he couldn't put people first. He committed suicide. When you don't grow up worshiping time, it can be difficult coping in a world that does.

Ann Landers wrote once that people who are always late don't respect the people around them. Well, maybe you're late because you do respect people. If somebody stops you and asks you a question, you take the time to answer. The people you are with at the time are the most important. You live in the present. You don't get rich, but you stay healthy.

Elders are important to us. They tell us stories; they believe in the old stories. They say that if an owl visits you, it will take somebody in death. Sometimes an animal will decide to sacrifice his life so that a human will live. I think there's some truth in this—it shows that we're all related. We give energy to each other.

From (telephone) interviews with the author, May 20, 1989, and September 1, 1990.

Editor's Note: In 1991 Lois Steele became chief medical officer at the Research Division of the Indian Health Service based on the Tohono O'Odham Reservation (formerly Papago) near Tucson. She also has an appointment as clinical faculty at the University of Arizona Medical School.

NOTES

1. Acronym for the Indians Into Medicine program.

2. For more on the values and responsibilities of an Indian woman physician, see Lois Steele, *Medicine Woman* (Grand Forks, N.D.: IN-MED, University of North Dakota, 1985).

3. The Assiniboine were originally part of the Sioux Nation. From the mid-seventeenth century on, migrations and relocations brought them to North Dakota, Canada, and Montana. They share cultural and linguistic traits with the Sioux.

4. The Sioux is whistling for a dog. According to Lois Steele, this is "a reference to the ritual eating of puppy by the Sioux."

17

Let Us Survive

ROBERTA HILL WHITEMAN
ONEIDA

Drive around the progressive Oneida Reservation in northeastern *Wisconsin, and you'll see Native people in suits, toting briefcases, going to work in an up-to-date computer center and industrial park. You'll also see Oneidas in jeans tending gardens. The tribe operates a tobacco business, a large hotel and a bustling "activity center" housing several casinos. Revenues from these enterprises have enabled the tribe to create new housing, parks, roads, and cultural and social service programs.*

The Oneidas are on the move, but just a generation ago, like other reservation communities, they were suffering from the loss of much of their land base and widespread poverty. For those Oneidas who had college degrees, there were few jobs on the reservation, and the surrounding white society was a hostile environment.

Growing up in the adjoining city of Green Bay, Roberta Hill Whiteman formed close ties to the Oneida community, which she renews on frequent visits to her relatives there. A poet, author of Star Quilt *and* Philadelphia Flowers, *she is a professor of Native American literature and creative writing at the University of Wisconsin. I asked her to comment on the place she considers home.*

MY HUSBAND ALWAYS TEASES ME ABOUT MY FAMILY. My sisters and I love to talk and tell stories. One of my cousins

194

has been tribal chairman at Oneida, one is an attorney, another one is a comedian. So we joke a lot about how much we all love to talk. [Laughs.]

There is a matriarchal tradition at Oneida. Women are prominent. One of our first tribal chairpersons in the 1940s was a woman; currently, Debbie Doxtator is chairwoman of the tribe. In fact, six out of nine council members are women. It seems to me that Oneida men are willing to give women space and a voice in political affairs.

Oneidas see all living things as interconnected. Every individual has to be responsible to every other being in order for life to continue. Oneida is an organic community. By that I mean that people try to keep within their own community the means of staying alive. When there's a good harvest, everyone shares. When I lived there, the tribe had a cooperative garden and a cannery so I could go and help with the process of planting and harvesting and storing. Now, the tribe also has a farm for raising beef cattle. But Oneida is back to back with a white population that basically wants to take over our land and make us a suburb, and this causes some tensions.

When there's money at Oneida, it doesn't necessarily go to individual tribal members; more often, it goes to the community as a whole. The casino enterprises have been helpful in terms of establishing services. A lot of the money used to develop housing, sewer and water systems, chemical dependency treatment programs, arts and education has come from bingo revenues.[1]

The federal government controls Indian gaming through a federal commission. To support this commission, Indian nations with gaming enterprises are assessed—this is not the case with other federal commissions. The commission is supposed to regulate competition from Las Vegas and other privately owned gaming corporations. But the head of the commission has ties to Las Vegas.

Native nations working to achieve some economic parity

with non-Indian communities around them encounter economic restrictions, not free enterprise. The government says: "We want you to have economic development, but this is the wrong kind of money, this is bad money, this may even be my money." I think federal supervision is a euphemism for control. Historically reservations were on unwanted land. Then, when resources were found there, these resources were and still are extracted without any concern for the Indian populations whose lives are hampered by so-called "development." Politicians manipulate the competition between Native needs and the demands of their non-Indian constituents, using the tribes as scapegoats to gain influence. They take a moral stance calling for regulation of Indian gaming while creating state-run dog tracks and lotteries.

It's a way of controlling whatever resources Indian people develop. Furthermore, it's one of the ways in which those in power suppress us and keep other Americans at a distance. By calling into question our ethical belief system, they attempt to delegitimize our social philosophy. If white people fully understood the profound social philosophies of Native people, they might question their own consumer society values.

White people look at the images of Indian cultures—the figure of Coyote, for example—they put on a jacket and sell it without understanding what Coyote means to the people. This trivializes the power of the symbol and its complex and important meanings. Besides, someone can make a buck in the bargain.

Once our symbols are diminished, it's easier for the government to continue the process of fragmenting Indian communities that began in the first encounter.

Historically, the Oneida have been part of the Iroquois or Longhouse Confederacy in upstate New York. In the 1820s and 1830s, the American government wanted the Longhouse People to move west. A charlatan named Eleazar Williams who spoke the Mohawk language was involved in moving the Oneida to Wisconsin. The Oneida chose to move, coming in several groups:

some were converts (Episcopalians and Methodists came first), some were "pagan." In Wisconsin, they established self-sustaining, organic communities.

After the move, some Oneida tried to hold on to their traditions, especially their language. But "Americanization" was government policy, and the old ways were forbidden. When you're oppressed and afraid you may be viewed as "pagan," you don't talk about your ceremonies; you keep it quiet.

Inside a sacred space
Let us survive.

When my father was growing up at Oneida, it was a Christian community. And it was very poor. He went into the army during World War II; then he went to college, and became a math teacher. He moved to Oneida and then to Green Bay hoping to teach high school, but not one school wanted to hire an Indian math teacher. So he found a job teaching math at the Wisconsin State Reformatory, where I'm sure he faced discrimination. Even though we lived in Green Bay, my dad stayed involved in the Oneida reservation community and was treasurer in the 1950s, when the federal government wanted to terminate us.

My parents wanted to buy a house in a middle-class area of Green Bay. My mother found one, and the realtor told her to bring her husband, and to make an offer. My mother was fair, my father was dark; when he appeared, they were told the house was sold.

My mother was part Indian, Choctaw from Louisiana. She died when I was nine so I don't know much about her. My father raised my sisters and me. I found out years later that the place where my mother grew up was called "the Choctaw Strip." I remember she liked to tell us stories while we ate breakfast.

Growing up in Green Bay in the 1950s, I felt alienated. Green Bay is a border town; the people there felt Indians were in the way. In school some of the white kids called us names. When we protested, we were the ones who were suspended. My father took my sisters and me home to Oneida often. We'd visit the "homestead," my grandmother's house. I was alternately fascinated and frightened because she had died, and the house looked forlorn. But the family had a sense of kinship, there were family gatherings where relatives teased and bantered with each other in a familiar yet ironic way so that folks could be discussing you, and you might not even be aware of the undercurrent of meaning.

When I was in elementary school, I asked my father to take me to someone who would teach me the Oneida language. He said that knowing it would only cause me suffering. Years later, from talking with elders I learned of the suppression of Indian languages in boarding schools. Some Indian people managed to keep their language, and searched out others who spoke it; some of the knowledge of language and culture was hidden within families; some was lost. When my father told us stories about the Oneida and about the Iroquois, we knew it was special, it was something for us to hold in our hearts, and to think about in hard times.

In the sixties in high school, I was trying to understand who I was, and how I fit into the world. I realized that in order to really understand the Oneida, I had to go away and see more of the world. After college I traveled, and taught at Sinte Gieske College on the Rosebud Reservation. In graduate school at the University of Montana, I met Indians from all over the country. We went to powwows; I felt less isolated.

After establishing myself as a writer, I went back to Oneida, and started writing an epic poem, "Under These Viaducts," which incorporates Oneida history up to the Revolutionary War. I'm continuing my research into more recent Oneida history. I want the next generation to grow up knowing what their people went through so they will understand why it's so important to recover their traditions and language.

I began writing a biography of my grandmother, Doctor Lillie Minoka-Hill. I used to love going to her house—I'd sit in her lap and listen to her stories and recitation of poems. She died when I was five, but after her death, I heard stories about her. All during the years I was growing up, when we didn't behave, my father would remind us of things Grandmother did and said so we'd follow her example. In a way, she haunted me. I started looking in archives and talking to people about her—each person remembered something—and I began piecing her story together. The people whom we love are not gone—you can find them again in the oral tradition.

Grandmother lived in an amazing period. From 1870 to 1950, so much was happening to change the face of the country. She was told she was Mohawk from Saint Regis. She was adopted by a Quaker obstetrician who put her through school, and she graduated from the Women's Medical College of Philadelphia in 1899. In 1905 she married my Oneida grandfather, they moved to his reservation in Wisconsin, and she became a farm wife. When Grandfather died, because she had no income she started practicing medicine. I think the women came to her with their childbirth problems because she was a woman. She met with some resistance to modern medicine and so she worked with the midwives using herbal remedies, but most often she used drugs because the dosage was more precise. I'm looking at the environment in which my grandmother lived and worked, and at her role in the community during this time of ongoing depression. People were hungry, and often sick; it was difficult just surviving.

The Oneida had their allotted farmland, but the farms were small and didn't support their families. They used to fish and hunt in order to have something to eat. The men worked in the cranberry fields or traveled around trying to find other jobs, and this split up families. People sold acreage to whites just to stay alive, and often were swindled. I've heard stories of Oneidas being driven out of their homes by the police for nonpayment of taxes they didn't know they owed. And there were foreclosures. In the 1950s, we had large acreage in timber, owned by the community.

Over the years, the lumber barons used the allotment system to manipulate the Oneida so they could take that land too.

I saw change taking place in the 1960s. Oneidas started trying to reclaim lost land. Realizing that our students were still facing the blatant racism I faced in the public schools, the tribe established its own school. Now, in addition to the regular curriculum, our students learn the language and traditions of the Longhouse People.

I've witnessed a wonderful change at Oneida: a rebirth of interest in our spiritual way of life. The Oneida seem to be tolerant and understanding of each other. Our elders who speak the Oneida language are Christian. A grandmother may go to a church service in the morning, and a Longhouse ceremony at night. She will be supportive of her grandchildren's interest in the old ways. I don't see any serious religious friction because all of us belong to more than one "group."

Our people have lived with many and varied traditions. The discussion and interest in them is beautifully chaotic. The seeds of ideas fly about in the wind. In time, we'll recognize which ones need to thrive.

Of course, the government may try to do all kinds of things again to divide us. They may try to destroy the economic development that has taken place since the 1960s. But the reality is it's not going to be able to do that.[2]

Changes come slowly in Indian communities. We know how to wait. Within Euramerican culture, waiting has a bad connotation, but in our communities, waiting sometimes means observing, understanding the way things are, grasping the moment. That's been our sense of how to survive. Without it, there might have been more hardship, more Indian people lost.

When the time is right, we advance. Now, all across this continent, Indian women are gaining power. They are supporting each other in constructive ways. They are recovering their heritage.

. . . We need to be purified by fury.
Once more eagles will restore our prayers.
We'll forget the strangeness of your pity.
Some will anoint the graves with pollen.
Some of us may wake unashamed.
Some will rise that clear morning like the swallows.

From an interview with the author, July 29, 1991.
Poetry segments from Roberta Hill Whiteman, Star Quilt.
(Minneapolis: Holy Cow Press, © 1984). Used by permission.

NOTES

1. An account of Oneida business ventures, and the role of women in the resurgence of the tribe, can be found in Patti Hoefft, "Gaming: The Oneida Experience," *Native Peoples*, Fall 1993, pp. 56–59.

2. For insight into the pressures resulting from economic development within the Oneida, Pequot, and White Mountain Apache tribes, see Erik Eckholm and Francis Clines, "The Native and Not So Native American Way," *New York Times Magazine*, February 27, 1994, pp. 45–52.

V

GO
SOMEWHERE ELSE
AND BUILD
A MCDONALD'S

"... We signed
no treaty What are you still doing here? Go somewhere
else and build a McDonald's. ..." ▽
CHRYSTOS
MENOMINEE LITHUANIAN

18

You . . . Who Have Removed Us: At What Cost?

WENDY ROSE
HOPI/MIWOK

For decades, one hundred human skeletons, most found during exca-
vation of Omaha earth lodge villages in Nebraska in the early 1930s,
were part of the University of Nebraska's collection. Harvard University's Peabody Museum displayed the Omahas' sacred pole and artifacts.
Following the Repatriation Act of 1990 requiring the return of sacred articles to the tribes, both universities turned the ancestral remains and
burial goods over to the Omaha, to be reburied ceremonially.

The appropriation by whites of the heritage and culture of First
Nations people remains a volatile issue. Collectors have plundered Indian gravesites, auctioning off their contents. Social scientists, considering Indian country their domain, have conducted long-term studies
of "the vanishing Americans." Many Native people consider scholars'
Eurocentric accounts of tribal customs and the unauthorized publication of sacred songs and ceremonies another form of plundering.

To be both poet and anthropologist seems like an oxymoron, but
Wendy Rose's life and work are filled with contradictions. Her heart
is with the Hopi, yet she remains on the fringe of that community. She
teaches Native American Studies and authors scholarly articles and
texts, but finds time to nourish her cactus garden at her home in the
Sierras. A much-lauded poet, her collections include Halfbreed
Chronicles, Lost Copper, and Going to War with All My Relations. Following one of her poetry readings in Minneapolis, I found

WENDY ROSE   *Photo by Pat Wolk*

*myself haunted by images of bones. Over lunch, I asked Wendy Rose
why she became an anthropologist.*

> *It was when my songs became quiet.*
> *No one was threatened, no eyes*
> *kept locked on my red hands to see if*
> *they would steal the beads and silver*
> *from museum shelves . . .*[1]

WHEN I WAS A GRADUATE STUDENT IN THE 1970S AT
the University of California, Berkeley, they were just developing

American Indian Studies programs. The topic of my dissertation was the sociological context for Indian writers—who are they, how do they relate to their communities, that sort of thing. The English and comparative literature departments didn't want to deal with that topic, so they said Indian literature is not American literature. It is about the culture of the storyteller.

I was stunned. That was a pretty racist idea—that our work is an anthropological artifact—that it doesn't stand on its own as literature, as art. I was shoved off onto anthropology.

There were a number of very strange experiences. I was told things about Indian people that were demonstrably untrue. Like one of the anthropologists said, "There's no pottery produced at Laguna Pueblo anymore." I said, "I know there's pottery produced there, by people I'm distantly related to." He said, "Well, I've found that Indian people don't really know as much about their cultures today as anthropologists do." Another professor said that California Indian women in the North don't wear basket hats anymore, and they don't tattoo their faces. Well, at that time, I went to a powwow or ceremony every couple of months. I went to the Miwok festivals, and some of the Pitt River Indians, the Yuroks, Tolowas and Hupas, would come down. And I'd see women with their chins tattooed, wearing their basket hats.

In the 1970s, there were attacks by Indians on museums that were displaying human remains. There was a demonstration in front of the Southwest Museum in Los Angeles. This was years before it was legally mandated under the Repatriation Act that all skeletal remains and grave goods be returned to the tribes from which they came.

I was working part-time for the anthropology museum at Berkeley. I remember overhearing the assistant director of the museum talking to the director of another museum about how they would hide any human remains that they had from Indian people. They would claim they didn't have them so they could keep them for "scientific purposes." I knew there was a huge storeroom under the women's gymnasium where these bones were stacked and stacked. So here I am typing away, and these anthropologists are standing right there talking about all this, as if I'm invisible.

I saw this as appropriation of the Native person, right down to our bones.

I've seen it in a number of situations. When Tellico Dam was built by the Tennessee Valley Authority, they had to remove the remains from several cemeteries, some white, some Indian. The white bones were reinterred in another cemetery; the Indian bones were taken to a museum and put into storage. This too is appropriation, like the "tomahawk chop." The bones become trophies.

I took a class on California Indians, and a film was shown of archeologists working in the late nineteenth century—looking for objects that would look flashy in a display case. They were tossing human bones over their shoulders. I remember getting up out of that class and walking out, and not being able to go back. The instructor got a long prose poem in which I told him that I felt it was my bones that they were tossing over their shoulders.

Working at the museum, Wendy Rose came across an invoice documenting the sale to the museum of "nineteen American Indian skeletons from Nevada . . . valued at $3,000." She wrote the poem "Three Thousand Dollar Death Song":

> *. . . You: who have*
> *priced us, you who have removed us: at what cost?*
> *What price the pits where our bones share*
> *a single bit of memory, how one century*
> *turns our dead into specimens, our history*
> *into dust, our survivors into clowns. . . .*[2]

In one of my classes, the instructor was talking about the Southwest. He said the Hopi were cannibals; when the Spanish went to their land, the Hopi ate them. That was too much. I guess

I had a warped sense of humor. I got together with another Indian in the class. For the next session, we sat in the front row—we each had a full dinner place setting with forks and knives in front of us, and we just sat there staring at him for the entire lecture.

I was becoming aware of the appropriation of Native American literature by non-Indians. Some white writers have published traditional oral literature while presenting themselves as spiritually Indian. If they had been accepted into a Native family, had taken on the responsibilities of that family member, then their work would have some legitimacy. But these are people who stand up and use their writing to say, "I can invent myself; I don't need to have a social or cultural context; I can have whatever I want." This kind of entitlement is just as ugly in my eyes as when a European decides he is entitled to take Indian land.

To take the words from a people is a sort of rape of the oral culture.

You have to be recognized by a community if you are going to speak for them. You don't become a traditional doctor [what some call *shaman*] by standing up and saying, "I can put words together in a clever way, I can move people emotionally." You can't be a traditional doctor or healer unless the community trusts you. It's the same with literature.[3]

If you take the words from a people, it will backfire. They forced all of us to learn English. Now, for the first time in history, Native peoples are united by language. That's permitted us to communicate with one another in such a way that the missionaries and the colonizers may someday come to regret. [Laughs.]

I remember Bea Medicine wrote an article about the dilemma of a traditional Indian woman becoming an anthropologist—one who goes around with a looking glass spying on people. There were people who were saying to those of us who were Indian college students, "Be careful. Don't let them ruin you." Students told me that they had been warned by older family members that they would become involved in witchcraft if they went to the university. So you had this sense that you were doing something dangerous, like parachuting.

I believe that for any Indian who goes through the American college system, there is the danger that he or she will sell out. For example, there's lots of money available to an Indian willing to become a mining or oil engineer, willing to support the exploitation of the land, the contamination of the air and water. You are, in a sense, put under a spell. You can have a nice middle-class life, a nice car. All you have to do is cooperate with the corporations and help them find the oil, then put in a good word for them with the tribal council. Sure, there is a real danger of being coopted.

> *Those quiet songs*
> *—I could tell you—*
> *simply expose the stone spirit*
> *of Warrior Katcina dancing sideways*
> *through the village . . .*[4]

I've always been a fighter. If they try to coopt me, I hope my fighting spirit is sufficiently awake and aware of what is happening to be able to counteract it. The spirit of the "katcina warrior" is with me, beside me.

In her poems, I observed, Wendy Rose contrasts white people's worship of technology with the Indian's worship of the land.

It's not like bowing down to a foreign idol. You're so much a part of the land, you could no more worship the forest than you could take your eyes out and put them on the table and regard them as separate from the rest of you.

I grew up in a white community in Oakland in the 1950s with my mom and her second husband. My mom is part Miwok, and part Northern European; she doesn't identify as Indian. There was a lot of abuse in our home. I locked myself in closets. I'd just sit there in the dark for hours, hiding.

My father was a traditional Hopi. I hitchhiked to the Hopi Reservation in Arizona where he lived, and visited with him a few times. Sometimes he would talk with me, sometimes he would act as if I didn't exist. He was in conflict, because if your mother isn't Hopi, you don't have any status there. He died last year.

I grew up feeling I was a mistake. I had a sense of being marginalized. I didn't really come to terms with that until I was in my forties. By then I had decided that we are part of an additional mainstream. We represent possibly the largest group in the western hemisphere, people whose heritage is mixed spiritually as well as biologically—we carry the blood of the oppressors as well as of the oppressed. That's what I meant in my book *Halfbreed Chronicles*. Sometimes halfbreed refers to actual bloodline, sometimes it refers to your position in history.

One of the poems is about Robert Oppenheimer, who lived across the street from us in Berkeley.[5] His involvement with the atomic bomb put him in an untenable position. He didn't really believe that the bomb he worked on was going to be used on anybody. He heard on the radio about the explosion in Hiroshima. I was told that he put his head in his hands and just wept all day. He never really recovered. His health deteriorated, until finally he died.

> *and nothing you can do*
> *will stop us*
> *as we re-make*
> *your weapons into charms,*
> *send flying back to you the bullets.*[6]

In my poetry witchcraft is a metaphor. If you tap into powers you can't handle, they will come back on you.

My poem about Oppenheimer is about what happened in Hiroshima, told from the viewpoint of someone who got up in the morning and thought it would be an ordinary day. It's about the people responsible for building the monster, about those who flew the airplane that dropped the bomb.

I tell my students there's a big difference between guilt and accountability. Guilt is nonproductive. Accountability is to recognize your part in something, to recognize who benefits, who suffers, and try to make amends. You try to find some way to balance it with something positive in your life.

When I started giving readings of the poems in *Halfbreed Chronicles*, I heard from concentration camp survivors, refugees from Southeast Asia and Armenia. They said, "I understand when you read that. I'm a halfbreed too."

If there is a North American tragedy it is the willingness of so many immigrants, whether they came here voluntarily or not, to cut their roots. The language is gone, the closeness to the church is gone. They have maimed themselves and their children and grandchildren. I had a student with a common German name like Schwartz, and he didn't know what country his family came from. I do exercises in my classes to sensitize non-Indian students so they will say, "This is my community, these are my people."

A Hmong student did a presentation on traditional Hmong culture—he wore the clothing, the silver, he showed a tapestry his mother had made. She's illiterate, but in the tapestry, she wove in family history: it showed their farms in Laos, the CIA coming, the airplanes, people dying in the war, their flight to America. She gave it to her son when he got married so his children and grandchildren will know who they are.

I identify with those who are a misunderstood minority in their own society, with political exiles, with those who have been colonized or caught up in war.

. . . Tie a yellow ribbon around the blood-spattered parade,
Around the bewildered mothers, lost and weeping elders,
lonely voices that cry
and beg for peace . . .[7]

From interviews with the author, July 17, 1992,
and May 6, 1993. Poetry segments used by permission.

NOTES

1. "How I Came to Be a Graduate Student," *Lost Copper* (Malki Museum Press, © 1980), p. 38.

2. "Three Thousand Dollar Death Song," *Lost Copper*, p. 26.

3. For more on this subject, see Wendy Rose, "The Great Pretenders: Further Reflections on Whiteshamanism," in M. Annette Jaimes, *The State of Native America* (Boston: South End Press, 1992), pp. 403–421.

4. "How I Came to Be a Graduate Student."

5. Robert Oppenheimer was a U. S. physicist who headed the Manhattan Project, which developed the Atomic Bomb. He advocated the peaceful use of nuclear power.

6. "Naayawva Taawi," *Halfbreed Chronicles* (Los Angeles: West End Press, © 1985), p. 35.

7. "Yellow Ribbons: Baghdad 1991," *Going to War with All My Relations* (Flagstaff, AZ: Northland Publishing, © 1993), p. 83.

19

We Have a Long History Here

CHERYL MANN
CHEYENNE RIVER SIOUX

As joblessness on reservations remains endemic, the migration of Indian people to cities continues. A traditional Navajo journeying from rural hogan to an urban "tract house" may be overwhelmed by rent payments, modern appliances, a computerized job market, taxes and hospital bills. The National Indian Youth Council, based in Albuquerque, provides support services for the more than thirty thousand Indians who have relocated to urban areas of the Southwest.

In the 1970s, the NIYC filed lawsuits for tribes seeking to halt strip mining and uranium mining on reservations. Cheryl Mann is the executive director of NIYC. As she explained, the organization's focus has changed, but it remains supportive of efforts to preserve the sanctity of tribal lands. She's lively and down to earth. In her late forties, she wears her black hair pulled back and dangling quill earrings. In her Albuquerque office decorated with portraits of Indian leaders, Cheryl Mann shared memories of her own migrations and gave her perspective on current issues in the Southwest.

I'M FROM THE MINNECONJOU BAND OF THE CHEYENNE River Sioux. One of my ancestors was a survivor of the massacre at Wounded Knee. Her name was Runs After Her Old Crow Woman.

The Sioux used to name you at birth. In puberty, they renamed you for something you did or accomplished. Well, each generation shortened the name. My dad's family name was Runs After Her, mine was Runs After. I married a man named Mann, so of course they called me Runs After Mann. [Laughs.]

During my childhood, we lived in Charger Camp on the Cheyenne Agency, South Dakota. We had no electricity, no running water, just kerosene lamps. We had family gatherings with people really talking to each other about the past. The young respected their elders. A son-in-law could speak to his mother-in-law only through a third person, and he never looked her in the eye. It kept the peace in the family. I think they should have kept that custom—you wouldn't have so many mother-in-law jokes. [Laughs.]

My grandmother used to tell us stories about the supernatural—I loved to be scared. I remember one time she said there had been a knock on the door and there were deer tracks all around the house, but no tracks leading to or away from the house. There were stories about owls—they were a bad omen. If they hooted by your house, that was a prediction a family member would die. That had happened to some people in my family's camp.

My father was an environmental specialist for the Indian Health Service, and he was active in tribal politics. He was the breadwinner, he turned his check over to my mother, and she took care of everything. We Sioux women are strong, vocal, we direct things—some call us pushy. [Laughs.]

The place where I lived as a child is now under water. The Oahe Dam and other dams flooded all the reservations from Pierre, South Dakota, all the way up and down the Missouri River, including their sacred sites, and the towns were relocated. The dams were necessary for flood control and for power, but why did they [the Army Corps of Engineers] have to build them only on reservations? I suppose they felt Indians were of no consequence, so why not flood their land!

I went to a Catholic high school on a scholarship. The school was on a farm in the middle of nowhere on the Lower Brule Reservation—I felt like I'd won a scholarship to prison. [Laughs.] There was nothing else to do but study, so I got a good education.

After high school, my father said, "Get off the reservation; there's nothing for you here." My parents wanted me be self-reliant in a world that was changing. So I went to UCLA and got my degree in electrical engineering. I worked evenings and week-ends for a company in Pasadena. They paid for my tuition and books so I could work on a master's degree. But the commuting, bumper-to-bumper traffic and the smog, I mean, I had tears running down my face. I said, "What am I doing this for?" and I moved to Albuquerque. It's close to mountains and the desert. I can go camping and fishing.

I completed my master's degree. I got a job as a TV news re-porter; the National Indian Youth Council was suing the station for discrimination in hiring, and I just fell into this job.

The NIYC was founded in the early sixties by young Indian intellectuals who were tired of having white people talk for us—we can talk for ourselves. They organized a leadership program for Indians in universities called the Clyde Warrior Institute. This was the period of Red Power. Indians were expressing pride in their heritage.

The NIYC began as a voluntary board working out of peo-ple's garages. In 1968, they "hired" Gerald Wilkinson. "If you want to get paid," they said, "you raise the money and pay your-self." He rented a small space and slept in a hammock in the base-ment, other people volunteered, gradually they got projects funded. We're still doing job placement, training and counseling, funded by the BIA and the Department of Labor. People have to be trained for jobs that exist. Albuquerque is big in the electronics field, so that's where the jobs are.

When people come here from other states, we help them find housing, medical care and child care. We need more parenting programs to relieve the child abuse and neglect that's prevalent in Albuquerque, but our client load is growing, and our funds are declining.

So far we have not had a problem with Indian gangs. The Pueblo Indians are a very peaceful people. After five o'clock, most of the Indians go home—most of the Rio Grande pueblos are within driving distance. That's a good thing; they can take part in the cultural life of their communities.

We thought we were making a change in the areas of civil rights and discrimination. We thought we had a friend in the court system, but we're repeating battles we fought twenty or thirty years ago. It hurts to think that the Indian wars are still going on.

The Indian Religious Freedom Act was passed in 1978. To have to have it written in the first place was a sign that the U.S. Constitution did not pertain to Indians. Why shouldn't we have the same rights as other citizens? Because of a lack of government support, and the changes in the makeup of the Supreme Court, we didn't stand much of a chance in court.

In the Lake Powell area of Arizona, that's in the Four Corners region, the Navajos were asking for a specific site to be set aside so they could have religious ceremonies there on Sunday mornings. They didn't want locals and tourists drinking beer there and despoiling the area. We went to court in Arizona, and we lost that case.

In 1987 Pope John Paul advised Native Americans to hold on to their culture. But the Vatican, in cooperation with the University of Arizona, supported construction of an international observatory on Big Seated Mountain [Mount Graham], home of the Apache Mountain Spirit Dancers considered by the San Carlos Apaches to be the source of their sacred songs and dances. Holy sites on the mountain contain medicinal herbs and water used by native healers for thousands of years.

Apaches and Zunis testified at hearings that this mountain was a religious shrine essential to the physical and spiritual well-being of Native people. But in 1988 the Arizona legislature authorized the project, citing "economic benefits to the state."[1]

That has happened in many states. In New Mexico, there's an effort to expand the Albuquerque airport right over our petroglyphs. The petroglyphs—drawings early Pueblo peoples carved into large boulders—tell stories about where they came from, their clans, their activities. There are images of animals, flute players, masks and headdresses. The petroglyphs are the writing paper, the diaries, the journals of the early Pueblo Indians. They spent a lot of time and energy creating them in order to preserve something important, something beautiful. This area is sacred to us.

The Petroglyph National Monument was established in 1991 and already they're trying to gouge pieces out of it in order to build a resort, and develop the airport. The city planned this expansion without doing an environmental impact statement. In hearings, Pueblo leaders said, "If you want to expand the airport, fine, but go around the site, don't destroy the history of our people, don't wipe out the past." The petroglyphs give us a sense of continuity, they show future generations we have a long history here.

Los Alamos National Laboratories, where Robert Oppenheimer built the world's first atomic bomb, sprawls across New Mexico's canyons and mesas. Not far away is Sandia Laboratories, also the site of nuclear testing and research. Elevated levels of plutonium have been found in nearby Rio Grande pueblos, but lab scientists monitoring waste disposal minimize the health risk to pueblo residents.[2]

The scientists buried radioactive tailings in the canyons and arroyos over the years, and have conveniently forgotten where. They have been leeching into the well water of the San Juan Pueblo. They have contaminated their water, and have caused health problems in newborn babies. They've had to shut down the water. It's a very poor community, and they haven't been able to tap into city water because of the cost. We have held hearings about this issue; there's been a cover-up.

Indians were heavily involved in uranium mining in the town of Grants. Now the mines are closed, but uranium tailings are blowing in the wind, contaminating homes as well as the water supply. At the Laguna and Acoma pueblos, which are near the Anaconda Mine, landfill used in the construction of an elementary school was found to cause birth defects.

We were involved for many years fighting the mining companies. We filed lawsuits, we put hundreds of thousands of dollars into court cases, but when you have one or two attorneys against a roomful of them, you automatically lose. They don't care about the health of Indian people. We couldn't afford to continue to lose, so we began moving in new directions. Now Indians are going into Congress. With Senator Daniel Inouye heading the Select Committee on Indian Affairs, I think things are changing. There's a proposal on environmental issues, and one on religious rights.[3]

At least once a year, the NIYC takes issues pertinent to different tribes to the United Nations. We're doing that for the Tohono O'Odham [Papago] Nation, which extends from Arizona into Mexico (there's an imaginary border). They're citizens of both countries and can go back and forth, but when they lost land to Mexico, they also lost services. Indians in Mexico are so poor, most can't go to school; they are treated worse than here. The tribe would like to get that land back, but feels it has exhausted its remedies with the federal government, so it has turned to the international arena. The United Nations has no power, but it is a place to talk and increase awareness.

It's a misconception that the U.S. government takes care of Indian people. A tribe is just like an organization—it has to raise funds to survive. Some tribes have turned to gaming as a way of helping their people. They're not gonna put a casino on sacred land, on a burial site. They're very watchful about that.

I believe there's someone watching us. Occasionally, if you turn quick enough, you might see them. People here at NIYC who have passed on, like Gerry Wilkinson—I feel he'll always run this organization, and I do things the way he would want them done. I think the spirits of the ancestors are with us every day, guiding us, reminding us not to be too selfish or greedy, reminding us to treat everyone the same. They help me remember that we're here to make life a little better for Indian people.

From an interview with the author, June 19, 1992.

NOTES

1. Following years of testimony by Native religious leaders and the enviromental groups supporting them, on July 28, 1994, a federal judge ruled that construction of the telescope must be suspended until environmental studies are completed. See *Americans Before Columbus* (NIYC publication), Fall 1991, p. 6, and *The Circle*, September 1994, p. 14.

2. See "No Peace on the Pueblos," *Sierra* magazine, March–April 1987, pp. 30-33; "Toxic Contamination Affects Indians," *Americans Before Columbus*, Vol. 17, No. 2, 1989, pp. 1, 6, 7. As this book went to press, the Mescalero Apache and other tribes were looking at controversial proposals to accept temporary storage of nuclear waste on their land. See Randel D. Hanson, "The Mescalero Apache: Nuclear Waste and the Privatization of Genocide." *The Circle*, August 1994, p. 6-7.

3. A broad coalition of religious and civil liberties groups called for new legislation to protect sacred sites, the use of sacred substances in ceremonies, and the rights of prisoners to practice their religion. On November 16, 1993, President Bill Clinton signed into law the Religious Freedom Restoration Act.

20

We Are
the Caribou People

SARAH JAMES
GWICH'IN/ATHABASCAN/
NATIVE ALASKAN

The *Chandalar River flows south from the foothills of the Brooks Mountains in northern Alaska. Just above the riverbank is Arctic Village, home to eight family groups of Gwich'in people who live in thirty small log homes; they have a school, a church, a post office, a general store, and a community freezer. Today the Gwich'in travel by snowmobile and helicopter, they enforce an alcohol ban, they send their children to public school, and a few go to college.*

Witnessing the social disorder that resulted when other Arctic villages formed corporations under the 1971 Alaska Native Claims Settlement Act, the Gwich'in resisted pressures for land sales and remained independent, preferring to live in the old way in what has been termed "the last fully intact ecosystem on earth." For thousands of years, their existence and culture have centered around the migrations of the Porcupine caribou herd. Following construction of the pipeline, oil companies sought the right to drill in the Arctic National Wildlife Refuge, the calving grounds of the Porcupine herd. The Gwich'in mobilized to protect the caribou, which are the center of their spiritual and cultural life, and won the support of conservationists, churches, and human rights advocates.

In the forefront of this continuing struggle is Sarah James, member of the Arctic Village Traditional Council, and spokesperson for more than five thousand Gwich'in peoples. She attended a UN Con-

SARAH JAMES   *Photo by Robert Gildart*

*ference on Environment and Development in Rio and a 1991 confer-
ence of Athabascan leaders in Alaska that resulted in a settlement tem-
porarily preventing oil drilling in the Arctic Refuge, but says Sarah
James, "The fight isn't over yet. The oil industry and the government
are thinking about oil and money."*

I WAS BORN IN 1944. MY MOM AND DAD LIVED OFF THE
land, way out in the country on our trap lines. We were isolated;
our nearest neighbor was about fifteen miles away. We traveled in

the area around the Yukon River, here and there, wherever my family could make a living. We went up the Salmon River in a wooden boat with an outboard motor. We had a little cabin my dad made out of logs that we stayed in, but when we moved from place to place, we used a tent.

We lived in harsh weather; we didn't have leisure time. The Aztecs, they had sunshine from morning to night, and abundant crops. They could build towers to the sky. Ours was a difficult life—we worked at survival. A woman had to learn how to hunt, get wood, bring in meat. If she waited for her man to do all that, she'd probably freeze. The man was out there hunting and trapping; if his boots were torn apart, if he waited for his wife to sew them, his feet would freeze, so he learned to sew his own clothing.

We all had chores. My father would get up around three or four in the morning, he'd take off with his snowshoes, gun, pack, he'd break a trail, he'd set traps, and hunt. By the time we got up, my mom had cooked us breakfast of eggs, oatmeal or pancakes, sometimes fried or boiled meat. One time, we ran out of everything, we didn't have sugar or flour, so she boiled meat, and we lived on the broth. We were hungry—it tasted pretty good. [Laughs.]

My mom did skin tanning, fur sewing, beading. She made all our clothes. I used to wear a caribou fur parka, with fur pants and boots that she made. I knew my life depended on knowing how to make the things we needed, so I'd watch her work. I'd ask questions, then I'd make a little fur parka. When my father was making a sled or toboggan, I'd make a little model of it, so eventually I learned how to do things.

The government said we had to go to school, so we moved here to Arctic Village and I went to a BIA school. I had a hard time talking English—I didn't know when to say yes or no, I didn't understand radios or TV or cars or traffic—it was hard for me to cross the street. When I was thirteen I went away to a boarding school, and I learned about the outside world. If you don't know the western way of life, you're considered dumb. I wanted to learn western ways so I'd be accepted in other societies. I knew that would help me to defend our way of life.

Our responsibility as Indian people is to protect our culture and environment. The Gwich'in lived on the land for thousands of years, hunting and trapping. My father wasn't out there trapping to get rich, just to survive. We always took just what we needed. But when the trappers came up the Yukon River, they killed a lot of fur-bearing animals on the way. They arrived here in the springtime, when migratory ducks and birds were mating—there was so much wildlife out there, it was so noisy, you'd have to yell to be heard. But the trappers were only interested in profit; they wanted the animals only for their hides. They put liquid strychnine on their bait, the animals ate it and died. People said that after that, the ecosystem got mixed up, the whole country just shut down within a year. It's never been the same since.

Our people had lived the only life they knew on the land, but there was nothing out there to hunt, and it didn't take long for them to starve. They spent so much time looking for food, their resistance got really low and when disease came, it killed them real fast. Many thousands of Native people died. If it weren't for the caribou that migrated from north to south through this country, we would have been completely wiped out.

My people have always followed the herds; we depended on the caribou for protein, for clothing, for tools, for trade. When we had to settle in one place, we came to Arctic Village because there were fish in the lakes, there was a trading post nearby in Fort Yukon, and the Porcupine caribou herd migrated here.

There was a time, the Gwich'in say, when all creatures spoke the same language; caribou and Gwich'in were one. There is evidence that caribou roamed the Arctic region fifty thousand years ago. Says Sarah James, "In a museum in Ottawa you can see a caribou leg bone scraper from Old Crow that is 1,350 years old. It is the same as the one my mother used." Today the Gwich'in hunt with rifles, not bows and arrows, but they follow ancient laws: no matter how hungry they are, they permit the first band of caribou that appears each spring to pass undisturbed; they kill a caribou only when in need.

We are "the caribou people." We do caribou dance and songs, we tell stories about them. They are sacred to us. The Porcupine caribou herd has gone to the same calving ground for thousands of years; we consider it sacred. We consider any place that is a nesting or spawning area sacred. If we don't take care of those places, they're not going to be there for the next generation.

In 1988, the State of Alaska pushed to open up the Coastal Plain to oil and gas development. They were supported by the Inupiat and other Native corporations. We opposed it, but we found they were going to go ahead anyway. The State of Alaska depends on oil—the price of oil affects the whole economy of the state. The Secretary of the Interior in Washington, D.C., and the U.S. Fish and Wildlife Service, they were all pushing for development.

We were just a small minority opposing it, and we didn't know what direction to take. We went and visited with the elders in other Gwich'in villages. They said, "In the past, when something threatened the nation, our people called all the elders together and decided what to do. Let's do that now."

So we called all the elders from seventeen Gwich'in villages together for a gathering in Arctic Village. I was on the International Porcupine Caribou Commission, and I helped organize it. Five hundred people came together here. That had not happened for a hundred and fifty years. Gwich'in came from other parts of Alaska, and from the other side of the Canadian border; they speak the same language, we all depend on the same caribou, we're all related somehow. The elders came because this was important to them. They wanted to take a stand for their beliefs. One whole family chartered a plane and came up from Fort Yukon.

The elders took control of the meeting. We had an agenda because the people who helped us with a little funding required that. But the elders threw the agenda away—they said that when they had gatherings a long time ago, nothing was written, and they wanted to take care of business in the old way. Nobody was allowed to take notes; only one movie crew was allowed in. They said that anybody who wanted to talk had to speak in Gwich'in. They presented a talking stick to the speaker.

We talked for three days. We had a translator for those who didn't know our language. The elders said, "This is important history being made here." Then they realized that it might help us with the outside world if we wrote something down, so the chiefs got together on a hill outside, and wrote up a resolution to protect the caribou calving grounds.

They formed the Gwich'in Steering Committee—they chose me to be chairperson. Our first goal was to reach out to all kinds of media, the next was to reach out to tribes across the nation, hoping they would join in our efforts to lobby Congress. We did it by making phone calls, publishing a newspaper, going to conferences to tell our story.

The federal government had to hold hearings. The hearings took place in Kaktovik, Anchorage and Fairbanks; they never held hearings in Gwich'in country, even though we're the people who have used the caribou herds for thousands of years. They just ignored us. So we got some money together (most families here earn very little money, but we pooled our resources), we chartered a plane from Arctic Village to Kaktovik, we took five people and we testified at the hearing. Then when there was a hearing of the House Subcommittee in Washington, D.C., we paid our own way so we could go and testify.[1] They gave all the time to the State of Alaska, to the oil company representatives, to the Interior Department. We were the last ones on the list. When we got up to speak, we were given only ten minutes, and by then, most of the committee members had left the stage. Even the movie camera was gone. They didn't care about us.

The Native corporations—they're our own people—they were there to support development, and they didn't want to talk to us. They claim that they can live a traditional life in harmony with the environment and do development at the same time. I don't agree with that. There's too much greed and waste out there.[2]

The government did an environment impact statement. There was a report from the Fish and Wildlife Service that said where there has been oil development, the companies have not followed government regulations about disposal of poisons. But that report was kept hidden.

Advocates for development claim that oil drilling in Prudhoe Bay on the western coast of Alaska has not affected the environment of the Central Arctic herd [a different caribou herd] which lives in that area. But in 1985, oil spills in the Prudhoe Bay region totaled 522, contaminating the water table with heavy metals.[3]

We've found information showing that the Central Arctic herd may be affected. The birth rate among the caribou is declining; some are in poor health; they're finding dead caribou. We don't want that to happen to our herd.

When they started the oil drilling in Prudhoe Bay, they said we'd get revenue, but we haven't seen it here in Arctic Village. A five-gallon can of gas for our snow machine costs $25. Industry is exploiting all our resources: timber, minerals, fishing. They send Alaskan salmon to Japan, then they sell it back to us in a can. They take gold out of here; it doesn't benefit the State of Alaska. The timber is shipped to Japan; then, we can buy Japanese furniture at outrageous prices. Our people here have the ability to produce their own furniture. People come up here from the lower forty-eight to work in the summer because they don't have to pay taxes up here, so they take jobs from our people. I know a lot of people who have big mansions down in the lower forty-eight.

People are raping the earth. Some get rich while others are homeless, and crime increases, alcoholism increases. Why don't we accept responsibility to save the earth for the next generation?

There are about two hundred Native villages like ours up here. They are mostly isolated, but we have telephones and television now. There are a few local jobs: fire fighting, maybe you can work in a store, a post office, at a school or clinic. But most of the people live off the land—that's the life they know and treasure.

It's all open country. It's beautiful. We have lakes and rivers with grayling, whitefish and lake trout. We have thick spruce forests, there are mountains all around. We have grizzly bear, rabbits, mountain sheep, ground squirrels, a lot of ducks and birds. We have a safe water system, but a lot of us still drink water from the river. One man who lives down there has a pump. I go down there and haul river water back up when I can. It tastes so good.

Our environment is part of our life. We celebrate Earth Day every day. We believe that we've always been here where we are today. We come from the land, and we're gonna go back to the land.

In this village, our families are very close; we're almost all related. We stay together—that's how we survive. We take care of each other. I know in western culture, they don't work that way—it seems like each individual makes out for himself. It's not like that in the Indian communities I see.

Some people have gone away to college, but they come back—they've got roots here. We're beginning to teach our language. We're going back to our religion. Indian people never gave it up—they took it away from us.

I travel all over, speaking about protection of the caribou. I've been to Washington, D.C., three times to testify, I've been to San Francisco, Mexico, Guatemala and Brazil. All these places have indigenous people, they're all my people. The thing that's most important to all of us is land. If we don't have the title to the land, we don't have anything.

People tell me I've accomplished a lot without a college degree. I always tell them that I only finished high school, but the teaching of our elders, of my parents, that's my degree.[4]

*From (telephone) interviews with the author,
January 27–28, 1994.*

NOTES

1. Sarah James testified before the House Subcommittee on Fisheries, Wildlife Conservation and the Environment, August 7, 1991.

2. Native corporations formed under the Alaska Native Claims Settlement Act are supposedly profit-making. They have business enterprises: an air service, a hotel, some are in lumber, oil, or mining; the villagers are the stockholders. But Sarah James told me, "These are a hunting and fishing people; they're not used to running a western-type business, and a lot of those corporations are going bankrupt. Then, if they sell their stock to non-Indians, they lose their title to the land. I think that was the intention from the beginning."

3. Oil corporations dispose of toxic waste materials by pumping them into the tundra. An 1989 Environmental Protection Agency report on Prudhoe Bay said, "The area around the drilling pads was found to be biologically dead; the tundra had been blackened" by chemical spills; vegetation and wildlife were depleted. Karl Guevara Erg, "Oil Threatens Alaska Natives," *Native Nations* (February 1991), pp. 4–29, and publications of the Gwich'in Steering Committee, Anchorage, Alaska.

4. For another perspective on Gwich'in lifestyle and culture see Robert Gildart, "Gwich'in: We Are the People." *Native Peoples* (Fall 1993), pp. 22–29.

21

They're Trying to Sell Our Treaties

ESTHER NAHGAHNUB
FOND DU LAC OJIBWAY/
CHIPPEWA

H*er Ojibway name is Ogimah-geshig-gwok-quay, which means "Head woman in the sky." She calls herself a grandmother and "a gatherer."*

At a recent Native American treaty rights conference in South Dakota, a tribal chairman introduced Esther Nahgahnub as "a lady warrior who fights for the survival of Fond du Lac." The Catholic Church considers her "a heathen," she says. An overzealous press sometimes portrays her wearing bearskin moccasins stalking the woods in search of prey.

The real Esther Nahgahnub lives on the Fond du Lac Reservation in northern Minnesota. Near the lake, across from a forest of pine and balsam trees, sits her white wood-and-brick rambler. Sculpture made from driftwood and moose horns welcomes visitors. Inside, a hunting rifle stands in a corner and a small dog plays on the floor. Deer skulls painted with intricate, abstract designs share white walls with dream catchers.

Esther Nahgahnub is an energetic woman in her mid-fifties with gray streaks in her black hair, "battle stripes," she calls them. Talking with conviction about her art and ideals, she seemed more like a peacemaker than a warrior. When she described the threats to the land and wildlife, as well as the schism within her tribe, she grew passionate, her anger tinged with sadness and irony.

I MAKE THE DREAM CATCHERS for children who have bad dreams. I make them out of feathers from birds that got killed on the road. I use everything: crow, hawk, everything. I even used the feathers of a tiny songbird the cat killed. You put them into the form of a spider's web; it is suspended near the sleeping child.

The good dreams know the way to get through the little hole; the rest of the web snares the bad dreams and holds them until they're dissipated by the first light of day. It works. Only once, someone told me his wore out from too many bad dreams. [Laughs.]

One of the dream catchers I made took me months and months to do, and it was composed of so many different birds and pieces of animals, I almost didn't want to give it up, but then a woman asked for it for a friend who was dying of AIDS and I thought, "Well, it couldn't go to a better home than that." So I let it go.

*One of Esther Nahgahnub's
dream catchers*
Photo by Vince Leo

Lately, I've been making dream catchers mostly for AIDS patients. If somebody needs one, they'll tell me and I'll begin to make it. It may take a few months. I won't force it. The dream catcher knows what it wants, it knows where it's going. Each one has its own personality. The image is already in there. I simply have to find it and allow it to develop. You have to hear with your heart what it's saying to you.

That fellow up there [she points to a small deer skull], he was a baby when they did him in. He's so small, he almost painted himself. I just held the brush. Now, this large deer skull over here is quite different from the other one in color and style. When I allow the deer to tell me what he wants to look like, I am honoring him.

I first saw him in a taxidermist's shop, hanging by a wire from the ceiling, ignored. He was full of cigarette smoke and chemicals. I felt sorry for him, so I had to buy him, I had to bring him home. Another time, I was in a shop with skulls, bones, claws and hides put there just to make money, with no feeling for the animal. There was a large head of an alligator turtle; there was such sadness about him. I remembered seeing a video about how they capture turtles—they go after them with an ax and break their shells, then, they drag them away still living. I bought the turtle head and took care of him. I still have him, and his sadness is gone.

None of these animals had the kind of quick, clean death they should have. The way they are killed is to me disrespectful. The same is true of the way trees are slaughtered. The trees or animals are just objects to be exploited. That's why this planet is so doomed. You can't keep on taking, taking, taking from the earth and not giving anything back. In this country, entire species of birds, plants and trees are forced out to make way for the new moneymakers.

Ours is gaming. I resent it when people call gaming "the new buffalo." That is so ungodly disrespectful. As if gaming were going to provide us with everything we need, including religion! The buffalo is sacred to many tribes! Gaming can be detrimental.

There are people elected by the tribes who are willing to sell our treaties for money. All of a sudden we can be powerful, we can have all the things we were deprived of as children, we can give things to our family. I've seen it here on the Rez, and on other Ojibway reservations where they're considering selling the treaties. Our people signed treaties in the nineteenth century so that when they were migrating, or ceding territory, we'd keep our survival mechanisms.

Some tribal leaders have negotiated settlements that in effect trade treaties for cash payments. One such proposed settlement was the 1988 Tri-Band Agreement involving three bands of Lake Superior Chippewa.[1]

When the state wants us to sell them a federal treaty, this is the way it works. Some Indian band of Ojibway exercises its treaty rights to hunt, fish and gather on ceded land. The Minnesota Department of Natural Resources arrests them for this; then the band sues the state for arresting them. But instead of a trial, the state says, "Let's settle out of court. We'll give you so many million dollars plus land and mineral rights to that land, and maybe an exclusive fishing zone on the biggest walleye lake in the world."

The band leaders say, "Hey, that sounds like a winner." The governor's salivating over this treaty buyout. He knows there's uranium and other minerals on that land. One tribal government said they were willing to accept four percent of the use of a lake, even though under the treaties they are entitled to one hundred percent.

If this treaty buyout goes through, the tribe will have sold its heritage; they can then be terminated. They will lose their very identity.

From the beginning, the federal government has been successful in dividing Indian people. Whites didn't like the fact that in our tribal councils, everybody got to speak; nothing was decided until consensus was reached, which could take anywhere from a day to a month. In 1934, when they passed the Indian Reorganization Act, they said, "You're gonna have a government exactly like ours. Then we'll know what you're up to." They made the word *band* interchangeable with *tribe* so instead of having six different bands in Minnesota that owe allegiance to each other, we have six different tribes. The tribes don't necessarily owe allegiance to anybody.

They diluted the chieftainship, encouraging the less effective leaders by giving them jobs, money and power. These people don't work for us; they're paid by the state, and the state is trying to get the treaties, so maybe the state will drag us down.

I mean, these white government men are not stupid. They know how to dismantle a nation.

Here at Fond du Lac, many of the traditionals still respect the land and the animals, they still believe in our treaties, they believe in the circle of life. But the Reservation Business Committee, as soon as their hand goes up and they take the oath of office, they become experts on everything. If they have enough relatives who vote, they don't have to ask anyone else what they want. It's like the people disappear!

I worked for the tribe as a bookkeeper. Then I took a few years off to complete my bachelor's degree and work on my master's. In 1988 when the RBC decided to sell the treaty, I felt panic—like somebody was grabbing hold of my heart. They acted like the treaty was something you could use in the outhouse. I felt betrayed. I said, "This is wrong. You can't do this to the people." We got together and organized a campaign against the proposed settlement. We fought 'em here on the Rez and in the legislature; we fought them tooth and nail.

The campaign was successful, and ultimately Esther Nahgahnub's band withdrew from the 1988 pact, but the issue remains explosive.

The treaty litigation is ongoing; some of the bands are for the settlement, some oppose it. We're under attack on every front. It's a war that is fought quietly indoors, not out in the open. Our group, the Anishinabe Liberation Front, is saying to the bands, "Look, you've got to come together. They can break one arrow, but if you've got ten arrows, you won't be broken."

That's when I started doing the dream catchers. I was spending money going back and forth to the legislature fighting that treaty sale, I was in debt, so I had to make some money. I thought, "Well, maybe somebody will appreciate dream catchers." And they did.

On December 19, 1989, officers of the U.S. Fish and Wildlife Service, aided by Fond du Lac Reservation game wardens and Duluth police, raided the Buffalo Bay Trading Company in Duluth. Tearing dream catchers made by Esther Nahgahnub off the walls, they stuffed them into garbage bags. The receipt identified the confiscated items as "art objects with feathers thought to be owl, crow or Canadian Goose." A few days later, Nahgahnub and the storekeeper Walt Bresette were arrested and charged with violation of a 1916 law prohibiting the sale of migratory bird feathers.[2]

I felt that we were set up because Walt Bresette and I are treaty protectors. They said we broke an international treaty protecting migratory birds. You see, white women used to wear all these feathers in their hats, and whole species of birds were literally exterminated, so the U.S. signed a treaty with Japan, Great Britain, Canada, Mexico and other countries agreeing not to kill those birds. They accused Walt and me of breaking this treaty. They accuse *Indians* of breaking a treaty. That's really funny!

I told them the truth. I said, "Yes, I made the dream catchers and the feathers are from a friend's molting bird, and from roadkill." I told them I had the right to use the feathers of these birds under our treaties. My own people said to me, "Why don't you just pay the fine and let it go?" I said, "Why should I pay a fine when my treaty rights back up what I'm doing? I'd be admitting that I didn't have those treaty rights."

Our case was tried in federal court in 1990, and we won it. It was a reaffirmation of our gathering rights. Feathergate became a precedent for all the tribes fighting against encroachment on their rights to hunt and gather.

Our Reservation Business Committee, which supported the state's claim, treated us like we had the bubonic plague. They were the people we had fought just a year before on the issue of selling the treaties. We had shown them the impact grassroots people could have, and they were angry. They told me I would never again in my lifetime hold a job here. Actually, they did me a favor by forcing me to live the way I should be living, the way my grandparents and their grandparents would have wanted me to live.

From then on, members of my tribal government would say to me, "You just want to cause trouble!" I'd say, "You aren't going to back us up to the wall anymore. We're going to be the kind of Indians our ancestors were."

My grandparents lived here, right down the road, around the bend. My grandfather was chief of the Fond du Lac band, the last chief. My grandparents had the best beach on this lake, Nahgahnub Lake. (It's called Big Lake now by the whites who live on it.) My grandparents eked out a living on that beach. They had a little shack right there, and sold candy bars and charged people a dime to swim.

Everybody was angry when my grandfather didn't want to let people put in electricity, but he knew that once we put in electricity, the whites would shove the Indians off the lake into the swamps and onto little plots of land here and there, and that's exactly what happened.

Still, we held on to our little piece of land until Northwest Paper reared its ugly head. The VP of the company wanted my grandparents' land. He hired bigtime attorneys to take it. People came and jacked up the house, put it on a trailer pulled by a tractor, and down that dirt road it went, followed by my grandparents. Some of the white people felt bad, but how do you fight big money?

It absolutely broke my grandfather. It broke that old man, tore his heart out. He was in his late sixties. A few years later, he lost his wife, my grandma, and he went after her as soon as he could, about three months later. They wouldn't allow him to be buried here because he wouldn't accept Catholicism, not even on his deathbed. They shipped him off in an oxcart to be buried in Wisconsin.

Once people got electricity, the whites started building their cabins and houses on the lake, and they are still there, pumping their body excretions into the lake. It's a tragedy. I wouldn't eat a fish out of that lake now.

My parents lived in Superior, Wisconsin, just across the bridge. When my mother was about to give birth to me, first she went to a Catholic hospital in Superior, but they turned her away. She would have come here where we had an Indian hospital, but there was a snowstorm, the roads were bad, I don't know if they had a car, so I was born at home. My mother died nine days later.

Some of the nuns from the hospital went to the home to save her Indian soul before she died. My dad threw them out by their habits, he sent them flying.

My dad was an ironworker and steamfitter. He tried to take care of us (there were three of us) after my mother's death. He said there was no way he would put us in boarding school or an orphanage. Well, he did put us into a sort of mission run by an old woman and her daughter.

They were Holy Rollers—you know, prayer meetings every day, no lipstick, very strict. They had a portable organ, and they would drag me around to jails and street corners where I would hand out these tracts about how God loves you. [Laughs.] I didn't mind the prayer meetings though because during them, I could get into the pantry and climb up to the top shelf where they kept the cookie jar full of great, big, chewy molasses cookies.

My father was a good worker. Eventually, he remarried and we moved to Billings, Montana, where he built us a home, so then we were together. Even after you move away from the circle, it's still a part of you. When you lose your parents or grandparents, you begin to remember something they said or did that influenced you, so they're still alive with you.

This incident stands out in my mind. One day when I was little, my grandmother unwrapped a brown paper bundle, very slowly she took out this red blanket and wrapped it around me saying, "This will take care of you." I thought, "I'd rather have candy." But I kept the blanket for many years.

Then after I had children of my own and we moved back here, I had a horse. One night I dreamed that my horse was going up into the night sky with my daughter. I went back to where my grandparents used to live, I sat by their pump—I used to sit there when I needed to talk with them—I told them about the dream, asked them what I should do. And then the memory of my grandmother and the red blanket came to me.

In a store downtown, I found a red blanket and bought it. I called my daughter, I unwrapped it and put it around her saying, "This will take care of you." She took it the way I did, like "Where's the candy?" Then a week later, she took my horse on a flying trip around the village. I mean, that horse was deadly, he could run like the wind. And she raced him, but couldn't stop him. They reached the blacktop, they spun, and rolled over into a ditch. When I heard about it, I knew my daughter was all right because she had that red blanket with her.

Esther Nahgahnub paused, reflecting, then observed the antics of a blue jay who'd come to call on her patio. The lines in her face softened. She laughed as his beak opened wide to devour the fat peanuts she had provided.

If you watch the animal world, if you watch the winged world, you'll see that they're wiser than humans. The only way we can gain that wisdom is by honoring these living creatures. When we hunt an animal, he knows that we are going to kill him and eat his flesh; he sacrifices his life for us. I make an offering telling him that I need his assistance to live. The skull and horns I save and paint is my way of honoring his gift.

Long ago when white people came to our villages, it looked to them as if we only worked when we wanted to, which was in essence true. You didn't have to hunt unless you wanted to eat, or needed something to put on when winter was coming on. But we had time for the necessary things: the development of the mind and the heart; we had the time to be contemplative. We had the time to see the relationship of all things to each other.

When you work in an office with forced air and you cannot feel the wind on your face, how can you understand the part it plays in our lives? How can you know the changes in the earth when you can't feel it through the soles of your hard shoes? If you can't touch the earth, how do you know it's living?

People pave over the earth and build parking lots, but what happens to what lived there? When you cage something, it begins to die. If people see a creek running, bubbling, singing over the rocks, they know it is alive, its spirit is there. But when that water is pumped into their toilet, it begins to die. Someone should declare the Earth a sovereign nation. Things of the Earth are living, and they need someone to represent them.

I know many of our old people were seers, and they saw what was going to happen to this land. They saw the treaties as a way of protecting both the land and future generations. The treaties are all that's between us and extermination of life as we know it.

From an interview with the author, May 25, 1993.

NOTES

1. For an inside look at the treaty rights struggles of the Chippewa of northern Wisconsin, see Walt Bresette and Rick Whaley, *Walleye Warriors* (Philadelphia: New Society Publishers, 1994).

2. For Esther Nahgahnub's article chronicling her encounter with the legal system see "Feathergate," *Artpaper*, February 1993. Ms. Nahgahnub and two other activists discuss Indian religious freedom and treaty rights in *Nokomis: Voices of Anishinabe Grandmothers*, a video available from Sarah Penman, P.O. Box 14322, Minneapolis, MN 55414.

VI

LOOK,
LITTLE ONES,
ALL THE PLACES
ARE HOLY

". . . Children, the wind in leaves
feeds fire
gives you dreams
and words
to move your lives . . .

Look, little ones
all the places are holy. . . ."
LINDA HOGAN
CHICKASAW▽

22

The Spirit
Takes Care of Us

VI HILBERT
UPPER SKAGIT

Wearing a mollusk-shell necklace and a shawl woven from cedar bark, her olive skin contrasting with her jet-black hair, storyteller Vi Hilbert told her tribal tales at Seattle's Native American Center. Later, I visited her modern home, which sits on a hill high above the Duwamish River valley. Looking down at us from her living room wall were her son's carvings. "These forms speak to us," she said, "reminding us that our sacred practices are a living force in our lives."

An honored elder in her mid-seventies, Vi Hilbert is the author of Haboo *and other books of traditional stories. She cofounded the Lushootseed language and culture program at the University of Washington and has published a lexicon and dictionary of the language.[1] On her desk sit a tape recorder and computer that she uses to preserve her people's songs and stories.[2] The spirit of her ancestors, she says, "speaks through the oral tradition. The wisdom is not all lost, it's sleeping. When it's time for it to be heard, it is awakened within us so others may learn."*

MY PEOPLE INHABITED THE PUGET SOUND REGION along its rivers, up and down its rivers. We were independent and lived wherever we cared to live. My tribe, the Upper Skagit, was located on the Skagit River, so I feel the river is my home.

VI HILBERT   *Photo by Len Bordeaux*

According to our legends, we were on this river from the beginning of time. It's where our world began—we feel it belongs to
us. When I lecture, I discount the Bering Land Bridge theory—our
legends give us proof that we've always been here. We know
where the first mountains came from, we know where the
mother came down from the sky world, pregnant with her child.
She gave birth, and this is what created the Sun and the Moon. It
is our epic story of creation. It takes one hour to tell. It's my way
of telling the powers that be that we've always been here.

I heard this story at home in the family setting, usually in the winter because then people were not out gathering food. My mother and father were storytellers. They were traditional people. They spoke the Lushootseed language.

We lived in dwellings on and along the riverbank. Father was a fisherman and canoe builder. For our transportation, he built canoes of cedar trees. There are few of those trees left now. It's one of our disappearing treasures. I'm sure my father said a prayer for the life of each tree he cut down, but he was a quiet man, and I didn't hear his prayers.

My dad was from the Upper Skagit Tribe. He was the historian of our people, and the respected carrier of our spiritual traditions. Because his father was head man of the river, he delegated fishing grounds to the people. That was a great responsibility; he had to know the waters, the ways of the fish, all the times of year that they traveled because that was a resource our people depended on.

I used to go fishing with my father, dipnetting for the salmon. I had to beg my mother to let me go—she was always afraid I might drown. We'd get in and he would pole the canoe upriver along the side of the river. We'd find a place where there was a deep eddy, a place where he knew salmon would come, and then he would tie the canoe to a limb. We would sit for hours with a dip net in the river to catch perhaps one unsuspecting fish. Slowly, he would pole his net—a dragnet—through the water like you would a paddle, over and over, so far down in this deep, still eddy. He did this until he could feel that some stupid salmon had gotten in the way, and then he would pull it up.

We just sat there quietly, waiting. I wasn't allowed to move or talk. I learned the meaning of patience. There was silent communication. There was time to enjoy the stillness and the beauty of the area. If my father was lucky enough to get one salmon, my mother literally kissed that fish.

I always loved the river. Some people thought of it as ugly and fierce, but I never felt that way. It's an active river. When the rains are heavy and it floods, it can become angry and muddy and full of debris. When there's not enough rain, it can become a sad little trickle and then the salmon runs are endangered. But to me it's beautiful.

We didn't sell the salmon commercially. It was for our own use. At that time, when I was a girl, the people were not allowed to use up that resource. Now, the resource is practically gone, so those who try to earn a living selling salmon are finding it a sad impossibility. The elders abhor the fact that there are very few left for ceremonial purposes.

My mother came from the union of a Samish[3] Indian woman and a French trapper. She was ridiculed by her peers because she had fair skin. But she was a survivor, bless her heart. After she married my father, as the wife of a head man she was expected to help others. People still come to me and say, "Your mother was so good to me."

In our family, decision making was mutual. My mother deferred to my dad, but he deferred to her in the speaking role. He'd turn to her and say, "You talk, Mama." She was very dramatic, very emotional. I think my mother considered my dad boss, even though she was.

When my father wasn't fishing, he supplemented his income by working as a logger. My mother worked in restaurants. I helped by working in the berry fields in the summer—I earned money for my school clothes—I hated it. My mother gathered and dried one hundred quarts of blackberries for our use during the winter, she carded wool and knitted socks to sell for fifty cents a pair. That's how we earned our living, a very rich living. Anything we had, we shared. When there was money, it was for all of us. I remember when I was very small, my mother gave me six or seven dollars to go out and buy groceries for the month. She trusted me to know what to buy. We had no overhead, no electric bills, no taxes to pay. There was pride in doing what the ancestors taught our parents to do.

In later years, my parents had to go to work pulling weeds in the berry fields. During the Depression, there were no other jobs, so they joined the rest of the people in the fields. In her old age, my mother inherited property in Nooksack country, and there my father built her her first and only home which was her "palace." They lived there till they died, and then I gave it to my grandson and his family.

All of my ancestors were spiritual people. My mother's grandmother was a medicine woman—Tsi-ska-tial was her name. Tsi-ska-tial had many, many children who had many children. That makes many of the people in the Puget Sound area my relatives. I met my great-grandmother when I was a little child. She was an ancient woman, with a wrinkled face and eyes sunken into her head. I remember I was in awe of her. She was one hundred and four when she died. She must have passed her knowledge on to my cousin Minnie, who was very observant.

You would have loved my cousin Minnie. She had a quality we respect—the ability to look with eyes and ears and hearts that can see and imprint information you will need at some time in your life. She was a strong woman, she didn't tolerate nonsense, and she loved and indulged me.

The medicine women were respected just as the medicine men were, but I don't think they needed as much recognition as the men. I think they felt stronger within themselves.

The expectations for women were never spoken, but understood. I was to carry the truths of the culture with honor and respect. This was part of my intuitive knowledge all the time I was growing up. I could never disgrace my parents or community by doing anything other than the proper role. I think there were high community expectations just because my parents were leaders. In our family, a child who disobeyed was quietly put in another room, out of sight. When I made a mistake, I was forgiven. Dad only had to look at me with disapproval—that was punishment enough. My parents never raised their voices to us. My children tell me I never raised mine.

I felt I was loved by everybody. I was made to feel that I was the most important, the most intelligent person on the face of the earth. Mother said to me, "You're ugly—that's why you lived." As a child, I didn't understand why she said that. But now I think she said it to protect me, because if you thought you were beautiful, it would be taken away from you.

I didn't feel beautiful; I never have. I felt then, and I feel now, that I am appreciated for who I am and what I do. In public school, I was picked on by the white students. If I complained, Dad would say, "If you complain I'll put you in a gunnysack." He felt I should learn not to bow to people who were prejudiced. I knew he meant it for my good. To this day, when people say things intended to make me feel bad, I think of my dad, I think they are just ignorant, and I don't let it affect me. So mingling in the white world made me stronger.

I didn't have a coming-of-age ceremony. Menstruation came as a big surprise, and I had to learn from my peers. Sexuality was a taboo subject. We were expected to preserve our womanhood until marriage. I was chaperoned everywhere. If a young man came to call, if he was not from a family of equal status, he was sent promptly away. It was taboo to speak of status—you just knew when somebody was not from the right kind of family.

I married two Indian men. The marriages didn't work out. So I married my German husband, and he helped me raise my children. When there were problems, I didn't go to family members for support. I was taught to keep my emotional life in perspective, not to let my feelings take over. So much happens to Native Americans. You can't let everything affect you.

We have our ways of expressing emotion. During the time of death, there is a coming together, a support system that is unique. We cry together, we help each other overcome pain. The entire extended family is there to support you. It's a blessing. But I didn't have that attitude when I was young.

Mother was a ritualist and she would take me to homes where

there had been death. As soon as you got to the door, you started crying. Usually the body was there in the home. And everybody would sit down and cry—you'd cry all your tears together in a circle. You'd share your grief. A wash pan was sent around and you washed your face to refresh yourself, you wiped your eyes, and sat in silence. As others came in, they joined the group and everybody wept again with them. People stayed with the family until the burial, usually a few days.

I had to go every time there was a death. I remember how frightening that was. You didn't show this kind of sadness in ordinary life. But now I'm glad my people took me. It's beautiful that people were able to expel all their grief—it all came out.

When I was a young mother, I lost my first son. People came to my mother's home, and I knew I was expected to prepare food for them, but I was just worn out from grieving. I didn't appreciate the presence of all these people, and I didn't deal with it too well. Mother said, "They're here because they love us, and want to comfort us. We thank them by preparing food for them." Now that I'm an old woman, I've learned to value the gifts that are given in this way.

After the burial, there was a burning, not in the cemetery, but in another place where not everyone has walked. Sometimes the burning was done at the home of the deceased. They'd gather all the clothing and objects cherished by the dead person, they'd put them on a fire, and those things went with the spirit of the deceased, who needed them in the other world. The Salish people believed that the only way these things could go to the spirit of the dead was through fire. We also burned food for the spirit of the one who had just died, and for others from our family in the other world. And then there was food for all who came. These practices have been ongoing, and are still done today by those who have a ritualist. There are a few ritualists left. I don't consider myself a ritualist.

The ritualist calls the spirits of the dead to come to a feast. Each ritualist has his or her own way of doing it—there is no right way. The spirits know that the feast is being prepared for them. My cousin is our ritualist. He has the power to call the spirits; he hollers in a spine-chilling way, and you can sense when the spirits are arriving. The ritualist calls to each individual by name, and you feel their presence. In the minds of our people, death is a part of living, and we respect the spirits of our dead who are still here.

There's a big revival of our Naming Ceremonies. Once your ancestors decide you are worthy of carrying on an ancestral name, they give it to you. You must lead an exemplary life, and never tarnish this name. Mine is—taqʷšoblu—it's written in the orthography of the Lushootseed language, and it's untranslatable. I've had the special function of giving every member of my family his or her ancestral name. To validate the names, you call witnesses so people will know you've done the naming properly—the best speakers and historians from the area give advice to the person who has been given a name. Before there were newspapers, this was our way of honoring people, and spreading the word.

You make or buy as many things as you can afford for the witnesses at a Naming Ceremony. The chanting of the prayer songs takes place—these are family spirit songs given to the family by the spirit—the words are never allowed to be published.

Then there's our ceremony for the salmon. We respect the salmon, we call them "Salmon People." The ceremony was not practiced for about one hundred years, but about ten years ago, my cousin Harriet Shelton and my uncle Morris Dan re-created it drawing on the memories of the elders. The people gather with their ritualist in the longhouse at the Tulalip Reservation. This is a re-creation of the ancient longhouse which rotted and had to be rebuilt. (I remember being in the original one when I was a child.) It's a big wooden structure, oblong, about one hundred feet long, in a beautiful setting. Open fires provide light and heat. The people sing the old songs. Each one carries a hand drum, and they drum to the beat of the song they are singing.

Then a young man comes in to announce that a guest is arriving, our guest is coming ashore. So the young people bring the King Salmon, the first salmon of the season, to shore on a canoe, lying on a bed of ferns or spirea. They carry him to the longhouse. They circle the longhouse four times—that is a magic number in our culture—chanting:

> *. . . This is King Salmon*
> *Upland it goes,*
> *Upland it goes.*
> *King Salmon this is,*
> *King Salmon this is*

Then we go into the dining room[4] and have a feast honoring the spirit of the salmon. After the feast, the skeleton of the salmon is put back on the bed of ferns and returned to the waters, to his people. It is said that the spirit informs the Salmon People that it has been treated respectfully in Tulalip so the salmon will return another year to be food for the people.

I was brought up with these ceremonies. They have survived despite the intervention of the church and government.

In the late nineteenth century, our ancient Longhouse Religion was forbidden. The priests felt threatened by the strong doctrine and practice of our people and forbid it as "heathen." The Bureau of Indian Affairs jailed those who practiced it. It was in 1903 or 1904, right around there the people decided they were going to argue to get their religion back, and were not going to jail. There's a story some of the elders tell that the BIA agent came to the old smokehouse at Tulalip to talk the people into accepting the controversial 1855 treaty. Tribal leader William Shelton said, through an interpreter: "If you let us do our ceremonies, we'll call it Treaty Day." Then the old medicine man Elzie Andrews sang his spirit power song, and at that moment, a cougar appeared in the smokehouse. The agent was so taken aback he said, "Go on, practice your religion."

You know, the presence of the spirits is something tangible for us. A few years ago, I was asked to call out the names of the signers of the 1855 treaty, and I did that, and then the spirits of the signers were ritually fed—food like salmon, clams, venison and berries was placed on a fire while their names were called. And my students who came said they could feel the presence of the spirits coming to be fed.

It's a lifelong process to become a member of the Longhouse Religion. There's much to learn. Both my parents were trained in the tradition. My father was sent out when he was young to quest for his spirit song, he received his spirit power and became a medicine man. Today people are sent to college to get a degree. Both have the same purpose—to prepare you for your life's work.

In the years I was growing up, when our religion was forbidden, my parents practiced as Shakers so the spirit power would continue.[5] When a person became a Shaker, his or her spirit guide was indoctrinated into the Shaker religion. So the spirit power song became a Shaker song, with a different tempo. At the same time, the Shakers used some Christian ritual. We practiced in a church—there's an elected head of the church, ministers and bishops. We used candles and crosses, there were bells on the altar— we'd ring them while singing.

In the winter when there was only an occasional salmon, my father and mother were called on as Shakers to help sick people at home, and I went along and observed. They would go into a trance. They'd look for the reason for an illness. It could be an outside spirit that had come to make the person ill; their soul could have been taken from them. Soul loss can cause lethargy and illness.

I saw all kinds of dancing as a child—quiet moving, shuffling of the feet, some more active jumping up and down—it depended on how the spirit moved the healer. The Shaker is given the ability to see through spiritual eyes what is causing an illness, to remove it and restore health. It's a gift. You have to have faith.

My dad wouldn't let me become a Shaker. "My daughter, you want to join just because you're curious. When you're older and you want to join the religion to help people, then you can join."

Both our religions have survived and become stronger. I go to the Shaker church. I don't practice the Longhouse Religion because that's a full-time job, and I can't do it and also do the work I do in the community. But I feel I'm a part of all of it. I go to every traditional ceremony I know about.

Tonight, there's a ceremony on the Tulalip Reservation, one which will initiate dancers into the spirit world of the Longhouse. The tables will be loaded with food to feed hundreds of people. There will be something going on almost every night. The young people don't practice exactly as our ancestors did. My cousin says, "They just go through the motions." But they are learning from those who have practiced all their lives.

The elders do not usually talk to white people about their religion. They can talk in a general way as I'm doing, but to talk specifically about what they do and how is forbidden. If anyone violates this taboo, they will be ostracized. Once I brought some students to observe, and people said to me, "Don't bring those white people with you again."

It's comforting to know that anyone can get in touch with the spirit. I think I've always had this awareness, and it has given me strength. Even the death of my child I came to accept as I got older—there are always reasons.

There have been changes in the lives of our people since the days when we inhabited the Skagit River. They decided to become a reservation, because then they would receive a little more help than those who live independently. They formed the Upper Skagit Reservation, and now have a tribal base near Sedro Woolley, Washington. They have a tribal center so people of all ages have a place to gather. This keeps them together. Some of the elders are on welfare, some have social security. The spirit takes care of us.

When we moved to the reservation, we lost the independence

of mingling in a world that was our own. But I'm realistic about that. Dad said it wasn't always peaceful; the tribes fought among themselves for power and territory. That was human, he said. And there were Indians, the Kwakiutl and another tribe, who came in canoes from the North and raided our villages. They took slaves. I never liked to think about that.

I live in Seattle, but I don't feel cut off from my people. My spirit guide says I have to work to help keep a roof over our heads. I have responsibilities here. I speak in many places. I'm taking part in the governor's summit meetings on ecological issues. I'll talk to them about taking care of our resources. If you kill them off, there's no way future generations can survive. I'll speak to them from my respected position as an elder in this community, I'll say: "If you study what the Creator has put here on earth, you will learn many things. The earth has much to teach us. The way a blade of grass grows, the way the saltwater, streams and rivers talk to us, the way the wind acts upon the waters and upon the trees, the way the clouds drift in the sky—these things are stories that you can study and learn from."

As a great-grandmother, it's my responsibility to pass our heritage on to our young people. It's a gift from the Creator. It's their path into the future.

From interviews with the author, November 1, 1989,
and August 20, 1991.

NOTES

1. Lushootseed is the language of Skagit people in Washington State's Puget Sound region. It is part of the Salish language family. For her life-long work as conservator of her language and culture, in 1994 Vi Hilbert was awarded a National Heritage Fellowship by the National Endowment for the Arts, and given a place in a national folk arts hall of fame.

2. Written symbols have been developed for the sounds of Lushootseed and have been incorporated into a computer program.

3. Another Salish-speaking tribe from the Puget Sound region.

4. Once cooked over open fires, food today is usually prepared in modern kitchens and served in a dining room adjacent to the longhouse.

5. In the 1880s, John Slocumb, a Washington State Indian, claimed to have "walked and talked with God." He developed the Shaker religion, an amalgamation of Catholic ritual, Protestant austerity, and Indian religious practices, and it spread in the Northwest. Says Vi Hilbert, "He taught us to practice healing, a gift from the Creator, using our spirit songs and prayers in our own language."

23

There's Some Kind of Healing Force Here

ROSE MARY BARSTOW
WHITE EARTH OJIBWAY/
CHIPPEWA

Wearing a floral print dress, her gray hair hanging loose around her face, Rose Mary Barstow met me at the door of her senior citizen high-rise apartment. Despite the three strokes she had suffered, at age seventy-three she had just a few lines in her face and she was alert and spirited. She looked back on a full life: she had helped found the St. Paul American Indian Center and served on the Minnesota Indian Affairs Commission. For years she taught classes in Ojibway language and culture at the University of Minnesota. Currently, she was taking part in demonstrations for the reform of tribal government on the Cass Lake (Ojibway) Reservation.

"I'm glad you're here," said Rose Mary Barstow as she served tea. *"I've so much to tell. I've been trying to write my memoirs, but the typewriter won't cooperate."* Then, in an almost unbroken narrative spanning three days, she poured out her personal history, alternately laughing and crying as she relived emotionally charged events. Her parakeet, a constant companion, flew in and out of its cage and perched on the tape recorder, punctuating her story with squawks and a flurry of flapping wings.

I'D LIKE TO TAKE YOU TO THE PLACE WHERE I WAS born. I'd like to show you my rock. When I was little, I used to slide on a rock down the hill behind my house. I played in the woods with imaginary people, a little boy and girl. They came to me when I was alone. They had little green shoes. We used to eat out of cups made of dandelion leaves. We sat at a table made of birchbark, and ate real food. If I hurt myself and cried, they comforted me.

We used to have clear, running water. We ate gooseberries, blueberries and currants. There were grasshoppers and butterflies, there were rabbits and chipmunks. A few months ago, I went back there and now the grasses are dried up, you fall over underbrush. The berries and the butterflies are gone. The earth has become uninhabitable for animals because of all the development and the chemicals. It's chaos in the woods.

I was born in Onamia (on the Mille Lacs Reservation), right where Lake Onamia ends and the Rum River begins—that's the birthing place. It was August 25, 1915. My grandfather presented me to the world. He thanked the Great Spirit and accepted responsibility for raising me. I think I was one of the last ones they did that for.

My mother had been converted to Catholicism, and she convinced my dad to convert. I think he did it just to marry my mom. I was baptized when I was six days old. They called me Rose. We had a log cabin in Onamia, just one room with two beds, very simple furnishings. It was built by my grandfather. He raised his family there. When my grandparents were relocated to the White Earth Reservation, my parents inherited that cabin, and we lived there until my mother got sick.

This part I don't like to talk about. Mother had something that causes pressure on the brain, kind of like epileptic fits. When I was very little, she had a stroke. She must have been twenty-three. She was paralyzed on her left side—she could only use her right hand. But I remember she made sure that I had a ribbon in my hair every day.

Father was very supportive of Mother. He was a jammer on

the river, he'd split logs at the old lumber camps, he worked from six in the morning until six at night. But when he was home he carried her around and kissed her a lot. He'd carry her across mud puddles so she wouldn't get her feet wet. I remember he was always brushing her hair. It hung down below her knees. She braided it or she wore it in thick buns in back. It was beautiful. It smelled good.

When I was around three, my mother went to the hospital—I didn't know why. My father tried to take care of me, but he didn't have the patience to brush a little girl's hair, to get all the snarls out. My aunt came to take care of me. She hugged me, and I cried. She said my mother had just had a baby, so I had a baby brother. They took him to an orphanage, so I didn't see him for many years. Mother came home, but she often had to go back to the hospital because she was sick.

I was about three or four years old when I discovered that all my peers had had naming ceremonies—a woman would give you her name, and gifts. So I found this lady I really admired and I asked her to give me an Indian name, and she took me to her home and had a benediction service just for me. We had a feast. She cooked some rice with raisins, she put maple sugar, fruit and candy on it—she called it a spirit dish, and then she prayed. She said, "I will give you my own name, Majigikwewis. It means "naughty little female spirit." So then I was content. I had an Ojibway name.

One day when I was visiting Mother in the hospital, she combed my hair, she braided it, and she whispered to me: "You're going to have to go away to live with relatives because I can't take care of you." She told me not to cry. So I got in the car with my aunt and uncle and we took off. We went under a railroad bridge—there was a long tunnel. When we went into it, the sun was shining, but when we came out, there was a storm. And I thought it was kind of like a prediction, because a storm clouded my whole life on the White Earth Reservation after that.

The aunt I went to live with at White Earth was mean—big bust, big skirts. In her house, I had to eat on the floor with the cat. I slept upstairs on a braided rug covered up with an old black coat. The wind used to come right through the eaves. I'd go down and sneak over by the stovepipe, and keep myself curled up by the heat.

After my mother died, my father gambled all over the Mississippi and Montana. But he heard how I was being treated, and one morning, he came. He pushed my aunt aside, he raised up the lid of a trunk, and there was all my stuff—my red velvet dress my mother had made, stockings, quilts, blankets. Father took me to Grandma and Grandpa's house. They had a hotel in White Earth with four bedrooms and a large kitchen.

I was five or six that summer, and I stayed there till I was eight. I was a tomboy, but I got a lot of culture there. The essence of home life was mutual respect and cooperation. I had responsibilities, I learned the proprieties. People would come from far away on foot or on horseback, and Grandma taught us how to cook for them.

At seven or eight, we were trained in birthing. I helped in a birth, I held a blanket for the baby to drop into. Giving birth was considered a woman's sacred role. She attained dignity in the process of giving birth, no matter who she was. Even if a girl was known to be irresponsible, if she married someone more respected than she and then gave birth, she'd redeem herself.

We were taught that our males are strong because of our strength. If we do not allow them to be strong, ours is wasted.

People who were different were accepted so long as they were headed for a meaningful purpose. If you were a gossip, you were left out, avoided. Retarded people seemed to me to be specially gifted. They gave so much without thinking of themselves. Homosexuality? I never heard about that until I came to the Twin Cities.

Grandma took us out into the woods to identify the plants

used for healing. "You never take the roots that grow from the North or the West—those are living spirits, and benevolent. You take those that grow South and East. When you take these medicines, you put tobacco in the dirt surrounding the roots to thank the Great Spirit." We chopped up thorn-apple roots, and mixed them with other ingredients for diarrhea. Snakeroot is used to retard fever—you break out in a sweat, and the sweat heals.

Grandmother used to go and pick lily pads, take off the tops, and the roots of the lily pad were made into a little ball like soap. We used it to shampoo our hair—our hair was so soft. To an Indian woman, hair was precious, and she took good care of it. We'd guard that little ball with our lives—one would last me all summer. We learned that there were opposing elements in the world—evil forces as well as good. Evil forces might gather your hair into a nest, and you'd be susceptible to constant headaches. But most of the time, the good would prevail.

We learned how to make utensils. We learned how to dig up turtle eggs. We learned how to freeze meat and fish, how to can vegetables, how to tan hides. Teachers came from all over to give us survival training. The girls were given blessings; then we were taught to fast, carry stones in our mouths, stuff like that. We learned how to make a fire in all kinds of weather. They'd lose us in the woods and we'd have to find our way home. They'd put us on a lake and we'd have to learn to paddle. They'd direct us from the shore: "Aim your boat for a birch tree, do it again until you get it right." The training wasn't easy, believe me, but if we made a mistake, we usually weren't chided.

In the spring, we had a feast to thank the Creator for having kept us safe all winter. It was an offering so we would have a bountiful harvest. See, everything was planted for our use—the berries, currants and other wild foods—the animals held back until we'd taken what we needed. We asked for blessings. We thought the Creator listened to our plea.

This happened in 1922—I remember because 1923 was the year I went away to school. Sioux families came to White Earth to honor the drum that had been given to the Ojibway when the two tribes made peace in the nineteenth century. We had a powwow that lasted for thirty days and nights. My dad did the hoop dance—he went through two hoops at the same time. It was really something. The women cooked for the entire community. For supper, we had kettles of food all mixed together—soup, rice, raisins, maple sugar. There'd be chunks of meat in the soup, fruit and candy on top. The candy always stuck in my pocket. [Laughs.]

My dad and my mother's relatives were part of the Midewewin Lodge.[1] Some of them are still in it. My dad was the pipe bearer. When there were special events, he'd pass the word around. My aunt was initiated. It takes a lot of your own initiative to put together the materials you need for a sacrifice, a giveaway, so you will be able to receive spiritual benefits. As you advance in the Midewewin Lodge, you gain strength.

I used to question Grandpa about the spirit world. "Grandpa, has anyone ever seen Manitou?"[2] He said, "There is a spirit in the lake, but no one has ever seen it." I was puzzled. During a storm, Grandpa would send me out with cut plug, a form of tobacco, and he'd tell me to put it in the stump of a tree. I'd go inside and watch to see if Manitou accepted the tobacco. After the storm I went running out, but it was still there. I thought I had done something wrong, a sacrilege; I thought Manitou didn't want my offering.

All of us camped in the open country, then we dressed up to go in a caravan to see a circus. Grandpa said we were going to see Manitou. In a big tent, there were stinking animals, jugglers, clowns, aerialists. Afterwards, I wouldn't talk to anyone. Grandpa said, "What's wrong?" I said, "You promised we'd see Manitou." He answered in Chippewa, "You did see Manitou."

One day, Grandpa was sitting on the woodpile. I got his pipe, cleaned it, put in fresh tobacco, he took a few puffs and told me to sit down by him. Pretty soon he started to talk. He said, "You know, when you were born, I offered you to the heavens and to the earth below to make all the spirits aware that you were endowed with spiritual meaning. Your name, Rose, symbolizes peace. You should never question the existence of the spirit world. The Great Spirit lives in you."

Then Grandpa said, "You have a memory bank which is called a brain, which stores all the information your senses pick up. Because you ask questions, I can tell your brain is big. Someday, you will use all your knowledge." I thought, "Oh, Grandpa, I feel so stupid." But through the years, I kept going back to that talk on the woodpile. I learned so much about the birds, the animals, the spirit world, the poetry of life.

That spring—I was eight years old—my lessons got more concentrated, as if Grandma and Grandpa were in a hurry to fill me up. I learned about medicines and about nursing, I learned to study the sky and clouds. The chattering of birds in a certain way means it will storm. But I felt a sense of impending doom.

In the fall, we moved to ricing camp. The older people did the harvesting and winnowing, we kids played tricks on each other, and caught up on the news: "Where do you find birchbark? Where is the best place to find raspberries?" The older kids paired off, leaving us little brats to get dirty, and catch heck for jumping into the river.

Grandma told us how to dig a large hole for the winnowing basket. My cousin and I were running around with our digging sticks, I bumped into her, and my stick cut her on the back of her head. I thought maybe I had killed her, so I ran into the swamp and stayed there all day. I could hear them hollering for me—I imagined myself going to jail, I could see the ball and chain. But when it got dark, I got hungry, and crept over to my cousin's camp. Grandpa saw me, he put me on his lap, they gave me potatoes and wild rice, they kissed me and put me to bed.

A couple of days later, Grandma washed my hair, braided it, put on my good stockings and high shoes and ribbons, and had my suitcase packed. Grandpa put me on his lap and said, "My girl, you are going to a place your mother chose for you so you can get an education." My dad took me in the truck to the Sister School, Saint Benedict's at White Earth. A sister showed me around the church. When we came back, my dad was gone. "Daddy," I yelled, running after him, but they caught me and brought me back. I felt really lost. The sisters cut off my long braids.

They put me in a kindergarten class because I could speak only Ojibway. A little Indian girl wrote something on the board, and I guess she made a mistake, because the whole class laughed. Sister had her hand over her mouth, but I could tell she was laughing too. The girl sat down, she put her head down, her shoulders slumped. I thought, "How rude these people are." I knew etiquette. The way I was raised, you don't make fun of people who make mistakes, you help them. If they're slow, you leave them alone. After that, I zipped up my mouth, I made sure they weren't going to make fun of me. The rest of that year, I never said a word.

We had a numbers class which I never spoke in. They put me in a high chair in the corner with a dunce cap. One time I was looking out the window watching a squirrel with an acorn in his mouth. I heard the teacher say, "If I had four apples and I gave you one, how many would I have left?" I raised my hand and I said, "Shame on you, Sister. You should give me two apples. When you share with a friend, you're supposed to go half and half." I was surprised that I was talking. Everybody was still, and the sister's mouth was open. Since then, I haven't been able to keep my mouth shut. [Laughs.]

In the fourth grade, they were studying a book on colonial history. It had pictures of warriors with almost bald heads, and a strip of hair down the middle. One was holding a woman by the hair and was stabbing her with his knife—she had a baby sucking at her breast. Oh, that just sickened me. Sister came and sat down by me. I said, "These are awful people." She said, "Why, my girl, you're one of those savages. We came here to civilize you." I grabbed that book and threw it as far as I could, and I ran to hide behind the juniper trees. In the shade there, I cried and cried. I thought, "There's no way my grandpa could be one of those horrible people. White people come to visit us—farmers and businessmen—Grandma always serves them tea and fresh-baked biscuits." I just cried and cried.

They didn't find me until nine o'clock. I wouldn't eat for four days. Finally, the priest came to see me, he brought me an orange and shared it with me—God, I was hungry. He comforted me just like Grandpa. He said, "You know those are lies about your people. Try to forgive." In the summer when I went home, I told Grandpa about that book and he said, "Now, Rose, I want you to learn English, I want you to learn all the words in the dictionary. Someday you will be a teacher, and you will write the truth about our people."

I resigned myself to school. I went to Flandreau Indian Vocational High School. One day in class, the sister went to the board to diagram a sentence. She dropped her eraser, she bent down to pick it up, and when she came up, everybody drew in a breath— she came up bald. She felt the breeze on her scalp. Deftly she picked her wig up, and put it back on her head—with the bun in front. I was seated in front because of my mischief. I tried not to laugh, but I couldn't help myself. Sister just stood there with a grim look. Well, she sent me to the principal's office, and I was so nervous, I couldn't stop laughing. I thought they would give me an F, but they didn't.

I graduated high school in 1934. I wanted to go to a teacher's college, but I didn't get a federal government grant because my father had no collateral, so I didn't go on to college. I had an offer to teach at the Institute for American Indian Arts in Santa Fe, a BIA school. It said in the contract that if you disapproved of any of their programs, you wouldn't be allowed to say so—that was just like white people—so I refused the offer, and gave up on being a teacher.

That fall, after ricing season, I went to Saint Ben's College in Saint Cloud for a while—I thought I would be a nun—but after they found out that my dad didn't go to church, that he was a fallen-away Catholic, they threw me out and erased my name from the records. It made me feel like a nonentity.

I went home to White Earth. I started going with a guy from another reservation, and on the Fourth of July we went to Red Lake for a powwow. We must have been charmed by moonlight—we messed up—and I got pregnant. I didn't want him to know because he was in school at Flandreau, doing postgraduate work to get his mechanic's license, and I didn't want to interrupt his schooling, so when I was four months pregnant, I went away and had the baby. When I came back, I got a job at a youth program they had like the WPA. I used to take my baby with me.

There was another guy I knew, Lawrence, and I didn't like him very much. He was always hovering around, asking me to go out with him. Well, my grandpa said, "That young man likes you. He's about the only decent man around here." I said, "Grandpa, you don't know him—he drinks. He hasn't got a job." Grandpa said, "You'd better go out with him." So I had to. We went back to his house to listen to ghost stories on the radio, and he kept me there all night—he wouldn't let me go home. The next morning when I went home, my grandfather threw out two bundles: one was my baby's with fruit juices and diapers, the other was my clothing. He said he was doing this "because of where you spent the night. I don't want another little bastard running around."

So I had to go back to Lawrence's place. I didn't know what else to do. His father moved out, and left us the house. I had to clean for two weeks to make it livable. He beat me. More than once, I tried to run away, but he always caught me and brought me back. When I tried going back to my grandpa's, they always sent me back to him.

Years later, when Grandpa was on his deathbed, he told Grandma he was sorry he threw me out of the house. When he died, Grandmother and I created a mound of dirt for his grave—that was the custom. Then I did it for her when she died. I hope they're happy together.

I kept Lawrence out of my bed for months—I never did find anything interesting in sex without love—but eventually I gave in. I was pregnant with my second child. The nurse said I couldn't have my baby out there in the woods, so they took me into town to the hospital. They didn't know if my baby would survive. She was sick and tiny when she was born, and I was afraid—I cried so much. I didn't want Lawrence around, and the nurses tried to keep him away, but he came anyway. I was still in bed, but he made me come home. I lost my little girl.

Father Leo came from the parish and he said, "Your marriage banns have been announced in the church." I said, "Who authorized you to do that? I didn't. People are trying to run my life!" I didn't want to marry Lawrence. But soon after, he tricked me into going with him to the welfare office to get some help. The social worker said if I wanted any financial support, I would have to sign an application for a marriage license. So under duress, I signed. We got married, and that was the last time my husband went to church.

I resigned myself to marriage, for I was raised to observe the commandments of the church. I tried to live the life of an Indian woman. We had eight children. Every fall, I took my children into the fields to pick potatoes, until machines put an end to that. I made quilts to sell to tourists. I braided and crocheted rugs using traditional patterns Grandma taught me—the log pattern, geometric patterns—and some I invented. Each piece was different, and they really looked nice. I hung them up on trees outside the house, I put up a FOR SALE sign, and people stopped and bought them.

There was no doctor nearby. When my children cut themselves I ran into the swamp and pulled blisters off the bark of a balsam tree. You boil them in water, mix it in lard and put it on a cut so it doesn't scar. I made cough syrup out of balsam bark. You take a strip of the bark, cut it into half-inch squares, boil it in water, strain it, then you add one quarter cup of brown sugar and one quarter cup of maple sugar. You cool it and boil it, and you have cough syrup for the winter. You use a snakeroot concoction to bring down fever. Most of my children survived.

One time when I was pregnant, my husband almost killed me—he was just mean. So I left my children at a neighbor's, and I went home to Grandpa's. I cried all the way. Lawrence came to get me; he said it wouldn't happen again, and he took me home. Well, it did. Finally, my dad realized I had to get away. He said, "We'll fix up that cabin we occupied when you were little. There's a stove in there. I'll provide wood for you, and if you need money, welfare will help you."

So I left my husband, but wherever I went, he'd follow me. He'd make promises, he'd appeal to my pity, and I'd take him back. During the Depression he earned forty-five dollars a week working for the WPA, but we hardly ever saw the money. My boys got jobs, but he took their money when he could get his hands on it.

One night my husband came into my house drunk; he was violent, and I threw him out. Then he came at me, swinging. I picked up a big bottle and I said, "You come close, and I'm gonna hit you." He lurched at me, and I hit him with the bottle. He was badly hurt, but he didn't die. Once my grandson asked me, "Are you sorry for what you did?" I said, "It was self-preservation. You struggle so long, and then there comes a time when you explode."

I'm telling this now because I want my children and grandchildren to understand what I went through. I'm not proud of that one moment, but I don't feel I need to apologize to anyone but the Great Spirit.

The next day, my children came home from church, we had Sunday dinner, and the sheriff came for me with a warrant for my arrest. At the hearing, I told the judge, "All those years he beat me, I never touched him. But this time, I lost my cool. He'll never touch me again. Nobody'll ever touch me again!" From the back of the courtroom my twelve-year-old son spoke up. He said, "I've seen him beat her. She kicks him out, and somebody always comes along and talks her into taking him back. If she doesn't kill him, one day I will." The judge understood, he ruled that it was self-defense, and I didn't go to jail.

But welfare came and took my children away from me and put them in foster homes. It took me two and a half years to get my kids back. I had no control over them during the most important years of their lives.

When I finally did get the kids back, we moved to the Twin Cities. By then, they were in school. I worked in a laundry, I cleaned homes for rich people. I worked in a hospital ward. I began putting money in the bank. When we ran out of money, we went on welfare. It was a hard life, and it took its toll on the kids. My youngest son became alcoholic. My daughter disappeared at age sixteen, she didn't return until she was twenty-one. Now she tries to be close, but it's too late for a relationship. I've had to face too many perils by myself.

I never gave up on getting an education. In the 1960s, there were government programs to help Indian women go to college. As they became independent, a lot of them divorced their husbands. Some Indian men don't like to see women more successful than they are. In the 1970s, I think there were more divorces than marriages.

I attended college on a Martin Luther King Fellowship, but there was almost no support money after the divorce, so I left school to go to work. I was a teacher's aide in the adult education program of Saint Paul Public Schools. I taught in a pilot program for reservation Indians relocated in the city: we taught them how to read with comprehension, how to manage money, how to pay for insurance and medical care. I began teaching in the Indian Studies Department at the University of Minnesota. I developed textbooks containing dialogues which are still used in schools to teach conversational Ojibway. A few years ago, I retired from teaching. I wish I hadn't. If they asked me to go back, I'd go.

When I was young, people said I would be a teacher—a catalyst for Indian people. They told me that the power of the white man is print; through this medium, we'd have the power to change the lies being printed about us. Now, I feel if I don't get this narrative down in writing, I will not be doing what I was assigned to do. My dream is to leave behind me something that people will remember, that will help them understand my life, and Ojibway people.

I've lived apart from the tribal community for so many years. I used to feel I didn't really belong. But Grandpa used to tell me, "Never forget who you are or where you come from, and then, no matter where you go, you will be accepted." He taught me such powerful stuff, and over the years, I began comprehending it. It's all coming back. I've used so much of that knowledge, my storeroom is almost empty. One of these days, I'll be flying around here empty-headed. [Laughs.]

When I left the tribal group and went into the world, I took the knowledge the elders gave me, and used it to survive, and I'm still doing that. We still try to do our medicine picking. We have our ceremonies in the Midewewin Society. The members still have their traditional roles, though some are symbolic. The ceremony includes initiation and renewal of vows. It's an affirmation of faith, like confirmation.

As a child, I learned Indian and Christian ways, and I could always see parallels. This little bag I'm wearing around my neck, an Ojibway elder at Cass Lake gave it to me to guard against evil influences. I don't know what's in it. It's like the Saint Christopher medal which Catholics say will protect you when you travel. I grew up in two worlds, the Indian and the Christian, and I can walk either path with dignity.

The great mystery is apparent in all things.

After all those years of trying to find a place, I feel that I walk within the sacred hoop of our people. And I consider myself part of a larger hoop presided over by the Great Spirit. Walking within that circle gives me a feeling of belonging to some greater force, a sense of being equal to others within the universal circle. Many of our elders pray for all humanity. Many of our young people today don't understand this. If you don't know the language, you lose meaningful things said in the prayers.

The silent spirits of people who are gone have helped me through my life. I feel I've been fortunate to get blessings from them. They're all around; they're in the air, you know, and every so often, they come by. Someone was here this morning before you came and blessed this place. They put their perfume here—the scent of cedar. I'm blessed by Catholic spirits too. So I never feel alone.

My children are growing up. Most of them have quit drinking, they're getting college degrees, they're becoming responsible. My granddaughter is competing for Miss Teenage Minnesota. But one of my grandsons committed suicide last year. We had a giveaway ceremony to keep his memory alive. It seems as if kids today have such a hard time.

My other grandsons come over, they bring me the fish they catch, they give me so much love and respect. They'll say, "Watch out, Grandma, don't fall." I say, "Don't make me sound so helpless." [Laughs.] Sometimes, one of them will come here and ask, "Grandma, do you mind if I stay over? Out there, it's crazy. When I come here, it's comforting and I feel sane."

So I guess there's some kind of healing force here.

From interviews with the author, May 5, 10, and 16, 1988.

Editor's note: I last saw Rose Mary Barstow in the hospital in December 1988; she had suffered another stroke, from which she never fully recovered. Not long after that, she died at a nursing home in Onamia, near her childhood home.

NOTES

1. Alternate spelling: Midewiwin. Ancient, secret society of medicine people dedicated to the use of plants and prayer for healing. A man or woman must be invited to seek admission; initiation is possible only after years of tutoring, meditation, purification rites, and demonstration of good character. Integrity is the primary qualification, according to Ojibway author Basil Johnston in *Ojibway Heritage* (Lincoln: University of Nebraska Press, Bison Books, 1990), pp. 80–93.

2. Kitche Manitou, the Ojibway name for the Great Spirit. The alternate spelling is Gitche Manitou.

24

You Defend What's Sacred to You

JANET MCCLOUD
TULALIP/NISQUALLY

The road from Tacoma, Washington, south to Yelm is lined with tall stands of pine and fir. Yelm, with its old homes and groves of trees, is on the outskirts of the Nisqually Reservation, a patchwork of fenced-in farms, small houses, and mobile homes. There, on a quiet street near a small general store, I located Janet McCloud's frame house thanks to an orange mailbox and a gold Subaru, which, she told me, "will be in front if nobody's borrowed it." The house sits on a large wooded lot, with a ceremonial tipi and sweat lodge in the backyard.

A direct descendant of Chief Seattle, Janet McCloud was active in the Northwest tribes' drive for fishing rights in the 1960s and seventies. She helped organize Women of All Red Nations (WARN) and the Northwest Indian Women's Circle.[1] In 1985 she traveled to Nairobi, Kenya, for the United Nations World Conference on Women. At age sixty she is a magnet for Native women seeking spiritual awareness. I found her in her kitchen, making pies from huckleberries.

HUCKLEBERRIES GROW ON TOP OF THE MOUNTAINS here. It's a real sacred food, beautiful food. You make jam out of them, and pies. It's real nice to go up in the mountains and pick the berries. I have a hard time, sometimes, because I'm diabetic. I get up in the altitude and it's smoky—but I don't care, I struggle along anyway.

I remember one time, I was up in the mountains with a couple of friends and one said, "If I die, I want to die in the mountains." The other one said, "When I die, I want to die by the ocean." I was young then, and I thought, "Well, I'd like to live in the mountains, I'd like to live by the ocean, but I'm not ready to die anyplace yet." [Laughs.] But now I'm getting old, and last time I was up there, I got winded, my heart was beating and I thought, "This would be a nice place to leave the world."

On the living room wall is her son's carving of a holy man, which Janet McCloud terms "an icon." I asked if her son shows his work in a gallery.

Not everyone can be Van Gogh. We've always had carvers. They don't do it just for money. Everything in white society is money, money, money—it's the cause of so much injustice. Money is the white people's icon. The Hopis say, "Oh, the white man doesn't know how to spell very good. Look at what they have on the dollar bill: In God We Trust. It should be: In Gold We Trust." [Laughs.]

People are so far in debt, they can't catch up. Indians and whites are caught up in that—that's why there's all this gambling on reservations. At Tuscarora [the Tuscarora Reservation in New York], they were putting in bingo. The younger people said, "We need it; there's no jobs here." The traditionals told them, "There were prophecies that gambling was going to come to our communities and tear down our culture," and the traditionals fought against it. My daughter and her children were right on the front lines. There was shooting. One boy used a hose against his own mother.

There's a split between people who want what white society has, and those who don't. I saw it on the Hopi Reservation.

Young people had gone away to college, they came home and wanted paved roads, electricity and indoor toilets. Well, indoor toilets call for sewer lines. The elders asked me to come. I stayed there four days; I had to sit and try and understand. You know, they have the underground kiva that represents the womb of Mother Earth. They said, "When we dance in bare feet, we don't want these filthy sewer lines boring underground in our Mother Earth, our sacred church."

There are whites who feel spiritually impoverished, so they run around the world looking for spirituality. The wannabe Indians—they've got this whole shamanism business—I call it showmanism. They're the New Age profiteers. Shirley MacLaine, Linda Evans, they do workshops and retreats near here, channeling and all that stuff. You should see the traffic and commotion around that place. It costs more than a thousand bucks to get in there. People will pay anything.

That's against our traditions. Our healers are not allowed to charge. They accept love offerings, whatever people give them. And they're the most powerful healers. Of course, most of them are dead now, or keep themselves hidden. There are a few in the Northwest—most are men. My friend in Alberta, she's a Cree medicine woman—she does healing and counseling. She's worked with hard-core delinquents. She brought them here. These were kids heading for prison; I saw them grow into young men and women with some direction in their lives.

I don't call myself a healer. I do counseling. I feel I'm a caretaker of this place rather than its owner. We have a sweat lodge and ceremonial grounds in back. I was trained by elders, and now I'm trying to pass on what I learned to the next generations. Whatever you call that, I don't know.

Once this man called me a "militant." I said, "I don't like labels. I'm not going to wear them—they're like barnacles on a ship. They weigh you down." You just do what you have to do to make sure your children and grandchildren will have a decent life.

JANET McCLOUD   *Photo by Dick Bancroft*

I always felt I was guided. Even as a child, I was searching for religion. I never found it in any of the boxes I was put into— people try to program you with their beliefs and stuff. But I knew things I had never learned in any book. I had an internal knowledge which helped me survive.

I was born on the Tulalip Reservation in Washington. My father was alcoholic, he and my mother divorced, and Mother remarried. My stepfather drank too. I'd get left with my three younger sisters and cousins while my parents were out drinking. The drunks knew we were left alone, and they'd come to sexually molest us. There was no one to go to for help. No place to go. My mother's mother died when she was five.

When I was seven, I started organizing the cousins. We'd find a corner in the house, we'd make beds on the floor and would put all the little kids behind us. We'd get axes and knives, and when the drunks came, we'd go after them and run 'em out. So that was my first organizing.

We moved all over with our stepfather, just like gypsies. We'd get a place, he would drink and never pay the rent, we'd be kicked out right on the street. When he came home drunk, he'd whack me around. So that's the childhood I had. It's the kind of childhood a lot of Indians face today.

Church people would take us off the reservations to retreats. Well, I knew all about sexual abuse, right? So here we are praying and praying, and these preachers and other staff people are feeling us up. I thought, "Well, hell, I can get this from the drunks at home," and I didn't go back.

I ended up in foster homes. Some were pretty nice, but I'd get lonesome for my sister and cousins, and I'd worry about my mother. So I went back home when I could. I used to sit and plot with my cousins how to murder my wicked stepfather. Isn't that awful?

I didn't talk about being sexually molested for years. People used to say, "You can find help in Jesus," and they took me to their churches, but praying didn't help. I went to a Christian Science church, and they'd say, "Pain is in your head. If you have faith and pray, it will go away." But it didn't. I went to church with this girl who was Pentecostal. They taught me psalms. I got up before all of them and sang, "The Lord is my shepherd/I shall not want . . ." Once I made a speech. So I guess I've been making speeches a long, long time. [Laughs.]

The Pentecostals talked in tongues. I'd try. I'd pray and pray, hoping to save myself. I'd get down on my knees—they still hurt when I think about it—but nothing happened, nothing. I thought

I was such a terrible sinner, God didn't want anything to do with me. There was a woman preacher who wanted to wash my feet, but I kept my distance. If anyone touched you, it hurt.

I blamed myself for being molested. I tried to commit suicide when I was twelve.

I went to school. I didn't read or write very well, but I loved to write rhymes. I wrote one for my mother's birthday because I didn't have the money for a card. Once I wrote three poems about spring. The teacher and principal sat me in a chair and demanded that I tell them what book I copied them out of. I said, "I wrote them," but they didn't believe me. I didn't write poetry for years.

I left school in the sixth grade. All it prepared me for was to clean houses for white people. I went back in junior high, but no one talked to me. I could have dropped dead in the middle of the hallway, and nobody'd notice—I was invisible.

I got married very young just to get away, and I got divorced very young. My second husband, Don McCloud, was a truck driver in Seattle, a teamster. We had two children, and were expecting a third—there were no birth control measures then. And then my daughter fell out of a second-story window.

She lived, but I could see the city was no place to raise children. So we bought this land, ten acres. My husband couldn't get a job here so he took up fishing. We smoked salmon. We sold fish, we bartered some, we gave some away. We had eight children to provide for. I learned how to grow a garden. We had an orchard.

When we first moved here, the house was just a long room built on logs with an old well under it. We struggled to make fifty-five-dollar payments each month, then we got a mortgage. I said, "I want my children to have someplace to come to if they need it," so my husband added on the rooms as we needed them. The kids come and live here when they're out of work. We never turn our kids out. It's a little hard on your nerves sometimes.

[Laughs.] They work in the garden, cut wood, get the sweat lodge ready. I don't ask them for money.

If I have money, the power company takes it, the telephone company takes it, the tax people take it, the grocery stores take it. None of them are owned by us. So why should I accumulate money and make them richer? I grow my own food and dry it. That's my money.

In the 1960s, we were having a hard time making ends meet. I was working on the waterfront here at Nisqually [the Nisqually River], and I thought we should develop our fisheries. Most of the men here were veterans, but they had a hard time getting loans because they were Indian. I thought if we could get loans, we could buy a fleet of boats, get our own hatcheries, get a smokery and cannery goin' and the whole community could become self-sufficient. We started trying to get the BIA to support us.

Then the state moved in on us. They had no jurisdiction—we had treaties guaranteeing our right to fish. But they had plans to make Washington State a sportsmen's paradise. So they took the most impoverished tribe, the most socially disorganized tribe, Nisqually, and they came in with an order to restrain us from fishing.

There were two violent incidents in 1965. On October 9, the state came to the river, they beat up Indians and bashed their heads in. We sent a telegram to the state, we got the support of the press, and said we were going fishing. We were on the river fishing in a little boat—my husband and me, our two sons, and two reporters. My mother was on the bank with the younger children and elders. And the state unleashed all this police power against us. High-powered boats, there must have been a hundred and fifty of them, came out of the bushes from every which way, and they just rammed our boat. It was frightening.

We knew we had to fight back. We organized through the sixties, and the celebrities began to come, Dick Gregory and others. I decided to keep a journal so I'd have a record of what was happening. I went to a secondhand store and got an old mimeograph for fifteen dollars. You'd have to feed the papers one at a time. I think it belonged to Benjamin Franklin. [Laughs.] But I couldn't make it work. My husband was real good at tinkering, he fixed it and we published a newspaper. I had tutors for my children, so I'd go to the tutor's office to have my grammar corrected. They'd say, "You need to put in a period, don't run everything together." Here's a copy of one of the first newspapers we did. It contains my affidavit of what happened at Frank's Landing during one of the demonstrations. The game wardens were beating up people on the shore.

> "The children were hurt and scared, trying to get free. I grabbed the warden's arm and said, 'Let go of them. You're hurting them.' A game or fish warden grabbed both my arms from behind—sticking their knee in my back . . . Wardens were everywhere and they all seemed to be eight feet tall— they were shoving, kicking, pushing clubs at men, women and children. We were vastly outnumbered yet we were all trying to protect one another. . . ."[2]

Both Don and I were arrested. Another time, Don was jailed for thirty days, and the women and I went fishing.

When there were no fish, we fished in defiance of the state. The problem became acute for us financially—we almost lost our home, there wasn't enough food, the children suffered. Well, my mother used to say, "You make do with mildew if mildew's all you got." We'd never go to welfare. We just survived any way we could.

I thought all we had to do was get the word out to Christians about the fishing, and all those people who were close to God would rise up in indignation that we were being mistreated, and they would put the state where it belonged. The rude awakening came when I found out all these people beating us, and the judges, were deacons in their churches, they were pillars of their communities.

With other Native people, the McClouds formed the Survival of the American Indians Association. This experience helped Janet McCloud resolve her identity conflict. "I had been ashamed of being Indian," she told me, but "working with traditional Indians, I learned about my culture." They battled federal and state officials until the fishing rights issue was settled in court.[3]

I had a hard time after my husband died of cancer. I mean, we were together thirty-five years. We went through a lot, we struggled together.

I got involved in a spiritual unity movement, part of the American Indian Movement. Traditional people would get together and we'd tell our stories and network. We made a journey around this Turtle Island [North America] to find out which tribes were still holding on to their land and original instructions. In 1978 we had The Longest Walk.[4]

When we got back we organized Women of All Red Nations and the Northwest Indian Women's Circle. We were tired of the sexist macho stuff we got from the men in AIM. We needed to do something for the women. We are the backbone of our communities—men are the jawbone. [Laughs.] A few years later we had the International Year of the Child, and to this day we have gatherings right here in my backyard.

You progress, you move on to new things. I wanted to attend law school. I studied law; someone trained me to do affidavits and write briefs. I did some work for a citizen's advocacy group. I was on a task force of about forty Indians from around the country trying to find solutions to our problems. There were big bets going at the time that forty of us who were so diverse couldn't be in the same room without killing one another. [Laughs.]

I became the official spokesperson for the Nisqually Tribe. From the time I was seven, I had been protecting the younger children in my family. You defend what's sacred to you, but not with guns. I used what the Creator gave me—my voice. I was a messenger. I met with other Indians, we shared ideas, we agreed that white people had messed up our minds so that many Indians have severe psychological and medical problems. We agreed there had to be a healing process, but that wouldn't happen overnight. You can't just go around doing an Indian chant and everything's going to change. You can't heal the pain in the world with a Valium or a shot of penicillin. There's no blueprint for happiness.

A few years ago I met some people from Tibet, the Dalai Lama's people with their sleepy eyes. They asked me through an interpreter if I had children. I said, "Yes, I have eight." They said, "Oh, you must have strong karma!" Well, we lived off the land. We did all right. Now I have twenty-four grandchildren. My grandchildren have been here all summer. We have a basketball court, two sandboxes and apple trees. They play; they work in the garden or on the ceremonial grounds. You know, if the children are crying or silent, something's wrong. We try to make the world a better place for them to grow up in.

Some of our kids are discouraged about the future. I hear them talking: "I don't wanta be nuked, I don't wanta be vaporized." In the school system, racism is alive and flourishing. Some teachers I know are educated fools. We teach our children to love life; we teach them they are part of the natural world. But sitting in a classroom, they become alienated from nature. And they have to memorize all this stuff. School destroys your creativity, your ability to dream.

I believe in learning whatever you have to learn to survive: how to find food and medicines in nature, how to fix your car, how to use a computer—these are the skills I teach women. You too. [Laughs.] But don't neglect the spiritual part of your life. If you get all locked up in the white man's world, you'll start to wither inside. People turn to drugs or alcohol because their spirit isn't being fed.

We've had a sweat lodge here for twenty years, and we use it all the time. We don't try to convert anyone; this is just what helps us. When you're part of a sweat, you're connecting with the living laws of the Creator. You're the first person I've told about this, outside of someone I'm taking inside. We didn't used to talk about it at all.

All the symbols—earth, air, fire and water—are sacred to us. The sweat lodge is built in a circle. When you go in there, it must be dark—we think of it as going into the spiritual womb of the Great Mother. (The men use Grandfather, but I believe all the power is feminine.) So you're sitting upon Mother Earth and the hole in the center is the belly button. You build a fire, using wood from the plant kingdom. This fire represents the fire within each of us, a creative, spiritual power like the sun. You pour water mixed with herbs onto hot rocks. The stones represent mineral life and our own skeleton—one day, we'll become mineral life, one day we'll be stones. You sit there on Mother Earth thinking of being in the womb, breathing in the air of creation. The sweat helps you purify your body and mind.

We humans are linked together by the spirit of life. People say they're from different nations and put different labels on, but when I look, I see just another human being.

There's an energy in the universe that links us to all other life forms. We are all children of the Earth. We have these earthquakes and other natural disasters because people are poisoning their Mother the Earth, they are poisoning her bloodstreams and cutting off her hair. They're not following the living laws about caring for the Earth.

All life is a precious gift. We're only here for a limited time. We need to value life, we need to find joy in it, and give something back.

*From interviews with the author, November 1, 1989,
and September 5, 1992.*

NOTES

1. McCloud was a galvanizing force for the women of AIM who formed WARN in the late 1970s and the Northwest Indian Women's Circle in 1981. In an open letter, McCloud acknowledged "the sacrifices of the young [male] warriors of the American Indian Movement." But she and others said that because of what "colonization" had done to the men, it was time for the women to join together to salvage what was left of their communities. For more information, see M. Annette Jaimes, *The State of Native America* (Boston: South End Press, 1992) pp. 328 *ff.*, and Winona LaDuke, "In Honor of Women Warriors," *Off Our Backs*, no. 11 (February 1981).

2. Excerpted from a newsletter written by Janet McCloud during the 1970s, used with her permission.

3. The controversial 1974 Boldt Decision reserving half the catch for Northwest Indian tribes.

4. In support of traditional elders who rejected the tribal council structure imposed on the tribes under the Indian Reorganization Act (1934), hundreds of AIM members marched from San Francisco to Washington, D.C., in the spring and summer of 1978. On July 25, at a rally at the Washington Monument, they delivered a manifesto demanding sovereignty for all indigenous nations, which was subsequently read into the *Congressional Record*. See "The Longest Walk," *Akwesasne Notes* (Mohawk Nation via Rooseveltown, N.Y.: Summer 1978).

25

Our Cathedral
Is the Black Hills

CAROLE ANNE HEART LOOKING HORSE
LAKOTA[1]/ROSEBUD SIOUX

From time immemorial, the traditional camp circle united the Lakota Nation and symbolized its spiritual well-being. Families belonged to the tiyospaye,[2] or extended family unit, cooperating to ensure security and economic survival. In 1890 the massacre of over 350 unarmed Lakota men, women, and children by U.S. forces at Wounded Knee creek in South Dakota destroyed the nation's lifeblood and spiritual center. Survivors were confined to reservations, where their religious practices were banned. Those who escaped that repressive atmosphere existed in a diaspora where assimilation meant survival. Still, a small number of Lakota took it upon themselves, at great risk, to preserve sacred ancestral objects, language, stories, and ceremonies.

As the wife of Arvol Looking Horse, spiritual leader of the Lakota Nation and Keeper of its Sacred Pipe, Carole Anne Heart Looking Horse is at the center of the resurgence of Lakota traditions. She has a legal background and is an educator in her own right. She came to Minneapolis with her husband to help set up a chemical-dependency prevention program. With Arvol Looking Horse sitting in the background listening to her and assisting with the spelling of Lakota words, Carole Anne Heart Looking Horse gave her perception of what it means to be Lakota.

I AM A ROSEBUD/YANKTON SIOUX FROM SOUTH DAKOTA. My mother is Phoebe Standing Buffalo, a full-blood Rosebud

Sioux from a small community called Milks Camp. My father is Yankton Sioux. We lived with my mother's grandmother, Eugenia Stars, and all our relatives. Traditionally in our society, the man lived with his wife's family. That's still often a part of Lakota culture—the home is the woman's place; it belongs to her.

We believe that a woman is powerful. The central figure in our culture is White Buffalo Calf Woman, who gave us rules to guide human behavior. Our story about her is not a "myth," it's real. This is the story of how the Sacred Pipe came to the people.

There was a time long ago when Indian people were having a difficult time finding game. They sent two warriors out to look for game, and while they were in a field, sitting on top of a hill, they noticed a cloud of dust in the distance. They watched, and then saw that it was a beautiful Indian woman with long hair, dressed in white buckskin. One of the men immediately had bad thoughts; he wanted to take her for his wife. The other man sensed that she was a spirit woman, and told the warrior to leave her alone, but he didn't want to. The woman approached. She knew what the warrior was thinking, and she told him to come to her. As he did, a cloud like a tornado enveloped him. It is said that one could hear the sound of rattlesnakes; his bones then fell to the ground.

The spirit woman told the other warrior that he was pure of heart. She said he should return to the village and tell the people that she was coming, and would bring them a gift. The man hurried back to the village and told the people. They prepared a sage altar for her, and sat in a circle waiting. She arrived carrying a bundle wrapped in white buffalo-robe skins. Laying it on the bed of sage, she opened it up, and the people saw that it was a pipe. The stem was made of wood; the bowl was made of pipestone. The spirit woman gave instructions to the people: she said that the pipe should be used to pray for health and happiness, but not for materialistic possessions. She taught them how to conduct the ceremonies we still practice today. Upon leaving the village, the people say, she rolled over and turned into a buffalo calf. Each time she rolled over, they saw four colors: red, yellow, black, the last being white. That's why

CAROLE ANNE HEART LOOKING HORSE   *Photo by Bryce McDermott*
AND CHANTE

she's called the White Buffalo Calf Woman, and those colors
and the pipe are sacred to us today.

My family had a Naming Ceremony for me, with prayers and
a feast. They named me Waste Wayankapi Win, which means
"when people see you, they see something good." My grandmother chose that name for me because she wanted me to be a
good woman. She wanted people to see not only my exterior, but
my interior. It's a name I have to live up to.

In Lakota, the word for children is *wakanyeja*. The literal
translation is *sacred beings*. I really got a sense, from my great-

grandmother and other relatives, that I was a sacred being. I never got a spanking. I don't remember anyone being mean to me during my childhood. Never. We were given a strong sense of identity and self-esteem.

In the evenings, the relatives would all get together and play cards, laugh and joke. Our parents were loving and affectionate. They didn't have to discipline us because we knew what was expected, and we did it. If someone got out of line, the aunties, uncles or grandmothers would do the disciplining. It's disrespectful to answer them back, it's terrible to snap your eyes at them—I wouldn't even consider doing that.

When I was little, I was very close to my great-grandmother. I remember she would buy us fruit, she would peel grapes and feed them to us. She treated us like we were precious little things. I remember she would always burn cedar and sage on the stove in the morning to purify the air, to purify us, and she would pray. We used to make spirit plates—you get a little plate and prepare some food to offer to the spirits. It's a symbolic way of remembering that the spirits who have gone before us need nourishment.

My great-grandmother used to talk to me all the time in Lakota, so that was my first language. She died when I was six, and it was so devastating to me that after she died, I refused to speak Lakota with anyone. To this day, I understand the language and can speak it a little, but I don't speak it fluently.

I remember the day my great-grandmother died. It was in the spring, and I could hear the wind blowing. Still whenever I hear the wind blowing, it reminds me of her. When they came to get her, I looked out the window and saw a big black hearse leaving the house, and I had the feeling she would never come back. They took me to the funeral way out in the country. I went up to the coffin and spoke to my great-grandmother, and I couldn't understand why she didn't speak to me and wouldn't get up.

I went to a Catholic boarding school on the Yankton Reservation until eighth grade. I got straight As. In class, when nobody knew the answer to a question the teacher would say, "Carole Anne, you tell them the answer." I hated that, because being held up to be smarter or better than others is a no-no in Indian tradition, so I hardly had any friends.

Even though my relatives were full-blood Indians who never spoke English, they took on Christianity and I was baptized. In school, they told us you wouldn't enter the kingdom of heaven if you weren't baptized. I'd say, "Excuse me, what about all the Chinese and African people, and our relatives that didn't get baptized, none of them will be in heaven?" I thought if my relatives aren't going to heaven, I didn't want to go either. I got into deep trouble. The nuns would send me to Father Connally, he'd try to explain why things were the way they were, so I had real intellectual conversations with this Catholic priest.

I went to high school at Saint Francis on the Rosebud Reservation, where I am enrolled. There were these little doilies at the door that we'd have to put on our heads when we went to church. One time when I was late there wasn't a doily, and the nun tried to make me put a Kleenex on my head. I said, "You know, Sister, I don't think God would care that I don't have a doily on my head. I think God would just be happy that I'm here." Well, she sent me to talk to Father Connally.

I didn't have a Womanhood Ceremony because I was in boarding school. But as I approached puberty, my grandmother started teaching me about my role as a female. Up to then, I was a fast runner, I played softball with my brothers and cousins, we wrestled and boxed, and I beat them up. But when I turned twelve, Grandmother said, "Carole Anne, no more wrestling with your brothers and your cousins. No more. You have to sit here with me now." I wanted to be out there playing. She kept strict control over us girls. We weren't allowed to date. Later I understood that it was a good thing. This is a time of transition in your life; you're becoming a woman. You're assuming a different role, you have new responsibilities.

My grandmother said, "We're choosing somebody in this family to go to college because no one's gone before." So I was like the little scout that was sent on ahead, preparing the way for the others. She told me I was not going to better myself personally, I was going for all my people.

In college, I realized there was a total void in the teaching of the history of Native people. I read every book in the library about our history. When I read about the massacre at Wounded Knee, I went home and got all my relatives together—I wanted to tell them about it. But they already knew. I said, "How come you guys didn't tell me about Wounded Knee?" My grandma said, "Well, we didn't want you to know about all the terrible things that happened to us. We wanted you to have a positive attitude." So you see how loving these people were? I understood then how they had been guiding me, preparing me to be a positive person.

I got a degree in psychology and zoology. I went to law school because it seemed to me that the legal process was critical to our survival; I felt this would be a way I could make a change. After my second year of law school, I went to Washington, D.C., and worked for the Office of Trust Responsibilities. People in the city seemed isolated; they didn't look at each other, they'd step over a homeless person rather than help him. What I missed the most was humor—Indian people are so much fun. All my relatives could be stand-up comics. I'm a little crazy myself. [Laughs.]

I returned home to the Rosebud Reservation. We wrote a proposal to create the Office of Water Resources for the tribe. We developed the Missouri River Basin Tribes' Water Policy Coalition that now works to protect the water of twenty-six tribes on the upper Missouri River Basin. I appeared before the State Water Commission [she was the first Indian to do so] over the issuance of water permits within the boundaries of reservations.

In 1978 I was part of a social group of women who, like me,

had left the reservation to get educated, and had come back. We were concerned about domestic violence. The belief then was that what happens in a man's home is his business. Well, domestic violence wasn't part of our traditional culture. Most traditional Indian men didn't beat their wives. Even though we always lived in close quarters, if you're brought up to respect other people, you will not take your anger out on another person; you will not violate the boundaries of another person. But ours was a society in transition.

I saw a lot of my friends having trouble. I would say, "Hey, if he doesn't want to change, leave him." I wrote a proposal for a program on domestic violence for the Cheyenne River Sioux Tribe, but they didn't want to deal with it then. So we said, "Okay, let's do it on Rosebud." We had to go through the tribal council and tribal court. We had to gather statistics on assault and battery in the community. Getting a male-dominated tribal council to agree to this was really something. I was in court, and Indian males would say things like, "Who do you think you are, interfering in our lives! You think you're smart since you came back to the Rez, don't you?" Finally we got our proposal funded, we got an old boarding school converted into the White Buffalo Sacred Calf Woman's Domestic Violence Shelter, and we hired staff. The shelter gives support to a lot of women.

I began working at the United Tribes' Indian Technical Assistance Center in Bismarck. I met my husband, Arvol Looking Horse, in 1987 at the National Indian Education Conference. Arvol had been invited to do opening prayers because he is spiritual leader of the Lakota Nation. We had a dance. This song came on that I wanted to dance to, and I went over to Arvol—I didn't know who he was—and asked him to dance. As far as I knew, he was just a guy from the Rez. He had short hair like a cowboy, he had on a black cowboy hat, black leather vest, tight white shirt, wranglers and boots. That was his uniform. He danced with me.

And then, all my friends asked him to dance. They were fighting over him. [Laughs.]

Later my friend told me that he was Arvol Looking Horse, the Keeper of the sacred White Buffalo Calf Pipe for the Lakota Nation, the nineteenth generation. I about fell over. I could hardly believe it. I was embarrassed about asking him to dance. But I was really honored to have met him. At the powwow, after the prayers, Arvol kept on sitting at the table with the speakers, he kept sitting there. I was the powwow coordinator; I wasn't sure what to do—you can't kick your spiritual leader off the platform, right? So I asked him all these deep questions. Later he admitted that he stayed up there because I was there.

He's this traditional guy. He was so subtle, I didn't realize he was interested in me; I was used to really aggressive men. But after a month, he came to my home to see me, and we started going out. He asked me to marry him a month after that, and I thought, "I don't know if I want to be the wife of a spiritual leader. It's a big responsibility. I'll have to live in a glass house." I had dreams that other medicine men were coming to check me out, and I do think they did. They'd look at me like, "What kind of woman is this?" I suppose they thought I was too contemporary, too assertive. Actually, I think a lot of the traditional women were like that. My grandmother was an outspoken community leader. The whole community rallied around her.

But no one prepared me to be the wife of the Keeper of the Pipe. We got married four years later. By then, I had come to realize that all my education, my legal training, my skills as a proposal writer and organizer prepared me for this role. Arvol's function is to preserve the culture of the Lakota. So we work together, doing what is necessary to heal the hoop of the nation. According to our prophecy, in the seventh generation, the nation's hoop will be mended. We are of the seventh generation.[3]

Our ceremonies were outlawed and suppressed by the government in the 1880s. We had no civil rights.[4] There was a Code of Regulations which specified that if our medicine men held ceremonies of any kind, they would be jailed, and they were. Some barely survived on bread and water. The media pictured our spiritual leaders as savages. Actually, they were like ministers, trying to hold on to culture and religion in order to keep the people strong.

Our spiritual leaders were murdered. Sitting Bull and Crazy Horse were murdered. The tribes were afraid they would lose all their spiritual leaders, so they hid the few who survived for many years. There is still that fear of reprisal.

Lakota spiritual leader Chief Sitting Bull refused to become Christianized, defied authorities, and was shot down at his camp in South Dakota in 1890. On the one hundredth anniversary of his death, December 1990, Arvol Looking Horse and Indians of many nations gathered at the place of his death—a sacred site marked by a symbolic death scaffold and red, black, yellow, and white tobacco flags. The air purified by sage, Arvol Looking Horse held an eagle-feather staff and offered the Sacred Pipe to the Four Directions, to Tunkashila[5] and to Mother Earth, then led his people on horseback along the 250-mile trail to Wounded Knee. There, at the cemetery, the spiritual leader offered the Sacred Pipe to the Four Directions, praying for the spirits of all those who have died in massacres, asking for "a new beginning" for the world's indigenous peoples.[6]

They rode twenty-five or thirty miles along the Big Foot Trail to Wounded Knee. I rode behind them in my white Cougar, with our little girl, Chante. You know, it's not just a bunch of guys riding a horse. Families gathered to welcome them all along the way. We prepared food for them. We were there to support them.

It wasn't until 1978, when the American Indian Religious Freedom Act was passed, that our people felt finally they could practice their ceremonies openly in this country. We are preserving those that survived and bringing back those that didn't. Most of them have to do with honoring our Mother the Earth. A woman can participate in almost all of our ceremonies.[7]

We have a whole cycle of ceremonies which are rites of passage going all the way to death. A newborn child is welcomed into the community and honored with a naming ceremony. We give the newborn a baby name suggesting qualities we want the child to possess. Our little girl's baby name was Chante—that's an Indian word meaning Heart. Now she's seven. Just this summer, she got another name in a ceremony: it is Kokikpapi Win, which means "They're afraid of her." She was named that because she'll say to people, "You shouldn't smoke. That's not good for you." [Laughs.] She's like a little grandma; she has the soul of a grandma.

Arvol and I thought for a year about the name—we wanted to give her one that would carry her throughout her entire life. Later we found out that this was the name of a baby daughter of Crazy Horse, so it's a good name for her. It's like saying to a child, "You're going to be a high-achieving woman. You're going to live up to your name."

For this ceremony, the whole family and community came to honor Chante. Arvol held a pipe ceremony, certain songs go with that, then we had a giveaway. We prepared for it for a year: we saved up money, and had star quilts made by Lakota women. We made or bought something for every member of the community: practical things like towels, fruit, packages of seeds, things they could use. That's the way we demonstrate generosity.

At the arrival of puberty, you go through the Womanhood Ceremony, called Isnatipi. In the past, a menstruating woman went away from the rest of the tribe and had her own tipi. As long as she was on her moon, the women waited on her, brought her food, it was a special time for her. Today, a menstruating woman doesn't interact with the rest of the family. She beads, she gets into herself. She is isolated because during the menstrual cycle, a woman is very powerful, and her power might throw off the balance between men and women. It's also a matter of respect.

The Womanhood Ceremony is a sacred ceremony that lets you know that now you are making a transformation from child to woman, you're able to bear children, you have to have respect for yourself, you have to be modest, you have to think about choosing the right husband. Older women, aunties and other respected elders, stay with the girl over a period of days, they speak to her giving her the knowledge of what it means to be female. Then she's brought out, the whole community comes to honor her, and the family puts on a feast and a social dance.

Once you've gone through the Womanhood Ceremony, you will respect the grandmothers and Mother Earth. Most likely, you will have too much respect for other women to go out with someone else's husband. You will be part of a society of women who support each other.

Pregnancy is part of the ceremonial cycle. A pregnant woman is treated as if she's special by everyone in the family. She is given really good food, people try to make sure that she is always in a good mood because she is the environment for this new being. When a woman goes into labor, the grandmas and aunties are there, and they choose a midwife they respect whose characteristics they want the child to take on. In my case, I was born at home; my grandmother on my father's side delivered me. I am honored to be like her.

We have the Hunka Ceremony. If there's a death and you've lost someone close, let's say an auntie or your mother, you adopt someone into your family and that person can take the place of the one you've lost. He or she will fill the vacant spots, and thereby keep your family strong. That practice is still with us today. In fact, I was just adopted last summer by one of my dearest friends, and I adopted her, so now we're sisters.

We give eagle feathers as a way of honoring someone. The eagle is the highest-flying creature on earth; the eagle can take your prayers to the Creator. We have purification ceremonies.[8] I look forward to them. Afterwards, I feel transformed: light, happy, accepting, relieved of burdens.

Men and women participate in the Sun Dance ceremonies for the well-being of the family or community. They fast, and dance for four days around the central Sun Dance tree. This experience takes you to a totally different plane of existence. Men pierce their flesh with leather thongs—these are attached to the Tree of Life, just as a child is attached to its mother. Women may make a small flesh offering, but they don't pierce deeply because they have their own suffering in this world; they bear children. Men and women do the Sun Dance so that the people may live.

Arvol and I think a lot about the impact of things we do. When Arvol was invited to speak earlier this year at the opening of the United Nations' Year of the Indigenous Peoples, we chose a grandma to come along to represent Lakota women and elders. Arvol spoke in Lakota, with a translator; I helped him write his speech. He told the true story of our people—how when Columbus landed here, there were seventy-five million Native Americans on the North American continent; now there are only around two million. People need to know about the mass genocide that occurred here so they won't let it happen again. Arvol said that our culture is very much alive.

We just came from a conference called Cry of the Earth. Arvol and Oren Lyons did opening prayers. Then we talked with indigenous people from all over North America: we shared our prophecies about what may happen to the earth if people don't learn to treat it with respect and let it heal.

I live and work in Bismarck. Arvol lives on the Cheyenne River Reservation where the Sacred Pipe is kept in a special place. This pipe—the Lakota word is *canumpa*—is ancient; it's wrapped in old wrappings. It's brought out only once a year; anyone who wants to pray is welcome to come to Cheyenne River. They may bring their own pipes.

All the pipes in the world are part of this pipe. The main pipe was made from the material we know as pipestone many hundreds of years ago; it's like the trunk of a tree, and the other pipes are the branches. The word for *pipestone* is *inyasa*: *inya* means Mother Earth, *sa* means red: we all come from Mother Earth. Inyasa is sacred because it is associated with the blood of our ancestors.

Pipestone is the cornerstone of our spirituality. To make people aware of that, we have a run every year around the state of South Dakota. All the tribes send their best runners, and we run in a circle through all the reservations, arriving at Pipestone, Minnesota, where the quarry is. We have a ceremony there to remind people that using pipestone for earrings, shot glasses and ashtrays is sacrilegious. It's like making earrings out of the host the Catholics use in church.

All sacred sites in North America belong to Indian people. The Pipestone National Monument; Wind Cave, which is associated with our creation story; Evans Plunge, which is the healing waters of our people, these are sacred sites where we pray. The Medicine Wheel in the Big Horn Mountains has been used for prayer by Plains tribes for ten thousand years. It is a circle of large stones shaped like a wheel which signifies the life cycle and the hoop of many Indian nations.[9] The area where the Medicine Wheel is located has been taken over by the National Park Service—they'll probably turn it into a tourist attraction. This is desecration.

In other countries, sacred places like the Wailing Wall are honored. In this country, white people believe they can own the land, they can own the air we breathe.

There is no word for religion in the Lakota language. Lakota belief is a way of life. We're teaching that to our little girl. She takes part in our ceremonies. I keep tobacco in my car. When Chante and I are out driving down the road, if we see a little animal that got run over, we stop and offer tobacco and say a prayer for the animal's spirit. If you believe in the Way of the Pipe, you try to incorporate spiritual ways into every minute of your life.

White people pray on Sundays in their big cathedrals. When the pope goes to New York, he travels with an entourage. For us, every day is holy. The Black Hills is our cathedral. When we go out to pray, we don't announce it to the whole village and have a marching band. We humble ourselves. Prayer is between you and the Creator.

When I think of home, of the Rez, I don't think of it as this isolated place. What I think of is how beautiful it is. On parts of the reservation, there are no houses, there are none of the markers of civilization, it's untouched. We were always taught to leave the Earth for our children in pristine condition, the way we found it.

I love to go home. Our home may be modest, we may not have the best designer furniture, but when you come into our home you feel like a part of the family, you feel alive, you feel the people's strength. At the core of tribal nations is not the individual but the family. Without respect for families and children, none of us will survive. We need to give people a sense of belonging. That's what makes a nation strong.

I would like to end by thanking all my relatives for supporting me, and for allowing me to be the person I am, for without them, I wouldn't be here.

From an interview with the author, December 19, 1993,
and March 3, 1994.

NOTES

1. The word Lakota refers to the western branch of the Sioux Nation (sometimes called Teton Sioux) and to the language spoken by this tribal group. See Royal B. Hassrick, *The Sioux* (Norman: University of Oklahoma, 1989) pp. 3–8.

2. The alternate spelling is *tiyospe*. See Hassrick, *The Sioux*, pp. 12–13.

3. The Lakota believe that when they were forced onto reservations, the Sacred Hoop of their nation was broken. Many Native people believe that "the seventh generation" is now born and has a special responsibility to lead their nations into the future.

4. Indians did not become citizens of the United States until 1924.

5. Lakota word for the Creator.

6. Said Lakota Birgil Kills Straight, who initiated the first Big Foot Memorial Ride in 1986 in response to a vision: "After the massacre at Wounded Knee our ancestors have never gone through the ritual that is usually accorded to the individual (or) the family that loses a loved one; until the time that takes place they are in a period of mourning." He went on to explain that completion of this ceremony will allow the people not to forget, but to move on and "build a better future for our children and grandchildren." See Sarah Penman, "Wiping Away the Tears of Seven Generations," *The Circle* (February 1991), pp. 14–15. See also video on the Big Foot Memorial ride, *Wiping the Tears of Seven Generations* (San Francisco: Kifaru Productions, 1993).

7. When asked if a woman can participate in ceremonies around the drum, Ms. Looking Horse said: "If she isn't on her moon, a woman can stand around the drum, but she doesn't sit with the males. Today, there are women's drum groups, but they're not mixed."

8. A reference to the sweat or sweat lodge, which usually precedes sacred ceremonies.

9. She elaborated: "Plains people who didn't have the wheel had an advanced understanding of how the solar system works. They knew that the earth was round and revolved around the sun. They knew that heavenly bodies are on a predictable course; they understood how that relates to natural cycles and planting seasons."

NOTES

P. XIII, From "The Women Speaking," in Linda Hogan, *Eclipse* (Los Angeles, California, UCLA American Indian Studies Center Press, © 1983).

P. 19, From a (telephone) conversation with the author, June 9, 1994.

P. 19, Ms. Alexie lives in Fort McPherson in Canada's Northwest Territories. The Gwich'in of Canada and Alaska are Athabascan people. The alternate spelling is Athapaskan.

P. 67, From "Anchorage," in Joy Harjo, *She Had Some Horses* (New York: Thunder's Mouth Press, © 1983), p. 15.

P. 99, From "The Trick Is Consciousness," by Paula Gunn Allen, in Rayna Green, *That's What She Said: Contemporary Poetry and Fiction by Native American Women* (Bloomington: Indiana University Press, © 1984), p. 18.

P. 145, From a (telephone) interview with the author, March 10, 1994.

P. 145, 1. Homes built by the Department of Housing and Urban Development.

2. Ms. Trusler heads Morning Star Enterprises. Her company hired so many Native Americans that the union instituted a reverse discrimination suit against them. "We proved that we hire a balance of Indians and non-Indians," she said, "and the suit was dismissed." In 1993 she received the Women of Enterprise Award.

P. 203, From "I Have Not Signed a Treaty with the United States Government," in Chrystos, *Not Vanishing* (Vancouver, B.C.: Press Gang Publishers, © 1988). Used by permission.

P. 241, From "Blessing the Children," in Linda Hogan, *Eclipse* (Los Angeles, California, UCLA American Indian Studies Center Press, © 1983).

Selective Bibliography

Cultural Studies: Native American Women

ALLEN, PAULA GUNN. *The Sacred Hoop: Recovering the Feminine in American Indian Traditions.* Boston: Beacon Press, 1986.

—— *Spider Woman's Granddaughters.* New York: Ballantine, 1990.

—— *Grandmothers of the Light: A Medicine Woman's Sourcebook.* Boston: Beacon Press, 1991.

ALBERS, PAT, and MEDICINE, BEATRICE. *The Hidden Half: Studies of Plains Indian Women.* Lanham, MD: University Press of America, 1983.

BATAILLE, GRETCHEN M., and SANDS, KATHLEEN. *American Indian Women: Telling Their Lives.* Lincoln: University of Nebraska Press, 1984.

—— *American Indian Women: A Guide to Research.* New York: Garland Publishing, 1991.

BATAILLE, GRETCHEN M., and LARIERSA, LAURIE. *Native American Women: A Biographical Dictionary.* New York: Garland Publishing, 1993.

BECK, PEGGY V., and WALTERS, ANNA LEE. *The Sacred Ways of Knowledge: Sources of Life.* Tsaile, Ariz.: Navajo Community College Press, 1977.

BOWKER, ARDY. *Sisters in the Blood: The Education of Women in Native America.* Newton, Mass.: WEEA Publishing Center, Educational Development Center, Inc., 1993.

GREEN, RAYNA. *Women in American Indian Society.* New York: Chelsea House, 1992.

JAIMES, M. ANNETTE. "Towards a New Image of American Indian Women." *Journal of American Indian Education* 22, October 1982, pp. 18–32.

KIDWELL, CLARA SUE. "Power of Women in Three American Indian Societies." *Journal of Ethnic Studies* 6, 1979, pp. 113–121.

LADUKE, WINONA. "In Honor of Women Warriors." *Off Our Backs*, no. 11, February 1981.

MEDICINE, BEATRICE. "Role and Function of Indian Women." *Indian Education* 7, January 1977, pp. 4–5.

WALLIS, VELMA. *Two Old Women: An Alaskan Legend of Betrayal, Courage and Survival.* Seattle: Epicenter Press, 1993.

AUTOBIOGRAPHY, BIOGRAPHY, AND INTERVIEWS

BRANT, BETH. *Mohawk Trail.* Ithaca, N.Y.: Firebrand Books, 1985.

—— "Grandmothers of a New World." *Women of Power*, Spring 1990, pp. 40–47.

BROKER, IGNATIA. *Night Flying Woman: An Ojibway Narrative.* St. Paul, Minnesota Historical Society Press, 1983.

BRUCHAC, JOSEPH. *Survival This Way: Interviews with American Indian Poets.* Tucson: *Sun Tracks*, University of Arizona Press, vol. 15, 1987.

CAMPBELL, MARIA. *Halfbreed.* Lincoln: University of Nebraska Press, 1982.

CROW DOG, MARY, with ERDOES, RICHARD. *Lakota Woman.* New York: HarperCollins, 1991.

—— *Ohitika Woman.* New York: Grove Press, 1993.

CRUIKSHANK, JULIE. *Life Lived Like a Story: Life Stories of Three Yukon Elders.* Lincoln: University of Nebraska Press, 1990.

HUNGRY WOLF, BEVERLY. *The Ways of My Grandmothers.* New York: Morrow, 1980.

KATZ, JANE. *I Am the Fire of Time: The Voices of Native American Women.* New York: E.P. Dutton Co., 1977.

KEGG, MAUDE. *Portage Lake: Memories of an Ojibwe Childhood*, ed. and trans. John C. Nichols. University of Alberta Press, 1991.

LINDERMAN, FRANK B. *Pretty Shield: Medicine Woman of the Crows.* Lincoln: University of Nebraska Press, 1972.

MANKILLER, WILMA, with WALLIS, MICHAEL. *A Chief and Her People.* New York: St. Martin's Press, 1993.

MOUNTAIN WOLF WOMAN. *Mountain Wolf Woman: The Autobiography of a Winnebago Indian*, ed. Nancy O. Lurie. Ann Arbor: University of Michigan Press, 1981.

SARRIS, GREG. *Keeping Slug Woman Alive: A Holistic Approach*, American Indian Texts. Berkeley: University of California Press, 1993.

SEKAQUAPTEWA, HELEN. *Me and Mine: The Life Story of Helen Sekaquaptewa as Told to Louise Udall*, ed. Louise Udall. Tucson: University of Arizona Press, 1969.

SHAW, ANNA MOORE. *A Pima Past.* Tucson: University of Arizona Press, 1974.

SWANN, BRIAN, and KRUPAT, ARNOLD. *I Tell You Now: Autobiographical Essays by Native American Writers.* Lincoln: University of Nebraska Press, 1987.

TICASUK (EMILY IVANOFF BROWN). *The Roots of Ticasuk: An Eskimo Woman's Family Story.* Anchorage: Alaska Northwest Books, 1981.

WONG, HERTHA D. *Sending My Heart Back Across the Years: Tradition and Innovation in Native American Autobiography.* New York: Oxford University Press, 1992.

ZITKALA SA (GERTRUDE BONNIN). *American Indian Stories.* Glorietta, N.M.: Rio Grande Press, 1976.

GENERAL INTEREST

BATAILLE, GRETCHEN M., SANDS, KATHLEEN, and SILET, CHARLES, eds. *The Pretend Indians: Images of Native Americans in the Movies.* Ames: University of Iowa Press, 1980.

BRANDON, WILLIAM. *The Last Americans: The Indian in American Culture.* New York: McGraw-Hill, 1974.

BROWN, DEE. *Bury My Heart at Wounded Knee: An Indian History of the American West.* New York: Washington Square Press, 1981.

DORRIS, MICHAEL. *The Broken Cord.* New York: Harper and Row, 1989.

JAIMES, M. ANNETTE. *The State of Native America.* Boston: South End Press, 1992.

LAME DEER, JOHN FIRE, with ERDOES, RICHARD. *Lame Deer, Seeker of Visions.* New York: Washington Square Press, 1976.

MATTHIESSEN, PETER. *In the Spirit of Crazy Horse.* New York: Viking, 1981.

—— *Indian Country.* New York: Viking, 1984, Penguin, 1992.

WEATHERFORD, JACK. *Indian Givers: How the Indians of the Americas Transformed the World.* New York: Ballantine, 1988.

—— *Native Roots: How the Indians Enriched America.* New York: Ballantine, 1991.

PUBLICATIONS

Akwesasne Notes
American Indian Quarterly
The Circle
Indigenous Woman
Native Peoples
North American Native Authors Catalog, Greenfield Review Press
Studies in American Indian Literatures
Turtle Quarterly

INDEX

ABOUT THE EDITOR

JANE KATZ has been a pioneering teacher of multicultural literature and a writer in residence in public schools. She is the author of a number of documentary books, including *Artists in Exile* and the widely praised *I Am the Fire of Time: The Voices of Native American Women*. She lives in Minneapolis.